QUEEN BEE
MOMS

&

KINGPIN
DADS

QUEEN BEE MOMS
&
KINGPIN DADS

**Dealing with the Parents, Teachers, Coaches, and
Counselors Who Can Make—or Break—Your Child's Future**

ROSALIND WISEMAN
with Elizabeth Rapoport

Crown Publishers
New York

Copyright © 2006 by Rosalind Wiseman

Library of Congress Cataloging-in-Publication Data
Wiseman, Rosalind, 1969–
Queen bee moms & kingpin dads : dealing with the parents, teachers,
coaches, and counselors who can make—or break—your child's future /
Rosalind Wiseman with Elizabeth Rapoport.—1st ed.
1. Parent and teenager. 2. Teenagers and adults.
3. Parents—Social networks. I. Title: Queen bee moms
& kingpin dads. II. Rapoport, Elizabeth. III. Title.
HQ799.15.W59   2006
649'.125—dc22   2005025030

ISBN-13: 978-1-4000-8300-8
ISBN-10: 1-4000-8300-1

Printed in the United States of America

Design by Debbie Glasserman

10 9 8 7 6 5 4 3 2 1

First Edition

To our mothers,
Kathy Wiseman and Mary Ann Rapoport,
and to our fathers,
Steve Wiseman and William J. Rapoport,
with love and respect.

Contents

Introduction   1

PART ONE

1. Perfect Parent World: Land of Perpetual Judgment   23
2. The Apple Doesn't Fall Far from the Tree,
   Part 1: Mom Cliques   36
3. The Apple Doesn't Fall Far from the Tree,
   Part 2: Dad Totem Poles   62
4. Turning the Lens on Ourselves: Understanding
   the Filters Through Which We View the World   84
5. Cracking the Code: Communication 101   102
6. Into the Muck: Confrontation 101   128

PART TWO

7. The Principal Will See You Now: How to Deal with
   Teachers, Counselors, and Principals   157
8. Field of Nightmares: Kids and Sports   192
9. "If She's on My Committee, I Quit":
   Parent Volunteering   219
10. You Are Cordially (Not) Invited:
    Coping with Kids' Parties   242
11. Sex, Drugs, and Rock 'n' Roll: Just Say, Oh No!   272

12. The Thick Envelope and the Thin: The Long
March from Gifted Preschooler to College Applicant   301

Epilogue   323

Acknowledgments   325
Index   329

QUEEN BEE
MOMS

&

KINGPIN
DADS

Introduction

How did it get to be Back-to-School Night again already? You can't believe another school year has begun so soon. Your daughter just started middle school, and you're excited to meet her teachers and hear what the principal has to say. But meeting the faculty is only a small part of the evening. You're embarrassed to admit it, but first you have to figure out what to wear. You want to look put together but you don't want to look like you're trying too hard. Should you dress more professionally? Maybe something more casual? Maybe jeans? But what if you're not taken seriously enough?

Three changes of clothes later, you walk into the main entrance. Where are all your friends? Everyone else is saying hello and doing the usual catching up. Well, not everyone—there are always those couples scattered around who never say anything; they all seem to be hugging the wall near the refreshment table. Why did you have to get here so early? Uh-oh, there's that woman you had the run-in with last spring when your kids both tried out for the travel soccer team.

"Oh, no!" you tell your spouse. "She's the one who screamed at the coach because her daughter didn't make the cut. I asked her to cool it and she totally went off on me." You round the corner quickly before she sees you.

Oh, look, there's the PTA sign-up desk. All the Power Moms—the movers and shakers on the school board, the PTA president and vice president, and the rest of the tightly knit group—are staffing the table, trying to recruit new families and encourage everyone to pay their dues. They're greeting some parents incredibly warmly; they're distant to others. They give you polite smiles, but the message is, "We don't know you; you're not one of the do-bees. We're reserving judgment."

At the next table, another team of women is aggressively recruiting for various committees. (You look around; no fathers seem to be manning these desks.) "We could really use some help on the Authors and Artists Event," calls out one of the moms. "May we sign you up?"

"Um, I'm not sure," you say. "Work has just been incredibly crazy, and I don't know—"

"Oh, that's okay, we understand," she replies, her demeanor cooling instantly. "I work, too. So does everyone else on the committee." That's code for "Hey, we *all* work hard. We're just not afraid to work harder—*for our kids*. Clearly, we're more dedicated parents than you."

There's Carly's mom, Denise. Carly and your Katie used to be such good friends, but lately things have cooled off—Carly didn't even call Katie back when she got home from sleep-away camp. Katie's hurt, but you're not really sure how to handle it; Denise is a little . . . intense.

"Hi!" Denise trills. "How was your summer? Carly had a blast at the Johns Hopkins lit thing. We went to Space Camp, too. How'd Katie do on that *Odyssey* paper? Carly had trouble with it at first, but I helped her out on the research and I think Mrs. Evans is definitely going to want her for the GATE class."

Was there a mailing you missed? Is your daughter going to be shut out of the gifted class because you buried some assignment in the foot-tall stack of old mail on the hall table? "*Odyssey* paper?" you ask weakly.

Denise's eyes widen. "Katie didn't do the *Odyssey* paper yet? They went over it last week at the GATE meeting. I was wondering why you weren't there."

"Oh, my God, we missed it!" you say. "Do you think it's too late? Katie should totally be in GATE."

Denise smiles soothingly. "Don't worry. Just talk to Rochelle." Rochelle. So Denise is on a first-name basis with the principal. You're not even sure how to spell her last name.

As Denise disappears into the crowd, a smiling mother holds out a flyer to you with one hand; in the other she's holding a clipboard and stack of papers. "It's about the new Kendall-McGee rubric. We think the principal is on completely the wrong track with the new curriculum. Did you have any questions before you sign the petition?" You have no idea what she's talking about, but you don't want to ask; you don't want to look like a clueless parent. "Let me get back to you on this," you say as the lights begin to flicker on and off. "Looks like they want us inside the auditorium."

On the way you pass the principal. She's already surrounded by parents who are hugging her and saying, "So, Rochelle, how was your summer? That suit looks fabulous!"

Inside the auditorium, there are more knots of parents getting reacquainted after a summer apart. It's immediately obvious which parents are new to the school. You and your spouse take one of the few remaining spaces up front. "I'm sorry," says a mother, smiling past your shoulder, "we're saving those." You apologize, blushing; you didn't know.

You've been at school ten minutes and already you've flunked.

Why are you worrying about what you're going to wear to Back-to-School Night like a fourteen-year-old before a school dance? And when and why did Back-to-School Night become a barometer for your own parenting and popularity?

Let's face it: Being a parent brings out our most nurturing, mature side, but it also taps our deepest insecurities, makes us question our every ability, and causes us to measure ourselves against everyone around us. In other words, it makes us feel like seventh graders all over again.

When I wrote my first book, *Queen Bees & Wannabes,* I wanted to help parents help their daughters survive and thrive in what I call Girl World, the social hierarchy where Queen Bees, Messengers, and Bankers (and their male counterparts) play pivotal—and often corrupting—parts in children's lives. My intention was to help parents decode Girl (and Boy) World so they would understand what their children are going through and could get advice on how to help their kids help themselves.

As I traveled all over the country and spoke to hundreds of parents, I learned that parents are also looking for another type of help. They want to know how to deal with the unspoken rules of Perfect Parent World, that mythical kingdom where all the other, presumably perfect parents live and rule, a world with a social hierarchy uncannily similar to that of Girl and Boy World. It's a world in which a few parents set the rules for all parental involvement, the standards are virtually impossible to achieve, and most parents feel frustrated or disempowered—including the parents who established the rules in the first place. It's a world that convinces parents to make decisions based on their fear of other people's judgments and leaves them struggling over whether and how much to get involved in their children's schools and social lives. In this world, many parents compete ruthlessly through their children, while other parents fear to speak out against them. And it has all of us reliving the traumas and dilemmas of our own youth, even as we're surprised to learn that those decades-old obsessions have returned or are still alive—if indeed they ever disappeared entirely.

In *Queen Bees & Wannabes,* I argued that the seemingly innocuous rites of passage that are dismissed with phrases like "girls will be girls" (gossip, cliques, competition for social status) teach girls how power and privilege work in our culture. I discussed how the "boys will be boys" mentality likewise teaches boys that might makes right. Both boys and girls too often learn to be silent in the face of injustice. It doesn't matter if that lesson is learned by a ten-year-old boy who is relentlessly teased by being called gay, or by a junior girl who thinks it's so important to be popular that she's willing to be physically tortured by other girls in a hazing ritual, or by a parent who doesn't think she can confront another parent about her child's cruel behavior. These experiences teach everyone involved that whoever has power and privilege in our society is permitted to do what they want to people who don't. If we don't confront this power system or if we buy into it ourselves, we can come across as unethical or cowardly and undermine our ability to teach our children a true moral foundation and feeling of responsibility to their community.

As the co-founder of the Empower Program, an organization dedicated to educating teens about the culture of violence, I work with more than ten thousand boys and girls and their parents, teachers, school administrators, coaches, and counselors every year. Here's what I've learned: Every Queen Bee girl or Dominator boy is hatched from a hive. The first lessons our children learn in creating their own social hierarchies are the ones they glean from us and the culture at large. The first step toward helping our kids cope with bullying in any form is recognizing the degree to which we're still immersed in those same battles for power.

I've written this book to give you, as parents, a different kind of power with your own children, other parents and their children, teachers, and administrators—power that is respectful of children's needs and desires and that changes their world for the good. Power that gives you the ability to look at your own behavior—without beating yourself up—and to understand how you can more effectively work with the other adults in your child's life.

Parents all over the country come up to me after my lectures to tell me stories—not just stories of how their daughters and sons have been victims or victimizers in their cliques and groups, but tales of their own experiences with parents, teachers, coaches, and other adults in their children's world.

> "I hate the PTA moms. They're on a first-name basis with the principal, and I know they pull strings to get their kids the best teachers. I feel completely boxed out."

> "My child was having a serious problem in school, but none of the teachers would listen to me. For way too long I played nice because I didn't want to come across as one of those crazy mothers, but nothing was happening to get my kid the help he needed. I can't tell you how painful it was to go through the process, because my child was suffering and I felt like no one was watching out for him."

> "My daughter had a birthday party and didn't invite a girl in the neighborhood who's been incredibly mean to her. Now all the other parents won't talk to me because they think we were horrible for not inviting this kid. I know this because a parent 'emissary' talked to me on behalf of the other parents. Now I'm avoiding almost everyone on the block."

The more stories like these I heard, the more I realized that I had underestimated how powerfully parents' social hierarchies influence how they guide their children's lives. *We don't leave cliques and peer pressure behind when we grow up or when we become parents; we just graduate to a new level with adults playing the roles.*

THE MYTH OF PARENTAL INVOLVEMENT

There are some accepted yet strange "truths" in our culture about today's parents. Parents are simultaneously portrayed as insanely involved in every minute detail of their child's life *and* AWOL—caught up in their own personal drama and/or professional ambitions. Is this true? How could it be true?

In my work, I see plenty of both. What I don't see is enough *sane* involvement. Instead, I see parents' actions dictated by anxiety, insecurity, fear—which is largely brought on by parents pressuring each other to be perfect or assuming that someone is accusing them of being a bad parent. To be sure, there are parents whose overstuffed lives lead them to overlook what's going on with their children, but equally troublesome are overinvolved parents who believe no one has the right to challenge their behavior. Over and over, I've seen parents use their children's lives as an arena to enhance their own popularity, prestige, sense of self-esteem, and entitlement—to their children's detriment.

Another popular misconception is that *parents* means *mothers*—as if they're the only parents who engage in this kind of socially competitive behavior. As I'll make clear, fathers are certainly no strangers to social pecking orders and competing for social power through their children.

Why are we so competitive? It's easy to see your child as an extension and reflection of yourself—if your kid is terrific, then you're terrific. Kids are the ultimate status symbol, and they always have been. It's unthinkable, unbearable, to have an ordinary, run-of-the-mill kid—so parents will jump in and "help" the situation in order that their son or daughter can have every opportunity to shine, even if it means spattering someone else with mud. I've been astonished at the number of parents who confessed to me the steps they'd taken to cement their own status by meddling with their child's. Some people may read this and say, "So what? Parents have always jockeyed for social power through their children." I don't disagree, but that's not the issue. We need to recognize that this kind of competition lays the foundation for adults mistreating one another—and our children—and we need to learn how to stop it.

I hope this book will help parents ask themselves some very difficult questions about their own need for social status. You may be reading this book because you've had experiences with other parents that made you doubt their sanity. While I'll certainly give you strategies for dealing with these parents, I'll also ask you to hold up a mirror and take an honest look at yourself. You may discover that you're more socially competitive than you realize. Or that it's harder than you imagined to admit when your child has made a mistake. Perhaps you haven't been as assertive as you needed to be with other parents and teachers or you've been too aggressive defending your child. Perhaps you'll realize that you've been over-protective of a child who needs to be more independent.

Drawing on my conversations and interviews with hundreds of parents, *Queen Bee Moms & Kingpin Dads* will spotlight how to recognize this kind of behavior in yourself and rein it in so that your son or daughter can thrive. Of course, I'll tell you how to approach the overbearing parent who screams from the sidelines, "For Christ's sake, what the hell are you doing out there? You're playing like a bunch of little girls" to the boys on the soccer field. And how to wrest the meeting away from the attention-hogging parent determined to use it as another private parent-teacher conference. But I'll also tell you how to figure out when your involvement in your son or daughter's life is actually teaching your child that he or she can't be independent and self-sufficient, or accountable for his or her actions.

This is tender territory. It's hard not to want to shield our kids from every one of life's blows. We don't want to see them get into trouble, and it can be extraordinarily tempting to minimize the consequences of their bad actions, or point the finger elsewhere, or work the system if we think they're being punished too severely. But when we do, we lose sight of our most important role as parents: to raise responsible, ethical kids who are well equipped to deal with failures and disappointments.

Not surprisingly, teens can be the keenest observers of parental behavior. I first began to appreciate how teens view their parents a few years ago when I found myself in front of seven hundred high school students in a cavernous auditorium in the Midwest. They were typical restless teens as

I began my speech, but they quieted when I said: "I don't know your particular school, so I won't assume I know what's going on in your lives. Instead, I'm going to share with you what I see all around the country. That social pecking orders create cultures in schools—even the 'best' schools—where no one is safe. Where some students are above the law. I'm not blaming people for the power and privilege that they may have in their school community, but if they're being cruel or bullying other people, they must be held to the same rules of accountability as everyone else. And the same should go for their parents—they shouldn't try to get their kids off the hook when they break the rules."

The room erupted in spontaneous applause. I was amazed. I realized these kids were sending me a powerful message: They understood how the pecking order of the school was impacting them and their parents, and they wanted to change it. They wanted the school to hold the parents accountable—especially when those parents threatened and bullied the school for trying to hold their kids accountable for breaking the rules.

THE BAD, THE UGLY, AND THE RIDICULOUS: PARENTS BEHAVING BADLY

I spend a lot of time working with teens, teachers, parents, and school administrators to curb everything from fifth-grade e-mail fights to high school hazing. As appalling as some teenagers' behavior can be, I think you'll be astonished to read how they're outdone by their parents. Or perhaps you won't be surprised in the least.

School Administrators Speak Out

School administrators are on the front lines of the nexus between students and parents. Here are a few stories they've shared with me.

- Setting: a northern all-girls Catholic school. A bunch of junior girls walk into the classroom and pass around photos of themselves drinking at a party. Their teacher confiscates the pictures and gives them to the head of the school. The head of the school meets with the offending girls' parents individually. One mother responds by demanding to know what proof the school has of her daughter's misbehavior. The head of the school shows the mother the incriminating photos of her daughter. The mother takes the photos and puts them down her pants and refuses to return them. The police are called, and eventually the girl convinces her mother to give the photos back.

- Setting: a southern coed middle school. Two girls are competing for power in sixth grade. An e-mail war escalates, and one girl alerts her mother. That mother decides that she could do a better job than her daughter of responding to the other girl and begins sending nasty IMs back to her.

- Setting: a small southern coed private school. A junior boy is the very popular, athletic son of the most respected minister in town. After repeated attempts to get his father's attention by driving drunk and breaking every school rule he can think of, he is resigned: "No matter what I do, I can't get kicked out of this school. He preaches all this junk and he is so hypocritical. And if someone's kid was in the same kind of trouble and asked him to intervene with the school, he would say, 'I'm sorry, I can't do that. My hands are tied.'"

- Setting: an East Coast middle school. Parents are brought into the school to discuss with the head of the school and a counselor their daughter's e-mail battles with another girl. In response to the accusation, Dad demands to see the evidence and the identity of the purported victim (Mom is present but silent). The counselor shows him a stack of e-mails that detail the vicious attacks by his daughter; the victim's name is crossed out. Instead of addressing his daughter's behavior, the father says, "I would never look at my daughter's e-mail because we have a privacy policy in this family." The counselor then shows the parents their twelve-year-old daughter's AOL profile. The girl describes herself as sexually promiscuous in the profile, something that anyone on the Internet could see—except her parents, because that would be a violation of their privacy policy.

- Setting: an urban school. Two girls write a "black book" that ruthlessly mocks the students and teachers in their school. They then post their "book" around the school—taped to the hallway walls, the bathroom stalls, and the walls of the cafeteria. When the administration investigates, one of the girls immediately admits her guilt, but the other steadfastly lies—and her dad is the head of the PTA. Both girls are expelled, but the parents of the girl who lied wage a write-in campaign among their friends to convince the principal to reverse the decision. Their friends don't want to write these letters because they think the girl got what she deserved (some of their children were listed in the book), but they all do it because they're too afraid to confront these powerful parents.

- Setting: a suburban northeastern public school. A group of senior boys are drinking and smoking marijuana when they're caught by local police, who take photos of the party scene. The police notify the boys' principal, who then calls in the boys' parents. After viewing the incriminating photos, one of the parents asks how the police and principal can be sure that it's beer in those cups and not urine. Another parent tries to negotiate the punishment: Could they fix it so that the son would skip graduation but be allowed to go to the prom?

It's easy to doubt the sanity of these parents. But while their behavior can't always be justified, each acted out of a powerful, even loving motivation. And if we look hard enough, we may even be able to see something of ourselves in them. If we want to help our children navigate the challenges of adolescence and become independent, moral adults, we must have the courage to look at our actions—especially in the moments when we think we are being our children's champions and advocates.

Teachers and Coaches Speak Out

We send our children to school to learn to think independently, follow a passion for a subject, reason clearly, write compellingly, and become responsible members of the community. And then we do their homework for them or we challenge teachers who discipline our children or do something else we don't like—such as giving our kids grades that are lower than we think they deserve. We send our children onto the playing fields to strengthen their bodies, have fun, and learn teamwork. Then as we watch them play, we stand back and say nothing as other parents scream at kids and referees, undermine coaches, or bully other parents. Perhaps we've even been in a few shouting matches ourselves. Here's what teachers and coaches have told me about parental interference:

> *"I got an amazing paper from a middling student that had clearly been edited by an adult. I asked my student about it, and he admitted he'd gotten a lot of help from his mom. When I called the parent, she flatly denied it and told me that if her child didn't get a good grade, she'd go straight to the principal. How can I help this kid learn to think and write if his mother is going to do his work for him? How can I deal with this mother?"*

> *"These parents keep trying to bully the principal into putting their daughter into all the accelerated classes. She has a mild learning disability and needs constant tutoring just to make average grades. I took her aside and she said she never gets to go to sleep before midnight because she's so overwhelmed by homework—and then she gets up at five-thirty every morning to finish it. I want to take the pressure off her, but the parents refuse to let up."*

> *"Silent Sunday is a gift from God. For one Sunday every month, the parents aren't allowed to shout at their kids from the sidelines. Last week I had to pull a parent off the field because he started to physically assault the ref because the guy had yellow-carded his kid. I wanted to scream, 'It's just a frigging soccer game. What's the matter with you people!'"*

Teenagers Get the Last Word

Sure, adolescence is a time when your child will be mortified by pretty much everything you do, no matter how you try to disappear into the woodwork or shrink down in the front seat of the car. However, kids are legitimately scandalized by how their own and other parents behave. Here are some of the stories they've shared with me:

- A shy girl confessed that her mother was still arranging her social schedule for her, even though she's fifteen. "She just wants me to be with girls she thinks are good role models. Guess what? I hate those girls and they hate me. The more she interferes, the lamer they think I am. I can't get her to stop."
- A boy on his high school's ice hockey team told me, "This kid high-sticked me during a game, and my dad went ballistic. He actually went up to the kid's dad and started punching him. They ended up having to call the police."
- A high school sophomore told me, "My mom is always 'just popping in' at the school 'to see how things are going.' She'll say she forgot to pack some of my lunch, or something lame like that, but it's completely obvious that she's checking up on me. I tell her she's embarrassing me, but I can't get her to stop."
- A middle school girl told me, "My mom volunteered to help out with the school carnival. She's a professional artist, but this major mom clique won't let her do any of the booths, even though she's ten times more qualified. She came up with some really cool designs, but when she showed them to the women on the committee, they said, 'We've got it under control. How about you bake cupcakes?' These mothers are meaner than any kids I know."

Even when they moan about their parents, teens look up to them and are desperate to have good models for how to behave. When parents act up or out, the short-term effect can be kids who follow suit. But the more long-lasting, devastating effect is that kids learn that their parents' family values are superficial. That doing the right thing doesn't matter when you're angry or frustrated. That in the moments when your ethics and morals are challenged, you don't have to abide by them—you just need to look like you do.

THE GOOD, THE BAD, AND THE FUZZY

Very often, parents' behavior is driven not by a Machiavellian desire for their children—and by extension themselves—to triumph but by a genuine though misguided attempt to live up to what they see as the impossibly high standards our culture sets for parenthood. Many parents see their role as helping their children navigate a world where the odds have been unfairly stacked against them, where the rules of the road are unclear or even just plain dumb. As I see it, sometimes they're right to worry, but at other times their actions are based more on perception than on reality. In any case, what's true is that they're genuinely confused. Here are just a few examples I've encountered from parents sincerely unsure about how—or whether—to step into their kids' lives:

- Tom has always been shy, but his friends finally convince him to go to a big party at someone's house. There's an illegal keg. The police bust up the party and the school is handing out suspensions to every student who was there. This is the first time Tom's ever done anything like this, and when he was caught he wasn't drinking. But the school's policy is that you can't be in the presence of alcohol without consequences. You think Tom's punishment is too severe; he got the same punishment as the kid who had the party, not to mention the kids who were actually drinking. Should you fight the school so that his record remains clean?

- Unbeknownst to you, Tara has slipped a Tylenol into her pants pocket because it's her period and she's feeling very achy. She takes it during gym class and gets busted. The school has a strict no-drugs policy, and that means *no drugs*—not even Tylenol. Tara is facing expulsion. Honestly, you respect the school's policy—who wants drug pushers sidling up to your son or daughter with roofies?—but this is going too far. Is the school really going to ruin your kid's entire life over a single Tylenol? What should you do?

- You used to be very close with the parents of Alison's best friend. The girls had a huge misunderstanding on instant messaging and things haven't really been the same since. You hate to admit this, but since then you've never spoken to Alison's parents beyond polite hellos when you run into each other. Do you accept that the girls' friendship may have run its course, try to get them back together, or try to repair things with the adults?

- The science teacher assigns a massive project that accounts for a huge portion of the kids' final grade. She assigns three kids to each team. The kids know exactly what this means: there will be an overachiever, an average student, and a do-nothing. Your middle schooler has always been so shy; now Charlayne's the overachiever, grouped with a girl she's becoming friendly with who's an average student and another girl she likes who's the do-nothing. She doesn't know how to tell them that they've got to pull their own weight on the project—what if they stop liking her?—so she sucks it up and does everyone else's work but becomes extremely resentful. You're furious, too. How do you handle it? Do you talk to the teacher? The other kids' parents?

I'll help you understand how to draw respectful boundaries in these kinds of situations and find a happy medium between overprotective parenting and frightened passivity.

The first step is acknowledging our blind spots. It's hard to appreciate them, but we all have them. While parents don't all react the same way to a given situation, they do have a few tendencies in common that get in the way of being effective role models.

I remember a clear example from the annals of my own parenting. When my first son was a year old, we went to a playground. He was playing with a little girl in the sandbox when suddenly she kicked him and snatched away his toys. Immediately my eyes narrowed: Who was this horrible, nasty child and where was her equally horrible parent? No sooner had I begun to look around for this disgraceful parent when my son hit the little girl back and threw sand in her face. And what was my reaction? "Oh, I need to get him home for a nap; he's really cranky."

As I walked away, child in tow, I realized that this dynamic was at the heart of most conflicts parents have with one another. It's natural to dislike or even hate the people who are mean to your child (even if they're much smaller than you). It's equally natural to excuse your own child's behavior. When he steps out of line, your first impulse will be to excuse his behavior because he was provoked, tired, or being self-assertive. Perhaps you blame someone else—the other child, the other child's parents, the school. (One of my favorite Roz Chast cartoons features a whirlwind of a little boy walking down the street, followed by his frazzled parents; the caption reads, "A boy and his spin doctors.") But you can't let these reactions guide your parenting.

So when do you step in and when do you hang back? I think a lot of parents would agree that the hardest thing we have to do is let our kids make mistakes and learn from them. We rush in for a million "good" reasons: We don't want to see our kids hurt; we think we know what's better for them in the long run; we want to protect them from a short-term mistake that will have long-term consequences; we want them to profit from our hard-earned wisdom. With the benefit of our maturity, we eagerly correct and help and fend off encroachers—and what our kids learn is that they're helpless and incapable, and that someone else will have to rescue them. When we shield them from the consequences of their bad actions, we keep them from developing the strong sense of morality they'll need throughout their lives and we send the message that we believe they aren't competent enough to handle things anyway. Frankly, while we intellectually know that we aren't our children and their actions do not necessarily define who we are as parents, our actions often contradict our better sense.

FATHERS ARE PARENTS TOO

Mothers buy most of the parenting books—even when the books are about fathers. If you're a dad reading this book, there's a good chance you saw it around the house and picked it up in a spare moment. Or maybe your wife urged you to read it. No matter why you're reading it, I want you to know that I'm not writing about fathering primarily to help mothers better understand what's going on with the fathers of their children—that's extra credit. I'm writing to fathers directly because I want to help you have equal involvement and an equal say in your children's lives.

During the fifteen years I've worked with schools, I've often wondered: When fathers see those flyers that begin "Dear Parent" stuffed in their kids' backpacks, do they translate *parent* as *mother* and assume the flyer isn't for them? Many dads do come to school events, but let's not kid ourselves: The vast majority of parents who attend school functions and parent-teacher conferences are mothers. Why do so many fathers think that the logistics of their children's educations and social lives aren't their responsibility or don't feel that they have an equal say? Aren't they influenced like mothers by social competition and parental peer pressure? In writing this book, I've drawn from conversations, e-mails, surveys, and focus groups I've conducted with hundreds of fathers to offer some answers to these questions.

I know that most fathers are passionately concerned about their children and their own parenting skills. Most tell me that they don't want to parent the way their own fathers did; they say and believe that they want to be equal parenting partners. They want to have close, meaningful relationships with their children. I'm not questioning that. But achieving these goals involves hard work and, frankly, a lot of them give up way too easily.

Why is this so? In part, because while many moms say they want their children's fathers to get more involved in their children's lives, when it really comes down to it, they often discourage even the most interested fathers' efforts—and then the men give up trying. We need to understand this dynamic. If women are territorial, it's often because they feel forced to defend their ability to do everything well and by themselves—achieving that ridiculous "balance between work and home" we so often hear about. If men give up and walk away too easily (or sleep on the couch), we need to recognize that in part it's because we let them get away with it. Fathers need to own this fact and we all need to change it. This isn't about blame—this is about taking ownership so that everybody can have more meaningful, supportive relationships.

For many of us, the roles for mothers and fathers have changed dramatically since the time we were raised. Fathers today are expected to (and most want to) not only support their families financially but also be more emotionally present. Instead of "ruling the roost," dads are expected to engage in give-and-take with their spouses. Giving up the traditional, authoritarian father role doesn't have to mean losing your authority. In fact, I believe it allows for men to be more respected—especially by their children. This book offers many examples of how men are embracing fatherhood in successful ways. I hope it will encourage fathers to think twice the next time the phone rings and it's another parent calling to discuss a problem with their children. Instead of throwing the phone to their wives like it is toxic waste, I hope fathers will hold on to that receiver and say, "Thanks for calling. How can I help?"

How to Use This Book

The first part of this book will give you a whirlwind tour of Girl World and Boy World, the places your kids live every day. We'll discuss what it takes to be accepted as a teen by studying the "Act Like a Woman" and "Act Like a Man" boxes. Then we'll explore how those attributes change—or don't—for adults. Because those cultures helped forge who you are and how you parent, I'll also encourage you to reflect on your own memories and experiences. If you want to understand your kids, you must remember what it feels like to be a teen, even if—perhaps *especially* if—that thought terrifies you.

If you can't remember what being in this often-harrowing world felt like, visualize this scenario: You're driving through a small town where you know everyone. You're singing along to the radio, the sun is shining, you're whipping along at a million miles an hour with the breeze in your hair. Suddenly you see a police car by the side of the road and a radar gun pointing directly at your car. You're busted. You're no longer in control of your day—the police officer has complete power over you. But that's not the worst part. As you sit on the side of the road, a million cars troll by, and everyone's craning their necks to see if they know you, and they're so glad they're not in your place. That's what it feels like to walk down the hallway of middle school for many boys and girls when people are gossiping about you.

Now fast-forward another decade or two or three, and welcome to Perfect Parent World. I'll help you understand how the lessons you've learned about social status and obtaining and maintaining respect in your community dictate your position in the social pecking order of this world.

In the next two chapters, I'll review the social hierarchies for mothers and fathers. Yes, they exist, and they have surprising similarities to—and crucial differences from—the carefully defined cliques of teenagers. I'll discuss the stereotypical roles mothers and fathers occupy, from the Kingpin Dads to the Starbucks & Sympathy Moms and the Invisibles. We'll look at how different types of parents interact with one another, and how the prevailing social hierarchies affect your relationships with other adults. Next, I'll discuss the various attitudes and experiences that affect how we interpret and respond to others—I call these our "filters"—and help you crack the codes other parents often use when they communicate. Finally, we'll talk about how to confront someone so you can have a productive exchange.

In Part Two of this book, I'll discuss common rites of passage for your child, such as getting invited to parties, participating in organized sports, or getting called to the principal's office. Of course our kids are at the center of these events, but in many ways they're rites of passage for us as well. What should *you* do and say in these situations? How does the way you handle them affect your child's behavior? When should you step in or hold back? How do you handle it when the problem is with other parents or adults? I'll give you very specific advice, including:

Landmines. These are words or actions you'll need to avoid because they'll cause other adults to shut down and tune you out.
Sample scripts. Ever wish life came with a script? In this book, it does. I'll give you specific scripts for handling particular situations—what to say and what *not* to say.

FOUR THINGS TO REMEMBER

1. You don't always have to like your child and he or she doesn't always have to like you. As I said in *Queen Bees*, you don't always have to like your child. You can even have moments when you question why you had a child in the first place. (One parent I know said, "I never stopped loving my daughter. I just occasionally loathed her. And by 'occasionally,' I mean for about two years straight.") And no one said that your child has to like you either. Many parents are afraid to do the hard stuff—such as holding their children accountable for obnoxious behavior—for fear that their kids won't like them or will stop talking to them. To this I say: Feel the fear and do it anyway. Your job isn't to be your child's best friend. Likewise, you don't have to be best friends with the parents and other adults in your child's life; you just have to learn to behave decently. And by the way, you can hold the line and your kids will still talk to you. If you don't know how, I'll teach you.

2. A little bit of paranoia and fear is a good thing. I'm convinced that someone has gone around the country in the last fifteen years and told parents that if they just teach their kids the right values and ethics, that will be enough to spur the kids to do "the right thing." This would be true in a perfect world—a place where no one I know lives. The truth is that teaching values such as respect and integrity are essential to good parenting—*but they're not enough*. Sometimes even the best kids need a little more motivation in the form of "If I get caught, I'm dead." Of course, I don't advocate physically or verbally abusing your children, but your kids have to know that you're serious about holding them accountable.

When my two boys are older, they may well be tempted to steal my car for an illicit night out—and this is not just any car. Picture the following: It's a beautiful Friday night and my husband and I are asleep. The keys to my 1963 electric blue Ford Falcon convertible are on the mail table and the kids' friends are waiting. After they quietly sneak into the garage and put the keys in the ignition, a thought elbows its way to the front and center of their brains: "If Mom finds out about this, we're dead." Which is quickly followed by "And no matter how we try to hide it, she'll find out." If this thought is in my sons' heads, I will consider my parenting a job well done.

3. This book is not *the* truth. What I am telling you is not the one and only truth—it's what I observe and experience in my work with adolescents, parents, teachers, coaches, counselors, and school administrators. Some of what I describe may resonate strongly with you; some might seem far afield of your own experiences. As you read this book, I'm asking that you engage with me in the process of understanding why we act as we do. If you read something and think, "Oh, I would never do anything like that," I'm asking you to question yourself closely before you read on.

4. Adolescence is tough; you need a theme song. Please go listen to "Isn't She Lovely" by Stevie Wonder while you read this book. (Feel free to substitute "Isn't He Lovely" if you have a son.) I defy you to listen to this song and not feel overwhelmed by how much you love your child, no matter how obnoxious he or she can be. Remember the feeling that song gives you when you're in a death match with another parent, because guess what? The other parent feels *exactly* the same way about his or her kid!

So take a deep breath and dive in. It takes a lot of courage to challenge yourself the way I'm challenging you, but there's so much at stake: your sanity, your child's health and safety, and the quality of the relationships that are most precious to you. When I work with adolescent boys and girls, I try to empower them to stand up for what's right—and I understand that doing this can be a terrifying and isolating decision. At its most fundamental, my job with young people is to tell them, "You can and you should defend every person's right to be treated with dignity." I want to offer the same gentle encouragement to you, but in all honesty, when I see kids in so much pain because they're being bullied or harassed while adults stand by succumbing to their own feelings of helplessness or condoning the bully's behavior, "can" doesn't cut it. I believe passionately that we *must* step up. When you see that bullying parent disrespecting that coach or teacher or kid, I hope you'll take action. When you see a principal or teacher turn a blind eye to cruelty in his or her school, I hope you'll do something—even if the target isn't your child. I realize that we all must pick our battles and that parents sometimes feel that if they say something, they'll just make matters worse for their child. But I believe that we absolutely must pick *something*, stand up, and let our voices be heard. This book will give you the skills you need to step up and demand more from yourself and all the people who touch the lives of the children in your community.

Part One

Perfect Parent World

Land of Perpetual Judgment

"You couldn't pay me enough to go back to seventh grade."

People love to tell me this. Teachers, parents, counselors, principals, people on the street, people at parties—everywhere I go, people tell me that they shudder at the thought of waking up one day transported back to seventh grade. But when I tell them I'm writing a book on parents' social competition, their eyes grow wide with delight or dismay—and always with recognition. "Do I have a story for you," they say conspiratorially. Clearly, few of us have left seventh grade completely behind.

My goal in this book is to get you to do *exactly* what almost no one wants to do: Go back to seventh grade and understand how the lessons you learned as a child and adolescent affect the way you parent. And when I say "parent," I'm not just referring to your relationship with your child. I'm including in my definition of parenting your interactions and relationships with other parents, teachers, coaches, school administrators, and children other than yours—any other person in your child's world.

You leave your adolescence with a sigh of relief—you think you never have to revisit it—but you're mistaken. You don't just relive it through your children; you also have countless opportunities to experience it all over again as a parent. These are the moments of growth that we all dread so much: You think you've gotten past your adolescent insecurities, but then you have kids and all your emotional maturity flies right out the window. Of course, parenting can bring out the best in us—but we also have to admit that it can sometimes bring out the worst. At the root of our actions lies a deep-seated need to belong. Let's take a closer look at this need.

BACK-TO-SCHOOL NIGHT: NIGHT OUT OR NIGHTMARE?

Let's review the rite of passage I mentioned in the Introduction: Back-to-School Night. I asked parents to tell me how they felt about that night, and you'd be hard-pressed to tell some of their responses apart from those of seventh graders.

Do Parents Worry About How They Look?

> *You want to look put together because you're going to see a lot of people you know.* Virginia, middle school mom

> *I got dressed up to the nines but one step down because I didn't want to look like I tried too hard.* Don, middle school dad

> *I don't need to dress up for Back-to-School Night because I work.* Alex, middle school mom (oblivious to the fact that she was dressed in her power suit)

Do Parents Worry About Running into Other Parents?

> *My daughter was in a special-needs class and I was apprehensive because I thought everyone would know she was the one who needs the extra help. I was embarrassed or ashamed that somehow it was a reflection on me as being a bad parent.* Jose, middle school dad

Do Parents Worry About Whether They'll Fit In?

> *What sticks out is how uncomfortable I felt. The teacher asked if there were any questions and I had one, but I didn't ask because I was worried that people would think I was an inattentive father.*
> Ronald, middle school dad

*I walked into the school and everyone else knew each other—except
for me. I just leaned against the wall and thought, "I'm sunk."*
Arlene, elementary and middle school mom

While there are parents who eagerly attend Back-to-School Night, most parents admitted to having some degree of anxiety about it. What's behind this discomfort? You've probably already intuited part of the answer: You feel like you're back in middle school. It's clear who's at the top of the social ladder, who's not, and who's waiting to climb up from the lower rungs. You probably have one of two reactions to the scene: You want to be part of it, you hope highly placed, or you want to have nothing to do with it.

Everyone wants to belong somewhere. There's nothing weak or pathological about it—it's a universal drive. It's just that our true character (individually and collectively) is revealed in the moments when that belonging comes at the cost of what we believe in and what we know is right, whether we're thirteen, thirty-three, fifty-three, or seventy-three. To my mind, becoming an adult is the process of understanding and holding on to our sense of self in the face of this drive, because belonging often comes at the cost of the values we stand for.

What groups do we want to belong to? Do those groups accept us? Why or why not? How do we decide where we want to belong? How do boys and girls, men and women attain and maintain respect in their community and in our culture? In turn, how is a social pecking order established through this process?

Writing this book has made me realize that there are many adults who feel just as trapped by the groups they are in, if not more so, than the teens with whom I work. Most parents become friends with other parents beginning in their children's play groups and then continue on through their car pools, athletic teams, and religious youth groups. To be sure, many people develop lifelong friends with people they've met through their children. But there are a lot of parents who are wondering how they became friends with these people and who can't wait for their kids to graduate so they and the other parents can quietly go their separate ways. Why? We chose to be with them on the assumption that we have similar values and because we've gone through similar experiences or rites of passage. But as we pass through parenting's rites of passage, it's easy to confuse partners in arms in a given situation or phase with people with whom we truly want to go through life and can depend on.

How do we know what we're looking for in each other? Let's start by looking at two definitions of culture: the one in Webster's dictionary and my own.

> *Webster's definition:* The customary beliefs, social forms, and material traits of a racial, religious, or social group.
> *My definition:* Everything we "know" about the way the world works but have never been taught.

Our culture makes us feel that we have to be and look a certain way so that we belong—regardless of whether we are poor, wealthy, or anywhere in between. It convinces us that we are "less than" unless we participate in the relentless struggle to keep up with or have more than our neighbors. But our culture is not a thing that happens to us. We are the ones who create and sustain it. If cultural values are handed down through generations, it's because we absorb them and act on them without question. Often we don't even realize the degree to which we're constantly pressuring each other to conform to cultural norms. Primed by these powerful cultural messages—in magazines, on television, in movies, in supermarket conversations, from our own parents—we can trick ourselves into believing that there's just one party to go to, one group to belong to, and that if we don't get in and stay in, we don't measure up or risk being thrown out.

As parents, we understand that the culture has great power over our children; they see the latest ad campaign for jeans and are convinced that their lives would be better if they bought them. However, we may not realize that we're no less immune. If you have a car, ask yourself what it says about you. In full, embarrassing disclosure, I bought an SUV because I couldn't tolerate the image of driving a minivan—which would have been a much better choice because they're cheaper and more fuel-efficient.

We also belong to microcultures where there are similar unwritten rules we "just know" we have to follow. Your children's school, your religious institution, your family—all have unwritten rules you must follow to be accepted, and there are penalties for the people who break those rules.

Cultural rule breakers can make others extremely uncomfortable, so most people don't want them around. These people are seen as "other," possibly tolerated but rarely accepted. Very often, rule breakers aren't respected, their opinions and experiences are easily dismissed, and other people don't want to be seen as associated with them, even when they think the rule breakers are right. If we grow up without learning to question the culture, we take a few lessons with us from our youth:

1. You should please the person who has the most power.
2. You should maintain relationships with the people in power.
3. The result of all this pleasing and maintenance will be that you won't say what you need or want.
4. Loyalty is defined as backing up your friends by saying nothing, laughing, or even joining in when their actions are unethical or cruel.
5. You should be silent in the face of cruelty so that the cruelty isn't turned on you.

So how does this affect parents? I think there is a parent culture that takes its cues from the overall culture, tricking us into thinking there is one best, most desirable way to be a parent. I call it Perfect Parent World.

WELCOME TO PERFECT PARENT WORLD

In Perfect Parent World, the kids are perfect. They do their homework without nagging, effortlessly get into all the honors classes, get elected to class offices, and give their parents a steady stream of bragging rights based on their scholastic and athletic accomplishments. In this mythical kingdom, the parents are perfect, too. They're financially stable, wear the right clothes, drive the right cars, never crack under the strain of car pool, offer our peers excellent parenting advice, and have great kids whose pockets are never filled with bad report cards, cigarettes, or Ecstasy.

Our family doesn't do average.
      Tammy, mother of a five-year-old, complaining because her
      son got an E for "excellent" instead of an O for "outstanding"

No one I know actually resides in Perfect Parent World, but most parents I've met—myself included—measure themselves against this impossible standard, and we imagine that the moms and dads with the most power and highest social status occupy that cherished real estate. But who decides who personifies perfection?

One of the primary ways both boys and girls and men and women define who has power and social status is by how our culture defines masculinity and femininity. Girls and boys are introduced to these cultural constructions very early in life. In middle school and high school they build groups based on how closely they perceive their fit into those cultural constructions, which I call Girl World and Boy World.

To understand more about how Girl World and Boy World evolve into their adult parallels, Mom World and Dad World, let's look at three definitions of the word *femininity*—the dictionary's, girls', and parents'.

Dictionary definition: The quality or nature of the female sex.
Girl World definition: You have a great body, guys like you, you're not a prude but you're not a slut, you're in control, and you're smart enough to get people to do what you want—preferably without them noticing.
Mom World definition: You have a relationship with a man, are thin, never had any doubts about having children, and are on top of all your thank-you notes.

Now let's look at how the same three sources define *masculinity*.

Masculinity: The qualities appropriate to, or usually associated with a man, or forming the formal, active, or generative principle of the cosmos. [I swear, my dictionary said this!]
Boy World: You control your friends with a look or a "hey." You effortlessly have the right style and a great body (if it's not effortless or you think too much about it, you'll be accused of being gay), you can laugh

off emotional and physical pain, the right girls like you and you like all attention girls give you, you're competitive about everything, and by five years of age you can discuss professional sports with authority (although it's permissible to trade knowledge of sports for expertise in martial arts or cars).

Dad World: You make lots of money and never worry about the money you spend, you're married and have a good relationship with your wife and kids, if you have a lawn it looks like a baseball diamond, you can fix things, and you're in shape but not *too much* in shape (because then you look like you're trying too hard), and you have a good sense of humor.

ACT LIKE A WOMAN: MOMMY'S LITTLE GIRL GROWS UP

When I work with girls, I explain my definition of culture and then I ask them what they think the culture is trying to persuade them they need to be and look like and what the culture says they shouldn't be. Then I ask them how a girl in their school earns high social status or low social status. I write their answers in for them as the "Act Like a Woman" box.

Shy	Right style	Fat
	Pretty	
	Thin	
Slut	Good hair	
	Popular	
	Nice	No friends
	Confident	
Prude	Money	
	Athletic and cute body	
	Effortlessly perfect	
Gay		Tries too hard

Copyright The Empower Program, 2004

What the girls realize is that their answers about what the culture wants and doesn't want them to be often mirrors the "Act Like a Woman" box they've said exists in their own community.

Now let's compare the girls' answers with the answers mothers told me when I asked them the same question—but directed to them.

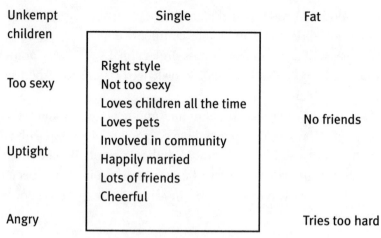

Unkempt children	Single	Fat
Too sexy	Right style Not too sexy Loves children all the time Loves pets Involved in community Happily married Lots of friends Cheerful	No friends
Uptight		
Angry		Tries too hard

Copyright The Empower Program, 2004

As I talked to mothers, it became clear that the unwritten rules were way too extensive for me to do them justice with a box. So here they are in full.

The "Act Like a Mom" Checklist

- She has the right style. She's cute. She stays on top of the latest trends but she's not too sexy.
- She's thin (no matter how many pregnancies).
- She's athletic (five extra points if that includes tennis).
- She's married to a caring, wonderful, wealthy, communicative, handsome man who always treats her like a queen.
- She's always loved having kids (no moments of hating them allowed) and her kids love her.
- She has lots of friends.
- She's involved in the community and is always available for a few more volunteer activities.
- She loves the family pets (no matter how much they shed because the house magically gets rid of all pet hair).
- She has a clean and organized house.
- She drives a family-friendly station wagon, minivan, or SUV that's immaculately clean, no sticky food allowed.
- She's cheerful, not hysterical and anxious.
- She's cooperative.

- She has great skin—no wrinkles, pimples, or the dreaded combination of both.
- She appears to achieve all of the above effortlessly.

Are you simultaneously laughing, cringing, and resentful? Me, too. And just as girls know they're held to an impossible standard of beauty but chase that ideal anyway, mothers know that this ideal is ridiculous but still stay up until 2 a.m. baking cookies for a bake sale instead of buying them on the way to school. The next day at school when someone remarks on what a Wonder Woman we are for baking the cookies, we shrug it off as if the achievement were nothing. Too often we exhaust ourselves trying to keep up, become intolerably defensive about our personal mothering choices, or attack other women by trashing them with our friends (or at least judge them silently) for not making the choices we did. Honestly, this is an old song and we need to learn a new one. So far we have been extremely resistant to change—we're invested in putting each other down. Why? Frankly, we've learned the cultural lessons too well. For the same reasons that we've been doing it since seventh grade, we're doing it now.

I would like to share with you one of my personal challenges in this department. We all have a perfect friend. She's the one who sends out thank-you notes written "by" her newborn within a day of receipt of the baby gift, hand-paints her furniture, makes her own duvet covers, curtains, and pillows, and has every family vacation documented in color-coded photo albums. This friend, through no fault of her own, makes you feel that you're a failure the moment you step into her beautiful, immaculate, and organized house. It makes no difference that you manage to do your job brilliantly on less than four hours of a sleep a day, that you frequently recall your spouse's name, and that you actually remembered to bring the juice and cookies on your kid's snack day—you still feel like a failure.

Do you have a friend like this? I do. Her name is Julie and she was my college roommate. Even then she was organized. Whenever you opened her closets you thought you'd been transported to a Benetton store, while mine looked like Filene's Basement after the Christmas rush. When I stay at her house, I immediately know where everything is; I have no idea where anything in *my* house is. Julie has an MBA and is currently staying at home with her two daughters. Her children's rooms are hand-painted with an exquisitely subtle bee theme in soothing sage, butter, and cream tones. All of the books are neatly arrayed on the shelves. The jigsaw puzzles are complete and stacked in a Montessori-approved set of drawers.

In all fairness to Julie, she's a great person and a wonderful friend. The reason she is both is because she's able to laugh at herself, especially when I point out how insane she is—seriously, getting a thank-you from her week-old baby on her own personalized stationery? I can also, without embarrassment, listen to Def Leppard in her presence.

Here's the thing about Julie: She's totally sympathetic, helpful, and nonjudgmental, yet when I walk into her perfect home I feel that I'm not a good mother because I can't keep it together like she does. Is that pathetic? Of course. Am I embarrassed about it? Absolutely. Would I like to be the woman who basks in her friend's maternal accomplishments without a jot of jealousy? Unfortunately, I'm very far away from the emotional maturity I would need to have that attitude. But admitting it does take some of the sting out. The point is that I'm just as intimidated and resentful of the women who personify that Super Mom image, and I work on these issues for a living.

Of course, I'm not alone. A woman recently admitted to me: "I'm ashamed to admit it, but I've secretly campaigned and strategized since my daughter was born that she would be popular. I'm ashamed, but I think so many of us do this but we won't admit it. I joined mothers' groups when she was three that I thought would start us off on the right foot—get us into the right groups. I arranged play dates and social activities so the right girls would play with her and I would get to know their mothers. Now my daughter is a cheerleader."

Part of the "Act Like a Mom" box is having a child that fits in the "Act Like a Woman" box, too, who reigns supreme in Girl World. Don't we all enjoy a matching set?

ACT LIKE A MAN: DADDY'S LITTLE BOY GROWS UP

When my colleagues and I teach Empower classes to boys, we ask them what characteristics the culture teaches them they have to have. What do they think they need for high social status and what characteristics get them teased? I've put their answers in the "Act Like a Man" box.

Gay   Poser   Weak

Strong
Tough
Funny
Right style
Money
Girls
Athletic
Independent

Sensitive   Not athletic   Like a girl

Copyright The Empower Program, 2004

Now let's look at how dads answered the same question directed to them.

Messy garage and
out-of-control lawn

Loner   Controlled
                                                          by wife
Fixes things
Funny
Can't take   Right style
a joke   Provider   Can't fix
                             Happily married   things
                             Athletic
Doesn't   Talks sports
provide   Mows the lawn   Fat

Copyright The Empower Program, 2004

There is no extended "Act Like a Dad" checklist; the dads I talked to said that the box pretty much summed up their unwritten rules. Why is the moms' list more complicated? As I'll explain in more detail throughout the book, while social pecking orders for men and women are equally powerful, women, like girls, have more complex rules and thus it is easier to make mistakes—which often you know only when you've broken them.

Permission Denied

Obviously we don't come out of the womb believing that being a good parent includes confidently wielding sports metaphors or maintaining a twenty-year-old's body even after we've given birth to three children. Wanting to be good mothers and fathers might be biologically natural, but the way we define good parenting comes from the culture. For example, our DNA doesn't program us to believe that we have to drive a SUV to be caring mothers or fathers, although it might well program us to desire safety for ourselves and our children. The media and what we tell each other convince us that the size of the SUV and the warm cup of coffee we drink while in the SUV signify safety. We have to be taught such ideas.

What is natural is that we want to belong, to feel respected, and to believe that our opinions will be taken seriously by others. The box exercises I describe above are my way of looking at how we are taught which people "deserve" to be treated with dignity or not because they bring to light our hidden cultural rules. They show how we are convinced that the more characteristics we have in the boxes, the more our opinion counts—especially when it runs counter to the opinion of someone with fewer of those characteristics. This dynamic is the basis for how discrimination works in any community.

Given the impossibly high standards of Perfect Parent World, is it any wonder that so many of us find it next to impossible to ask for the help and support we need from other parents? That we don't stand up when we see other parents bully us or others, including other kids, teachers, or coaches? Down deep we fear that the further outside of the box we are perceived by others to be, the less what we say and experience will be believed and taken seriously by others—and that's a frightening realization no matter what your age.

> I'm afraid that if I ask for help and admit my daughter has problems, then those parents will take it back to their kids. Basically, if I ask for help, my child will suffer.   Hal, middle school dad

Understanding these issues involves more than teaching your child to be nice to others or getting along with other parents yourself. They're really about how discrimination and social cruelty can influence your day-to-day life as a parent. In the next two chapters, I'll take a closer look at the adult cliques with which mothers and fathers contend so you can see exactly how you and the other parents in your community fit into Perfect Parent World.

The Apple Doesn't Fall
Far from the Tree, Part 1

Mom Cliques

It's my great privilege to travel around the country and speak to young people, parents, and teachers. When I'm picked up at the airport, I'm often met by someone from the school or organization where I'll be speaking. As this person drives me to my hotel, we talk about their community and my work. After a few minutes of pleasantries—whether I'm in Ohio, Georgia, California, or Australia—the same thing always happens: My driver lowers his or her voice and says, "You know, this Queen Bee stuff doesn't end in high school. Our faculty [PTA, staff, office] is so cliquey. You really need to write about how adults act just like they did in high school."

In fact, teen and adult cliques differ in important ways. Before we dive in, here are some important definitions of *clique:*

Webster's definition: A narrow, exclusive circle or group of persons held together by common interests, views, or purposes.
My definition: A group of people who band together like a platoon of soldiers to survive.

Survive what? Take your pick: adolescence, having children, raising children, working in an office. No matter what the age of the group, there's a chain of command, and from the outside they seem to operate as one. Individual survival is perceived to be and sometimes is based on loyalty to the most powerful member of the group. And just as teen girls refuse to admit that they have cliques but say they know lots of other girls who do, adults are in denial about themselves. Ask parents if parents are exclusive, gossipy, rude, and cliquey, and they'll launch into endless horror stories of *other* parents, but most will refuse to admit that they may be guilty themselves.

It's true that in general we've learned something from the often bruising experiences of our youth, and most of us have more wisdom and perspective. Adult groups can be more flexible on a day-to-day basis. The key thing is that cliques form when we feel pressured to bond to survive a stressful experience—and as I've said, there's not much that's more stressful than parenting. I want to focus on what being in a group or clique teaches us about when to speak out and when to stay silent. It's when conflicts arise between parents that we seem to time-travel back to middle school and become afraid to speak out.

> *What do you do when the other mother thinks that it's all my daughter's fault? What do you do if the mother has been my close friend since the kids were three years old? The kids have been best friends for years. What do you do when my friend gives my daughter a look of hate on a soccer field and my daughter sees this and confronts me? Any tips?* Jane, middle school mom

When a parent tells me pleadingly, "I just want my child to be accepted," it's easy to suppose that she's insecure. But who doesn't want their child to be accepted and popular? When I take my sons to school and see other children run to greet them, my heart swells with happiness. It's hard for us to admit that being popular is important not just to our children but to us, because popularity has negative connotations and the subject often evokes painful memories. But there's nothing wrong with wanting to be popular—to have other people think well of you. So first let's look at the dictionary definition of *popularity* and then put another spin on it.

The dictionary defines *popularity* as "the taste of the majority; widely accepted; commonly liked or approved." I have two definitions of popularity. The first is what girls call "good popularity": when people like you because you're nice to them, are inclusive, act generously, and apologize when you hurt their feelings. The second is what girls call "evil popularity": being liked because you're the powerful Queen Bee. (Picture someone who looks like Barbie and acts like the Queen of Hearts in *Alice in Wonderland*.)

Who, at any age, doesn't want to be commonly liked or approved of? Parents tell me that they despise kids' "popularity contests," but their actions often speak louder than their words. Let's be honest: when our kids are rejected, we often have four feelings, sometimes all at the same time: (1) How dare someone reject my child? (2) Can't they see how wonderful my child is? (3) What is my child doing that's causing his peers to reject him? (4) What mistake have I made that's caused my child to be rejected? Listen to this mother describing her agony and self-blame when her daughter was rejected by her friends:

> *I have spent hours going over the things I did wrong. I should have fired that one babysitter we had two afternoons a week — the one that favored her sister. I should have spent more time playing on the floor with her. I shouldn't have focused on teaching my kids the Broadway musicals I loved so much when the rest of the third graders were focused on the Spice Girls. The list goes on. Why didn't I force her to stay with swimming lessons? Maybe I should have chosen a different nursery school. . . . I used to forgive her shyness and speak for her on occasions when she seemed too quiet to talk. Maybe I should have practiced more "tough love" and forced her to handle certain things on her own.*
>
> *Or maybe not. The irony of her crisis of confidence is that it has become my own crisis. I was once a very confident parent, but I've now begun to question every decision I've ever made. Worse than that, I've begun to question my own daughter! I notice that I'm not only blaming myself, but I'm becoming her critic. What is she doing, I wonder, that would make people reject her? How has she behaved that has caused former friends to turn away? Maybe she's too self-involved. Maybe she's too desperate for friendship. Maybe she's kind of boring. Maybe she— What am I doing, for goodness' sake? She's my daughter and I love her. No, she's not perfect, and she never will be. Am I one of those thirteen-year-old girls myself?*
>
> Pamela, middle school mom

LANDMINE!

If you just read that quote and thought, "That woman just needs to get a life," be careful. Would you still think this is superficial if it were your child who was rejected?

Pamela's words are a great illustration of how many parents feel. We're wise enough to be able to articulate the problem but we can still feel overwhelmed by our own emotional reactions and powerless to make things better for our children. Having these feelings doesn't make us bad parents—it makes us normal parents.

Popularity conveys an illusory sense of power. Even the most level-headed among us catch ourselves thinking that if we achieve it, the skies will clear, the sun will come out, and everything will be great. Some of us become obsessed with it and take daily barometric measures of our popularity, issuing constant weather reports (e-mail and instant messaging help this immeasurably, no matter if you are twelve or forty). Some of us dismiss the issue entirely. Some of us feel left out and angry but deny that we do—which explains why we find ourselves gloating when a celebrity who seemed to have it all falls from grace. In all these ways we resemble teenagers. The difference is that we are less likely to admit just how much we covet it because, as adults, we're supposed to be above such immature longings.

How do we know who's in and who's out? The same way we knew when we were adolescents: We gossip. The dictionary defines *gossip* as "a rumor or report of an intimate nature." I define it as currency we can invest or speculate with in order to gain social power. Think of it this way: If capitalism dictates that whoever has the most money has the most power in the economic marketplace, our culture dictates that the person who commands and controls the choicest gossip has the most power in the social marketplace.

In my first book, I asked girls and boys to help me define the roles within their cliques. While any person's position within the clique is flexible—a girl might be a Queen Bee one week and be overthrown the next, or she might be a Sidekick at school and a Queen Bee at her church group—the positions themselves are well codified. They come from the girls' micro-culture—what they "just know" about the way life within Girl World works. Based on my conversations with parents and my own observations, one thing is clear: Many parents are in denial about their own contribution to the social pecking order and the roles they play. The fact is that many parents, especially in moments of conflict, assume roles akin to the ones they held in cliques when they were growing up. It's important for us to realize that although we can often easily see how other parents fit into these roles, we tend to be considerably more myopic or stubborn than teens in admitting where we fit ourselves.

In this chapter, I'll review the roles for women, which are similar to the roles girls assume before they grow up. I'll separate them into three groups, the Entitled, the Middle of the Pack, and the Left Out, and I'll break down the groups into distinct roles. I'll offer some parent personal-ity profiles—descriptions of particular types of moms you'll spot in the hallways at school. Finally, we'll eavesdrop on some moms dishing the dirt on the dads.

As in *Queen Bees,* I'm describing these roles in hopes that we can bet-ter understand what motivates us. If you identify yourself or someone you know in one particular role, it doesn't mean that you're doomed to stay that way for the rest of your life. However, I do think it can be difficult for adults to change—certainly more than most young people. As far as I can tell, the main reason is that we've mastered the art of rationalizing even our craziest behavior, and we're more fearful of giving up a prime posi-tion if we have it. Also, unlike young people, we don't want to admit to ourselves that we're still struggling with these issues; admitting it seems shameful, weak, and unforgivable.

When adults do change roles, it's usually because we've come to real-ize that they're hindering our ability to have emotionally honest relation-ships. Queen Bee Moms can decide it isn't worth being at the top of the social ladder because it means losing who they truly are in an effort to keep that ever-present smile on their faces and fulfill what they assume are other people's expectations of them. Those who have been Left Out can step into the limelight. No one likes being labeled—including me—but I believe that putting names to these cultural constructs can give us insight into group dynamics and into ourselves. Once you've figured out the emotional price you've paid for assuming a certain role, you can work on achieving three goals: reciprocal relationships with others in which you feel respected and valued, work inside and outside the home that reflects these relationships, and being an amazing parent. Life will still be messy—because it always is—but the process will feel a lot better.

THE ENTITLED

Queen Bee Moms

Queen Bee Moms, like their younger counterparts, appear to have perfect lives. They're socially intelligent and often very charming, and they really, really like being in charge. They're often the designated "spirit squad" of the teams, class parents, or heads of the PTA, school board, or class play. We may not like their naked grab for world domination, but let's be honest—we can't trash them outright. Queen Bee Moms are the ones who get the job done. I also want to be careful here, because not every PTA president is a Queen Bee Mom who'll hit you over the head with her clipboard if you challenge her. The hallmark sign of a Queen Bee Mom is not that she's in a leadership position; it's that she *has* to be in control. Here are some other telltale signs:

- She organizes her children's social activities 24/7. No free time is allowed.
- If other parents don't like her, "that's because they're jealous."
- If someone else is in charge of something, it's because the Queen Bee Mom has explicitly permitted it and even then, whatever "it" is, it has to be done her way.
- She's extremely skilled at telling confidential sad/bad stories about another parent, child, teacher, or administrator—but she doesn't see this as gossiping. She shares the hard-luck story with the understanding that the person in question should be pitied, but her not-so-hidden message is that the person is pathetic, incompetent, and/or a social liability.
- When she or her child includes you or your child, you feel like you're special, you've made it. On the other hand, if you or your

child has a run-in with her or her child, your dread of dealing with the situation propels you right back to junior high school.

- Her parenting philosophy is "Let's let the kids work it out"—until it's her kid who's being wronged. Then she's all over you like white on rice. When her child gets into trouble, this mom always believes her child's version of the story. There are no two-way streets in this woman's world; her child's spin is gospel.
- She won't apologize for her child's behavior. She sees other children as overly sensitive. The other child just "took it the wrong way." Or she excuses her child's bad behavior by saying, "That's just what kids do. All kids do that."
- If she or her child does apologize for something, a return apology is expected. When a Queen Bee Mom does apologize, she does it in a way that explicitly communicates that she's apologizing out of the goodness of her heart because you're so pathetic: "Well, I'm so sorry that *you* took it the wrong way."

Despite some similarities, Queen Bee Moms are not simply grown-up Queen Bee girls. Queen Bee Moms will band together to exert their power; Queen Bee girls tend to view their position as a zero-sum game— if I have power, you don't—so they usually don't team up. From what I've observed, Queen Bee Moms have it worse than adolescent girls because they feel like they have more to lose—their way of life will be taken away from them if they don't uphold the "mission statement" of the household. The threat of loss doesn't have to be explicit; it's the sense that they have no self-worth without these things. Queen Bee Moms believe that they *are* their mothering; it's what you are, not who you are. They're brilliant at rationalizing their Queen Bee behavior.

In fact, this very type of rationalization is a hallmark of Queen Beeism. Everything Queen Bee Moms do is based on a "higher" reason: acting in the best interest of their kids, upholding family values, and being a good wife and mother. The problem is that they convince themselves that this nobler reason justifies really obnoxious behavior. Queen Bee Moms are often their own worst enemy because they can't admit when they need help or feel overwhelmed. When Queen Bee Moms are happy, they're full of smiles and warmth. When they're angry, they're most likely sitting with arms tightly folded across their chests, legs crossed tightly beneath them. When they're sharing their opinion, their entire torsos are straining forward like they're about to spring out of the starting gate. These are postures of barely contained anger; Queen Bee Moms believe they can never be out of control. They don't allow themselves to be overtly aggressive in public, so their body language speaks for them.

Queen Bee Moms aren't dangerous to you or your child as long you don't challenge them. The problem, according to Nikki Crick, one of the foremost researchers on girls' aggression, is that one of the inherent characteristics of Queen Bee girls is that they perceive more hostile intent than other people. I don't think it's too much of a stretch to extend that to Queen Bee Moms. For example, if a Queen Bee Mom was watching her daughter play in a soccer game and another player accidentally kicked her daughter but didn't get a red card, the mother would be more likely to believe that the kick was intentional and/or that the referee was deliberately favoring the other team.

Sidekick Moms

Sidekick Moms, like their teen counterparts, define themselves in relation to a more powerful peer. Sidekick Moms are the second in command beneath the Queen Bee Moms and usually less socially intelligent (that's why they take their cues from the Queen Bee). Unlike girl Sidekicks, who can overthrow the Queen Bee and ascend to the throne, Sidekick Moms are much more likely to stick to their place. A Sidekick Mom typically:

- Organizes her child's social calendar so he or she is in the same activities as the Queen Bee Mom's child.
- Forces (she would say "encourages") her child to be friends with the Queen Bees in the class or the child of the Queen Bee Mom.
- Finds any and all opportunities to share her child's latest accomplishments but is careful not to overshadow the Queen Bee's child (unless she's staging a coup).
- Bases her parenting philosophy on "Let's let the kids work it out"— until it's her child who's being wronged.

- Won't usually apologize for her child's behavior unless the "wronged" child or his or her parents are considered to have higher social status or there is no social or other cost. Then she is graciousness personified, although with parents of lesser status she might excuse her child's behavior at the same time. She may rescind her apology if it becomes inconvenient or politically necessary.
- Is very focused on getting her child into the "right" class, with the "right" teacher, the "right" social activities, etc., and sees her motivation as solely based on acting in the best interests of her child.
- Joins in when other parents gossip about another child, parent, or teacher.
- Can start gossip but looks to the Queen Bee Mom for affirmation.
- Eagerly joins petitions to fight the school at the behest of more powerful parents.

Starbucks & Sympathy Moms, aka Banker Moms

Have you ever had someone approach you after you've had an unpleasant encounter with someone else and offer to be a source of comfort, agree with your assessment of the confrontation, and then turn on you at a convenient (for them) time? That's what Starbucks & Sympathy Moms—aka Banker Moms—do. They're very smart but also good at hiding it. Their strength is figuring out where people feel vulnerable, gathering information, and spreading it when it's most advantageous to themselves.

Queen Bee Moms also use gossip strategically, but they're more clearly trying to run the show; Starbucks & Sympathy Moms are happy to have their position based solely on their ability to wield power behind the scenes. What types of information are currency to Banker Moms? Try these: Who's starting on the team? Who got the lead in the play? Who really should have gotten the lead and why didn't they get it? Who got into which high school or college? How much money did the parents give to get said child into that school or college? Which girl on the soccer team has an eating disorder? Which boy was caught cheating? I am sure you could add a few.

While S&S Moms aren't as easy to spot as Queen Bee Moms, never underestimate them. They gain their status by spreading information in such a way as to create a generalized state of anxiety in which hearsay becomes fact and is acted on accordingly. An S&S Mom lets it be known that she heard that so-and-so's kid is a starter on the team only because his parents paid for the uniforms. Her rumor will spread virally to the parents of the other teammates. Some will find themselves wondering whether they should have ponied up money for new team sweats; others will start talking because they believe their kid is a better athlete and deserved the starting slot; some will begin to attack the coach's integrity. Soon the coach's authority and leadership are entirely undermined.

Starbucks & Sympathy Moms are sneaky—but you know whose radar they *don't* sneak under? Your child's—he or she is on to her.

> We all know which parents are gossiping about which kids are doing what. I don't think the other parents get it, but it can be just like when we were in sixth grade.   Jen, high school sophomore

> A lot of the rumors that kids pass around stem from things that they've heard their parents say. There are those parents who know everything about everyone and don't restrain themselves from exaggerating the truth at times. Often when two parents are mad at each other they begin to spread rumors about their opponent's daughter. They'll pass these rumors along when they're driving a car pool around, or when there's a group of kids over. Parents also fight by dropping little snide comments in public places that embarrass the other parent.   Naomi, high school sophomore

Middle of the Pack

Torn Wannabes and Desperate Wannabes

Wannabe Moms, like their girl counterparts, are looking for opportunities to raise their stock in the social marketplace—which often means selling someone else short. They're the ones who support you in private but say nothing or even take the opposite stance in public. They spread gossip for the same reason. The biggest difference between adolescent and adult Wannabes is that the adults can be more self-aware about their desire for higher social status and understand at some level that this isn't an attractive quality. On a conscious level, this causes them to behave in self-rationalizing ways. There are two types of Wannabes—those who know better but can't help themselves (Torn Wannabes) and those who don't know better and act just like they're twelve (Desperate Wannabes).

Torn Wannabes are unpredictable and frustrating, and usually everyone has a good friend who falls squarely into this category. She's the woman who privately supports you 100 percent when you're in conflict with another person but abandons you at the moment of confrontation. She never tells you exactly what she thinks. It's not that she's being deceptive (at least she doesn't see her behavior as such); usually she genuinely doesn't know what she thinks because she wants to please the person in front of her and/or the person with the most power in the room.

She's a great rationalizer of her behavior and gets herself off the hook when her actions don't match what she knows she should have done. Her words and actions are often contradictory, since she might know what the right thing is but then does what benefits her the most. She's a conflict avoider—at all costs. Still, one-on-one, she can be a great friend. That's why you're still friends with her, even if she's disappointed you.

The Desperate Wannabe is easier to dislike. Unlike the Torn Wannabe, she hasn't matured to the point where she realizes when her actions don't match her purported values. One bonus is that she isn't unpredictable. She will *always* please the person with the most power and she will *always* back that person up. The Desperate Wannabe can also come across as full of herself; she's not good at editing herself because she's so desperate for you to know that she and her family belong.

She frets a lot about whether she, and by extension her child, is keeping up. She's a name-dropper. Like the Torn Wannabe, she's a conflict avoider, but when she can't escape, she can be really nasty. You recognize that her anxiety over losing her position is what drives her crazy behavior, but you'll fail to empathize after she spreads gossip that is usually unbelievably exaggerated about you or someone you know—perhaps even your child. But one of the most obvious signs of her position is her need to be in the center of things.

This woman, who used to be my best friend, decided she was going to start a book group. And so she put out a list of people, and I shared with another friend that I'd been asked to go to this book group. And she said, "Why am I not on that list?" And so she asked the other mom, who said, "Well you're not a third-grade mom," which was a bunch of bunk because there were three or four women who were not third-grade moms. I wrote to this mom and said, "Why can't you put this mom on the alternate list if you have too many people?" She did not respond to that. I almost think I should call and say I can't go. You know I don't like this. But I'm curious. I'm obviously one of the cool moms since I was invited.   Hilary, elementary school mom

Steamrolled Moms

Unfortunately, the Steamrolled Mom acts pretty much exactly like her younger counterpart, the Pleaser. She sacrifices her needs and judgment because she wants to avoid conflict; she's the one who's always saying, "Whatever you want is fine" or "It doesn't matter to me." She's unlikely to stand up for what she thinks is right because she's afraid to offend and wants to be "nice." As an adult, she may be more reluctant to admit her situation because she knows it looks pathetic, but she's been so beaten down by the relationships in her life that she doesn't think she can speak out. When she does get up the courage to say something, she's likely to salt her words with apologies. She can't even imagine confronting someone directly. Steamrolled Mom can be so reluctant to disagree with anyone else that she gets rolled right over by other parents—and even her own kids. When she hears gossip from other parents, she'll stay silent even if she disagrees. Then on the drive home, she'll rehearse all the things she wished she'd said, continuing the conversation in her head while in the shower, when she puts her head down on the pillow, etc. She may take out her frustration over her own silence on her spouse, who will likely say with a mixture of love and exasperation, "Would you just either *do* something about this or be quiet!"

Floater Moms

Floater Moms enjoy the same freedom Floater kids do; they can move easily from one group to another without arousing resentment. They embody "nice popularity" in that they're genuinely liked for who they are. The Floater Mom dresses "appropriately"—she doesn't stand out. Ann Taylor and the Gap are her friends. If she has a lot of money, you wouldn't know it. Her house isn't over the top, her car isn't fancy, and she isn't buying her kid a car as soon as he turns sixteen. A lot of parents fall into this category, but here's the catch: You might assume that Floaters are generally the peacemakers, but I haven't found that this role is exclusive to them. In fact, I've seen Queen Bee Moms become peacemakers because they have the power to call an armistice.

So in spite of the fact that Floaters are genuinely cool, they rarely take a public leadership role. In fact, when you compare teen Floaters with their adult counterparts to see who's more willing to exert positive peer pressure, the young people pretty much win every time.

Why? Because Floater Moms have the understandable attitude that they went through this ridiculous drama when they were girls and they're not going to waste their time on a parent who still acts like she's running for prom queen. A Floater kid, on the other hand, has to be with other Entitled kids all the time—in class, assemblies, sports, student council, art class, lunch, gym, etc.—so he or she is more motivated to speak out.

Reformed Moms

Reformed Moms are moms who have done the necessary self-reflection to be able to analyze their behavior and make improvement when and where necessary. If they were Entitleds when they were younger, they've gotten over their sense of superiority. I love these moms—especially the ones who used to be Queen Bees—because they often have the best sense of humor. Reformed Queen Bees are great for a lot of reasons. They've kept all their positive attributes (they're charismatic, fun to be around, intelligent, capable, and able to make fun of themselves) and lost most of the attributes that made everyone (including themselves) miserable. Listen to two of them:

I was definitely a Queen Bee running the show. They called me Julie McCoy [from Love Boat*]. Now I feel less cool, that is for sure. If I was as cool now as when I was fifteen, I would be a terrible mother.*

Miranda, middle school mom

I was a Queen Bee when my child was in high school. I feel better now because I feel calmer, more sure of my friends, but I still need to make amends to a lot of people.   Daphne, high school mom

Reformed Moms aren't Floaters because they still hang out with pretty much one social group, and also they don't have to be Queen Bees. There are lots of former Sidekicks, Wannabes, and Outcasts walking around today who have become genuinely amazing women whom you want as friends as you go through parenthood. They can laugh at themselves while at the same time feeling secure in their core beliefs. They have strong convictions but are open to listening to others' opinions. They can look back and honestly take stock of what they appreciated and valued about their own parents while understanding but not harboring resentment over any failings.

This doesn't mean that Reformed Moms don't have moments where they revert back to old behavior, but when they're called on it, they can admit it, apologize if necessary, and move on.

THE LEFT OUT

Invisible Moms

Invisible Moms are good, well-meaning parents who try to attend all the school functions and never, ever say a word. They have a few close friends within the school and usually one or two close friendships with other Invisible parents. They need not belong to any particular race, ethnicity, or other grouping. Invisible kids can see their ability to fade into the background as a kind of superpower; they don't get picked on so much because no one notices them. However, adult Invisibles often seem more uncomfortable with their choice not to take on the more powerful parents. I've seen these parents so often, hugging the back wall in the auditorium, sitting silently. I've made direct appeals to them to speak out against the Entitled parents, but they let me know, mostly by downcast eyes, that they couldn't possibly imagine doing so. I once had an open confrontation with some amazingly powerful Queen Bee Moms. Afterward, two mothers approached me to say they were ashamed that the other mothers had spoken to me as they had. My response to them was, "Look, I had to deal with these parents tonight, but your kids are in this class, so you have to deal with them much more than I do. I can only do so much. If you feel so strongly about it, talk to the school, talk to them." Their response was "We just can't. It's too hard."

Outcast Moms

Outcast Moms are out of it; they don't live in the "right" neighborhood, don't go to the "right" church, or are raising their children alone. They might have been Targets as teens, but not always. As I'll discuss in Chapter 4, a woman who goes through a divorce, particularly when her financial stability suffers, can easily find herself an Outcast—especially when she previously enjoyed high social status. Outcast Moms and Dads would be invisible except that they have characteristics that highlight their difference or "otherness." They might be gay parents living in politically conservative communities, or people of a minority religion living in a community with a religious majority. But it's not just conservative communities who "other" people. Liberal, secular communities can discriminate against Outcast parents in exactly the same way. Conservative parents who send their children to more liberal schools because of their academic excellence or overtly religious people in a secular community can feel just as excluded and dismissed as their peers in the opposite dynamic. Like Outcast kids, Outcast Moms are vulnerable to dismissal or attack even if they don't speak out or call attention to themselves. However, like their younger counterparts, Outcast Moms can also enjoy the freedom of not having to worry about the social pecking order, which means they can sometimes take the risk of speaking out; what do they have to lose?

Socially Challenged Moms

As an educator, one of the more heartbreaking and difficult things to watch in school is a child with social skill deficits. For a variety of reasons, he or she can't read other people's social cues—cues that are obvious to others. Some of these children carry this problem into adulthood. You may have dealt with a parent like this—someone who stands a little too close when he or she talks to you, who interrupts and then monopolizes conversations, who doesn't seem to realize the seemingly obvious signs that other people are bored, irritated, or put off by his or her mannerisms or behavior. Children with social skill deficits can suffer horribly because other children often exclude or bully them. Parents with these issues usually fare better because other adults are more tolerant, but they are often still ostracized. A mother who falls into this category seems to suffer more than a father because moms are usually more involved in their children's social lives, so she'll have more opportunities to feel the sting of exclusion by the other mothers. A father who is awkward in this way is usually ignored or tolerated by the other fathers, who tend to write him off as that weird guy they don't have to take seriously.

The Great Mom Divide

I was a lawyer for ten years before stopping to take care of children and my husband is still a practicing lawyer. When I am advocating for my children, I prepare. [During a school meeting] I practice what I am going to say. I have points one, two, and three, the way I used to prepare for a judge and a jury. I wear darker, more serious clothes. I want them to know that this is a smart mom. But when I get there I quickly stray from my plan because all I want them to see is how I think my child is wonderful. . . . I can hear my voice on the verge of tears and I think to myself, "Get a grip, woman!"

I have struggled for ten years about leaving my work and staying home. . . . People say to me, "What a waste! Don't you want to carry the torch for your daughter?" As much as that makes me mad, I worry. When my eight-year-old daughter says she wants to stay at home when she's a mommy just like me, I tell her she can be anything she wants to be and I remind her that mommy was an attorney. But my being at home is what she knows.

Lily, elementary school mom

There's one issue that divides women as much as cliques: staying at home or working outside the home. This is something women love to talk about, but they rarely say what they really feel, and it's difficult for them to agree on anything here. When I speak to mothers from both groups, I'm struck by how fearful we are of being judged by others. We all suffer from it. The process starts during pregnancy. Many of our mothers nursed highballs and puffed away through their pregnancies, but we are hectored by an avalanche of how-to books promising the perfect baby if we reform everything from our diet to our birth plan. Don't get me wrong—I'm not suggesting we should cultivate unhealthy habits. But it's ridiculous to judge ourselves and each other so harshly if the lone piece of sushi, wedge of unpasteurized cheese, or sip of wine makes it past our lips. We lock ourselves into unspoken competitions about who can gain the least weight, eat the healthiest diet, have the most drug-free delivery.

But it's after our babies are born that we are at our most judgmental. It's then that the ultimate test of motherhood arrives: Are you a working mom or a stay-at-home mom? This is what I hear from women who work about women who stay at home with their kids:

- They live their lives through their children; it's all they talk about.
- They won't ever admit that staying at home can be boring and un-satisfying. Worse, they can be very irritating when they make comments about "how staying at home isn't a sacrifice." They "wouldn't miss out on these precious moments with their kids for any job in the world—because you know you can't get those moments back."
- They have too much time on their hands—which is why they get so worked up about small problems with their children.
- They're possessive about their husbands and have "traditional marriages" where the husband is the sole authority of the house.

And this is what I hear from stay-at-home moms about women who work outside the home:

- They look down on women who stay at home; they think whatever's going on in their lives is the most important—especially because they think they have so much more going on in their lives.
- They assume they should and will get their way because they're smarter and more capable than stay-at-home moms.
- They're scattered and anxious and are really self-righteous about it.
- They're irresponsible—always picking their children up late, giving their children too much freedom, letting them play at other houses unsupervised.

Of course, women in both groups harbor ideas about the fantasy lives they imagine the other women enjoy. Women working outside the home often believe that stay-at-home moms have much more intimate relationships with their children. Stay-at-home moms often romanticize the intellectual challenges of working life while privately fearing that lack of adult companionship has caused their IQs to drop. In reality, most women are ambivalent about the choices they've made (again, if they're lucky enough to have a choice), so we have that in common. Another commonality is that the conflicts we have with other mothers, regardless of the content of the conflict, are often made worse by these judgments. We assume the other mother doesn't respect our opinion because we don't work, or we are defensive because we assume the other mother thinks we put our job before our family. It goes on and on.

Can we please declare a cease-fire? Okay, here's the deal: If you work outside the home and you have a satisfying job—which I would define as having two or more of the following: being fairly paid, feeling encouraged for showing initiative, being creative, working with colleagues you respect, and being allowed to fulfill your family obligations without being penalized—this is good for you and your family. If you aren't in a job like this (and many aren't) or if you let that job take over your life to the degree that it's turned you into an anxious, self-centered mess who often thinks of herself as a martyr or the most important person in the room, this isn't good for you or your family, and it'll be hard for you to provide a positive role model for your children. You won't be teaching your children that women who work outside the home are worthy of respect. Plus chances are high that when your children are grown, they'll bring someone home who is very different from you and you'll take it personally.

If you stay at home with your children (and yes, I believe wholeheartedly that staying at home with your kids is work, but I'm not going to patronize you by being politically correct and calling it "work inside the home") and you explore activities that give you personal satisfaction and interact meaningfully with different people in your community, this is also a good thing and allows you to be a powerful role model for your children. If you live your life primarily through your loved ones, feel underappreciated and disrespected, are not intellectually or spiritually challenged, and believe that because you don't work and contribute to the family income you don't deserve to have as much authority in your marriage or as a mother, this is not a good thing. You're teaching your children that women who stay at home to take care of their families aren't worthy of respect. And I know you aren't staying at home because you want people to walk all over you.

So that's it in a nutshell. Both options for parenting can be great and both can spell trouble. The only way to be sure you've made the right choice—again, if you're lucky enough to have the choice—is to explore these very difficult issues.

ANN TAYLOR ANTHROPOLOGY 101: PERSONALITY PROFILES FOR MOMS

Many parents shared with me that one of the most helpful parts of *Queen Bees* was the parent personality profiles. Here I'll share customized profiles for moms with some valuable clues to their most common dress and behavior based on observations by mothers all over the country:

Tennis Skirt Mom

She seems to be the first that comes to everyone's mind. Many teens described this woman to me by saying, "From the back you can't tell if she's a girl or a mom." She's the one who always comes to school in a tennis outfit—no matter what the season, no matter what the time. On the rare occasions when she wears street clothes, she's dressed to the nines. She always has a sunny smile on her face and describes herself as "busybusybusy," caught up in a frantic whirlwind of activity—tennis, the gym, lunch, the nail salon. (If you happen to pick up your kids at school while wearing your workout clothes, that doesn't automatically mean you're a Tennis Skirt Mom. But if you're always wearing a perfectly coordinated outfit, with perfect makeup and not a hair out of place, I don't know what kind of workout you're doing, but you're a Tennis Skirt Mom. And don't use the excuse that you "like to look presentable." You know what I'm talking about.) She's a Queen Bee or Sidekick.

Hip Mom

She's so desperate to be liked that she lets her kids transgress every possible boundary, often helping them over the fence by allowing (or even providing) the alcohol ("Hey, they're gonna drink no matter what I say, so they might as well do it under my roof so I can keep an eye on them") or ponying up expensive gifts or bribes. The kids find her easy to manipulate and seldom respect her. The other parents know that when the cops pull up to bust the kids for alcohol, the lights on the squad car will be flashing in front of her house. She's a Wannabe.

Hovercraft Mom

"How was the party? Were they nice to you? Who was there?" "Excuse me, I just want to make sure my daughter signed up for the play [the right honors course, the soccer team]." Hovercraft Mom is convinced her child can't fly the plane alone and so she's constantly hovering nearby, micromanaging the kid's every move and checking to be sure every one of her directives was followed. She bristles when school administrators or friends suggest she might be a tad too controlling. Her anxiety guides every decision and all behavior. Teachers and other parents roll their eyes in annoyance, but the person who is most annoyed is usually her child. She's a Wannabe or an Outcast.

Proud-to-be-a-Pain Mom

"The school did *what?* And no one's doing anything about it?" "The coach said *that?* And no one's calling him on it?" "Those kids were making out in the *hall,* and no one's stopping them?" This mother is the one who steps up, especially when other parents are standing around dumbfounded, and takes action—"Well, we'll see about *that*"—even if her kids are cringing nearby: "Oh, God, it's Mom again."

One Proud-to-be-a-Pain Nebraska Mom told how she'd dropped in on her children's high school dance. The DJ was making out with his girlfriend while these towering midwestern dads looked on, obviously uncomfortable but saying nothing. The chaperone committee was oblivious, too, so the mother took it upon herself to march right up to the DJ and tell him that what he was doing wasn't acceptable. When he didn't stop, she turned on the lights and unplugged the music. Of course, her kids, blinking in the suddenly glaring lights along with a hundred of their peers, said, "It's *got* to be Mom."

The truth is, Proud-to-be-a-Pain Mom enjoys her role as gladiator. And secretly, her kids often enjoy it, too. Someone's got to do the dirty work. She's a Queen Bee or a Reformed.

Closed-Book Mom

You could be this woman's best friend and it's all around town that she and her husband are in counseling or that her daughter has an eating disorder or got pregnant—but you'll never hear it from her. I've found that many Closed-Book Moms learned not to trust other girls when they were teens and have carried that mistrust into adulthood. Closed-Book Mom believes that family problems should stay within the family, and she'll shut down your friendly inquiry with an icy stare or quick change of subject. Her kids learn that it's shameful to ask for help. She's a Banker and/or a Queen Bee.

Don't-Ask, Don't-Tell Mom

She just doesn't want to know. Not from her kids, not from you. She's just hoping for the best; what she doesn't know won't hurt her. This mom often feels overwhelmed because she lacks a strong support system within her own house, with other parents, or within her extended community. She feels out of control because she doesn't think she could handle the problem effectively. She's a Wannabe or Steamrolled Mom.

Benign Neglect Mom

She's so exhausted and distracted by work and other obligations that she's wildly inconsistent with discipline, rules, and enforcement. You like her because she's interesting and smart, but you hold your breath when your kid goes over to her house for a play date or a party. She's an Invisible or a Floater.

Spirit Mom

She lives her life through her kids. She constantly puts her kids' needs, and by extension the school's needs, before her own. She's the one filling out the roster for the travel soccer team, staffing the concession stand at the football game, and doing every other thankless task. She deserves gratitude for all the invaluable service she performs, but she runs the risk of overidentifying with her spirit activities and letting them be a stand-in for her self-worth. She's a Wannabe or a Sidekick.

The All-Boy Mom

There are two versions of this mom, strong and weak. If you're the strong version, I would walk down a dark alley or go to a Back-to-School Night with you anytime. A strong All-Boy Mom has sturdy boundaries with her sons and communicates directly, whether she's yelling up the stairs or chatting at the dinner table. She's straightforward and confident, has a good sense of humor, and is flexible. She usually has a supportive husband or partner or is parenting solo. Her sons are likely to grow up respectful and have a healthy fear of disappointing her; they'll make good boyfriends, husbands, and fathers.

The weak version is exactly her opposite: She has a really hard time standing her ground as baseballs are thrown around the house. She feels defeated when her sons break furniture, art, or walls or when they openly disrespect her, especially if the boys' father doesn't back her up. Then her boys have no respect for her—or any other women either. Strong are Floaters or Reformed. Weak are Wannabe Sidekicks.

The All-Girl Mom

It's her and the girls. The strong version of All-Girl Mom really enjoys all the fun girl stuff and is a great role model for her daughters. She can be a great confidante for her girls, and her daughter's friends are likely to come to her for advice as well. The weaker version has double duty pulling warring sisters apart. In fact, as her daughters grow, they can develop their own miniature Girl World within the family, where one girl can be a Queen Bee and another a Target. A weak All-Girl Mom can often feel helpless to stop the bullying or even recognize that it's a serious problem (which it is). Strong are Floaters or Reformed, weak are Wannabes and Sidekicks.

No-Privacy Mom

She's the one who reveals how she found dirty magazines under her son's bed or caught her daughter stuffing her bra. She invites dinner guests into intimate family disputes even as the kids cringe in horror or leave the table in fury. Her unbridled disclosures cross the line from typical parent chitchat to true invasion of privacy, making the listener as uncomfortable as the parties being tattled on. She's a Wannabe or an Outcast.

Sound-the-Alarm Mom

Even the most tolerant parents roll their eyes and groan when she opens her mouth. Her kid didn't get the right teacher, the school board has the wrong budget priorities, they shouldn't have changed the parent pickup procedure, whoever picked the upcoming class play was insane. She might have legitimate concerns, but her poor social skills make it impossible for her to be taken seriously. Sometimes a new or inexperienced teacher or administrator might take her too seriously at first; alternatively, she might be dismissed when there really is a problem because she's cried wolf once too often. A good head of school or teacher needs to work with her to give her the structures and skills to register her complaints and concerns properly. She's either a Queen Bee or an Outcast; it depends how much money she has.

Mousy Mom

She's prone to wearing baggy clothes and comfortable shoes that completely humiliate her thirteen-year-old daughter. She usually has a genuinely good relationship with her daughter but she can become a huge embarrassment when her daughter reaches adolescence, although her daughter can be very protective of her at the same time (sons often feel the same way). Mousy Mom has a few good parent friends in her child's class. When she was in middle and high school, she always thought the popular kids were on a different planet; she finds the popular moms just as alien. In addition, while she's often extremely intelligent, she's also self-deprecating. If she has time to help with school activities, other parents may completely take advantage of her so that she ends up doing all the work and getting little of the credit. She's an Invisible.

Best-Friend Mom

This is the mom who comes up to me at PTA meetings and parent coffees to brag that her kid tells her everything and would never do anything she didn't approve of and the two of them are the best of friends. She lacks the social intelligence to realize how annoying she is to the other parents when she confesses, "I don't know what we did to be so lucky, but we never have problems with our Sam." She's a Wannabe or a Sidekick.

Pushover Mom

"No . . . I said no. . . . I *mean* it, *no!* . . . Oh, okay." The kids congregate like sharks around this mother, and other moms are very wary of her, knowing that she's the rampart that will get stormed first when the kids

MOMS ON DADS

Mothers don't agree on much but we do agree on how the fathers of children don't do enough. When I get a group of women together to talk about these issues, first there are complaints all around—he acts like a child, he can't do the simplest thing correctly. Then, after all the complaints, one mom will say something like, "Well, he really does a lot of the housework and he's so good with the kids. I wouldn't have married him if he weren't so wonderful." And then all the other women concur.

So which is it? Are the dads unhelpful and incompetent or are they great husbands and fathers who really pitch in? Let's let some moms weigh in:

I don't let my husband organize the soccer schedules. I can't depend on him, so I don't. I'll be lying on my deathbed and I'll still be making plans.

My husband loads the dishes and then expects accolades. For what? He does it wrong anyway.

My husband can't even handle keeping up with my daughter's social life. For a little while my daughter gave him a scorecard of her friends—who was in and who was out.

Husbands and fathers get credit for doing the least little things. I went away for a week and while I was away the mothers on the block organized dinners for my kids. They threw a barbecue for him. Does anyone throw a barbecue for me? Then my husband told me he went to the grocery store with the kids and they were acting up and everyone was so helpful. If the kids had been acting up with me, people would have avoided me, left my line, or glared at me.

Men will do it differently. But we can't complain about them not doing their fair share if we won't let them. And we don't let them because we think we should be the ones who do it—whatever it is.

The last quote really helps me to understand what's behind women's contradictory feelings. The "Act Like a Woman" box teaches you to reject the image of the powerless housewife and mother but simultaneously tells you that a good mother is still in charge of family logistics and relationships. We can't let go or we think we have failed in our primary responsibility as mother—including the way we want the dishes stacked in the dishwasher. It comes down to this: If we want the men in our lives to do equal work, we have to demand it and then let them do it; even if that means they do it differently than we would. We also have to acknowledge how these dynamics are impacting our relationships with the men with whom we are intimate and raising children. Otherwise, we do a disservice to them, our children, and ourselves.

want something. On the other hand, she's the go-to girl for the doggiest of dog jobs connected with those annoying fund-raisers. She's a Wannabe.

Boobs-on-Parade Mom

Why oh why is she wearing that low-cut sweater to her son's basketball game? And why does she have so much mascara on? The mothers are suspicious of her, while the fathers scope her out (or so the moms think). Her kids are embarrassed; she's oblivious to their feelings, doesn't care, or maybe even resents her children for being too uptight. You catch yourself judging her harshly, thinking she's trashy, and then you wonder: Are you just jealous of her body? What's wrong with looking sexy? Since most moms can't tolerate the inner turmoil she generates, she's usually an Outcast.

Do boys and men belong to cliques? If so, can they even begin to approach the social sophistication of the ones to which girls and women belong? Absolutely, although the way fathers band together differs in some important ways from the way mothers do. I'll describe this in the next chapter.

The Apple Doesn't Fall
Far from the Tree, Part 2

Dad Totem Poles

Sweetwater Middle School wants to implement a new program as part of its seventh-grade life skills curriculum. As usual, the school has given the parents an opt-out option if they don't want their children to participate. But for a few parents, the opt-out isn't good enough; they don't want the program at all. The students are overscheduled as it is, and last year's test scores, which will determine their children's track in high school, were horrible—especially compared to those in Rosedale, the neighboring town. And how much does the school know about the counselor teaching the program anyway? What are her credentials? When the principal gets concerned phone calls from the usual parents on both sides, she schedules a meeting so that the counselor can explain the program and give the parents an opportunity to ask questions.

The morning of the meeting, the phone rings in the counselor's office:

DAVID SMITH: *Does the Board of Education know what you're doing?*

COUNSELOR: *Excuse me? Hello, may I help you?*

DAVID SMITH: *This is David Smith (pregnant pause because he assumes the counselor knows who he is, which she doesn't) and I asked you if the Board of Education approves of what you're doing. What is this life skills thing anyway?*

COUNSELOR (*making the mistake of thinking that this is a conversation instead of thanking David Smith for his concern and referring him to the*

principal): *Well, sir, this is a pilot program that the school is very excited about. Other schools in the area have used it with great success.*

DAVID SMITH: *Really? Which schools? I think it's obvious that those students are a little different than ours. And I want to know what gives you
the right to experiment on our children. What are your credentials that
you've been given the responsibility for teaching this program?*

COUNSELOR (*increasingly flustered*): *I have an MSW. . . . I've been teaching and overseeing enriched curriculum for more than ten years at
Sweetwater. . . . I've been— You know, you should talk to the principal
and come to the meeting tonight.*

DAVID SMITH: *I absolutely plan to be at the meeting tonight. I'm not going
to let some untested program waste Chelsea's time.*

Far more than the usual ten parents show up for the meeting that
night—and it's clear that battle lines have been drawn. The counselor
and principal scan the gathering for David Smith, but they're not sure
who he is because he's never come to a single meeting before; they've always dealt with Chelsea's mom, who seems quiet but nice. But there's no
mistaking David Smith when he arrives in his navy blue suit and power
tie. He sits down in the front row of the auditorium, ready for battle.
Some of the other dads know him and inwardly groan when they see him.
If they'd known he was going to be there, they never would have agreed to
come. He can be such a jerk.

After the principal describes the program, she asks if the parents have
questions and concerns. David Smith raises his hand and says in an incredibly patronizing tone, "I think we all want to know why on earth
Sweetwater is worrying about these so-called life skills when our kids' verbal and math scores are tanking. As I'm sure many parents here would
agree, I think I can take care of teaching my child life skills." As David
continues to hijack the meeting, the other parents say nothing. Not during the meeting, not after. Not when they see David at their daughters'
next basketball game. Never.

What gives the David Smiths of the world the right to be such bullies?
Why do they think they can get away with it? Why would other parents remain silent—even other dads? Do dads compete with each other through

their sons and daughters? Do they gossip about their kids? If dads are co-parenting more, then why do so few of them come to school activities? What experiences from Boy World do they take with them as they become fathers, teachers, and coaches? This chapter will explore these questions, and we'll also look at why dads can be so reluctant to get involved in the logistical and social problems of their children—even fathers who say they want to parent equally with mothers.

I'll admit that before I began the research for this book, I wasn't sure that the male half of Perfect Parent World had as complex a pecking order as the female one. After all, although dads do contact me, they do so in nowhere near the same numbers as moms, who constitute the vast majority of the audiences for my presentations and who e-mail me daily to describe the pain, anger, and self-doubt they feel when their children struggle with social problems. I've since reached out to fathers all over the country—asking them to fill out questionnaires, talking with them after presentations, interviewing them both one-on-one and in focus groups. Fathers do indeed have many of the same problems as moms. Perhaps I shouldn't have been surprised, because the boys I work with can feel just as constrained by Boy World as girls do by Girl World. While I still don't think most dads internalize the social problems of their children to the same degree as moms, they are certainly not immune to them. And what I've found is that how dads conduct themselves when their children are in conflict with someone else can have a profound impact on their children and their community.

In this chapter, I'll review the "Act Like a Boy" and "Act Like a Man" boxes, then look at the roles men assume when they grow up and draw some parallels to the roles for boys I wrote about in *Queen Bees & Wannabes*. Just as I did for girls and women, I'll separate men into three groups: the Entitled, the Middle Men, and the Left Out. Then I'll break down each group into distinct roles. These roles don't arise in a vacuum; they're a reaction to, reflection of, or rejection of the culture's expectations of men. I'll discuss how a father's position on what I call the Dad Totem Pole affects how he approaches conflict, and what men really think about stay-at-home dads. Just as I did for mothers, I'll offer personality profiles for fathers. I've included a "Bulletin from the Front" to showcase fathers' responses to the questions I hear most often from mothers.

Once again, a disclaimer: These roles are a way of naming behavior so that we can better understand why we act as we do. These roles evolve as a reinforcement of or reaction to what men learn while growing up in Boy World, and they influence the way grown men parent. These roles are flexible, especially if fathers reflect on why they're in a certain role and what it costs them in terms of their ability to be honest with themselves and one another. Middle Men can develop their courage and speak out to the people who intimidate them—especially when they choose to be role models for their kids. Dads who have been Left Out can do the same. While I hope that moms reading this chapter will better understand their husbands, I've written this chapter for the dads. You have a responsibility to figure out how the Dad Totem Pole influences your interactions with your child—otherwise you'll be less of a father and mentor than you want to be.

The Entitled

Kingpin Dad

The Kingpin Dad is the male equivalent of the Queen Bee Mom. His junior partner in Boy World, the Dominator, is the boy who embodies our culture's ideals: he takes risks (so long as there's little chance he'll get caught—or if he does get caught, he's nonchalant about the punishment) and he's good-looking, attractive to girls, and verbally persuasive—and therefore able to influence his friends' behavior. All grown up, Kingpin Dad is successful in the way that men in our culture are socialized to be. He takes pride in providing for his family, especially if he's doing a better job bringing home the bacon than other dads. The Kingpin Dad can be charming but, because of the power he exerts, he doesn't need to be. Unlike Queen Bee Moms, who often depend on their social intelligence and charm to consolidate their power, the Kingpin Dad relies on the appearance of financial success or professional standing.

Although the Kingpin Dad can be irritating and bullheaded, I do have a degree of empathy for him. Recall that in Chapter 1, I reproduced the dictionary definition of *masculinity:* "forming the formal, active, or generative principle of the cosmos." When I first read that, I saw it as yet another example of how sexist and oppressive to women the world is. But when I thought about it, I realized that this definition is at least as oppressive to men as to women. After all, if you're partly responsible for the creation of the universe, that sets the bar pretty high—you'd *better* be financially successful. So when we women criticize men for choosing work over time with their family, I think we need to realize the pressure these men feel. If we don't, we're likely to deal with them in ways that make them feel personally attacked, and they're likely to react to us by getting ugly or by dismissing us as unrealistic, naive, or weak—which, not coincidentally, fits many of the negative stereotypes of women. This isn't to say that we should let arrogant, presumptuous Kingpin Dads off the hook, but we need to understand where they're coming from.

There are two species of Kingpin Dads: the one who respects his wife as an equal and the one who doesn't. What both have in common is that they see their wife and kids as an essential part of their social status. The respectful Kingpin Dad usually has a wife whom he considers very successful either in her work outside the home or in running the family. The wife may manage the household herself, but this couple has the financial resources to hire other people to do the heavy lifting: cleaning the house, child care, etc. This means she's often something of a general contractor when it comes to the household business.

The Kingpin Dad who doesn't respect his wife as an equal partner generally believes that his wife shouldn't work outside the home because her job is to make things smooth for him. Although he puts her in charge of everything on the home front—caring for the kids, maintaining the social calendar, holidays, and family relationships—he doesn't put full faith in her performance. He's very invested in sticking with traditionally gendered roles within the family (although some Kingpin Dads with daughters may actively encourage them to "succeed in a man's world," for example, by going to business or law school). When the kids get in trouble or the parents are called on the carpet by the school, he believes that it's the mother's duty to handle it. If she doesn't achieve exactly what they've previously decided is an acceptable outcome, she's "failed." Then the Kingpin Dad swoops in to clean up after her because he believes he's ultimately the one who can get other parents, teachers, administrators, and coaches to do what he wants.

Both species of Kingpin Dad respond similarly when their kids get in trouble: When he's told that his child has committed a serious infraction or is facing a dire charge, the Kingpin Dad's first reaction is to demand the evidence and the identity of the people who got his kid in trouble. He justifies this by saying, "We have a right to know who our accusers are." When he has to deal with school administrators, he's likely to assume that the women in education are too emotional and the men aren't quite "real men." He conducts every meeting with administrators or teachers as if it were a business meeting or a court proceeding; he can be openly disrespectful and patronizing. If he's the kind of Kingpin Dad who doesn't respect his wife, he'll extend this attitude to her (or, God help her, his ex-wife). Here are a few examples of this kind of father in action:

> I had to ask a child to leave my school because she had choked another student. We had problems with this student for a while but this last incident was absolutely the last straw. When I met with the parents, it was horrible. The mom was quiet the entire time except once and then the dad told her to shut up and say nothing. I told him that I valued both Mom and Dad's opinion and he laughed dismissively while she looked at the ground. This family sued the school and I am still dealing with it.   Mary Ellen, head of school

> When his kid is in trouble, he always tells me, "I know the law."
> Ethan, middle school principal

Kingpin Dad needs to demonstrate his control of the family in any public meeting. If his child is in the meeting with him, the Kingpin Dad is likely to tell him, "Be quiet, I'll take care of it." With his son, he'll usually make this statement in a commanding and patronizing tone. With a daughter, he's likely to adopt a tone that implies she's Daddy's little girl— and if you watch closely, you'll see the daughter's smug smile just behind her tearstained, I'm-so-devastated expression. In both cases, this is how he shows his nurturing side. Here are other characteristics of the Kingpin Dad:

- He never attends any school or parent meetings unless he's angry about something or forced to go by his spouse, but he'll attend important athletic events and school fund-raisers—schedule permitting.

- He can be incredibly condescending to teachers—who often know more about what's going on with his children than he does.
- He talks to male administrators as if they're in this together against the emotional women.
- He believes that threatening the school with a lawsuit is an excellent way to resolve conflict.
- He believes that hazing on sports teams (especially with boys, and even more so if they attend his alma mater) is part of a valuable tradition because he wants to equip his sons with the strength of character to handle a tough world where each man is out for himself. He sees it as a positive, fatherly responsibility to encourage his sons to do the kinds of things that will build this strength. He believes that true friendships are formed through these difficult rites of passage. That's why he feels personally attacked when hazing and similar activities are questioned.
- He sees teasing as a primary way to connect with his children and/or wife. Harmless gibes too often become humiliating digs. If his loved ones don't respond positively, he feels rejected, but he shows his rejection by seeing them as "overly sensitive."

Sidekick Dad

In Boy World, a Backup or Sidekick is the second in command to the Dominator. He laughs at whatever the Dominator deems amusing, puts pressure on those who disagree with the Dominator, and bullies and silences other group members to maintain power and control. When I first started interviewing fathers, I wasn't convinced there were Sidekick Dads. One father, who was also a high school dean, laughed at me when I asked him; how could I not know?

> There is a Sidekick Dad. He's the one who hosts the after-parties. He lives beyond his means, he supports the team and the school until it's his kid [in trouble], and then he always puts his kid first. He wants to take more risks and he can undermine the school. He's not as talented or bright [as the Kingpin Dad] but he wants his kid to shine.

While his kids are having the party, he goes over to the Kingpin Dad
and smokes a cigar with him.

Al, high school dad

Here are some of the Sidekick's main characteristics:

- He's very impressed with the Kingpin Dad and will often try to belong to the same clubs or organizations.
- He directs his son to play "guy" sports.
- He feels the same way about hazing as the Kingpin Dad and considers it part of a valuable tradition that teaches his son to be a man.
- He's not as socially intelligent as the Kingpin Dad.

Banker Dads

Recall that a Banker occupies a position of considerable power, since you can enhance your social standing through the judicious storage and dispersal of gossip, the coin of the realm. And yes, boys gossip. In Boy World, topics of discussion are any risky activity: kids' perceived or actual sexual conquests, car racing, drinking, cheating on tests, vandalism, or drugs. Boy World certainly has its Bankers, but they're really tricky to spot since few boys are as verbally skilled as high-verbal girls.

While fathers aren't as easily perceived as gossips, there are indeed Banker Dads. Who got more playing time? Whose wife is difficult (specifically, whose friend is "whipped") and why does their friend put up with it? And just like Banker Moms, Banker Dads make other parents believe that innuendo and assumptions are fact.

I have a friend who's always talking about how our other friend is
completely dominated by his wife. He sort of draws me in to talking
about it because I agree with him.   Richie, high school dad

Bankers also talk about who earns the most money, and they're adept at picking up on the "tells" that indicate wealth or status: "Did you see the car that Henry's driving?" As one mother observed, "When one of the

guys on my block gets a new car, all the other dads come out and pet it."
One father owned up to the pressure he feels to earn social status among
his peers: "You have to have the latest truck parked in the driveway and
you have to keep your yard looking like a checkerboard."

MIDDLE MEN

Torn Wannabes and Desperate Wannabes

Like their female counterparts, Torn Wannabes know they're too status-
conscious but are embarrassed to admit it and can't seem to help themselves. That's what makes them so unpredictable and frustrating to be
around; their opinions change to fit those of the most powerful person in
the room. Above all, a Wannabe Dad is desperate for you to know that
he's one of the guys.

> *My big frustration with parents is, "How come you don't like me? How
> come the men aren't, 'Hey, it's Mark!'" And I say to myself, "I don't
> care. I don't want to be their friend anyway." But it sure would be nice.*
> Mark, father of teenagers

The Desperate Wannabe is much easier to dislike. He's a name-dropper
who's always keeping score, trying desperately to be sure that he's keeping
up. Like his female counterpart, he'll always please the person with the
most power in the room and be his backup. Just like a Desperate Wannabe
Mom, adulthood hasn't given Desperate Wannabe Dad the increased
social skills or understanding of social cues that many of us take for
granted. That's why he reminds you so much of kids you knew in high
school, why you think he's trying too hard ("Doesn't he know how he's
coming across?" No, he doesn't), and that's why you don't like hanging
out with him.

> *The Wannabe has complete hero worship. He's a notch below in earn-
> ings. He wants to vacation in the same spots as the Kingpin Dad and
> Sidekick Dad. My wife and I went to dinner with three couples and
> one of the guys had been a professional athlete. At one point, the
> guys went to the bar. The Red Sox were playing and the Wannabe lit-*

erally stepped in between me and the pro player. My wife was really upset but I don't really care. I just couldn't believe how obvious it was.   Stephen, father of teenagers

Caveman Dad

Unfortunately, Caveman Dad acts pretty much exactly like his younger version, the Stuck and Silenced—the boy in the middle who acts like a deer caught in the headlights. He's often paralyzed and silenced by the dominating members of the group and may rationalize or apologize for their behavior. Many Caveman Dads I've spoken to were raised by Kingpin or Sidekick Dads and promised themselves that they'd never be like their fathers. As a result, they tend to be emotionally engaged with their children and spouses. Unfortunately, it's difficult for these dads to find role models to show them how to express anger in appropriate ways, so they often sit on that anger until it blows up or they cave.

[My wife says,] "You wouldn't understand, so let me handle it." And I do every time. I'm not proud of it, but it's true.
                                    Frank, high school dad

Everyone takes advantage of Caveman Dad—the mother of his children, other parents, his own kids—because he's so reluctant to speak his mind. If this dad has a job or life situation that makes it more difficult for him to be a part of the day-to-day nitty-gritty of home and school, his guilt enables the mother to have even more dominion over the family (imagine a Hovercraft Mom married to this guy). He's usually motivated by good intentions; he respects the mother's dedication to the family and therefore feels he should acquiesce to her wishes because she knows more and she's putting in the time.

I would do anything to not be my father. He called me names, personally attacked me . . . I never knew what would set him off. I realized being the one who initiated the divorce that I'm guilty. I was the one that left, so I always say yes to my ex-wife and my daughter. I often wonder, do I have the right to have any feelings because I'm not there every day? My daughter doesn't respect me because I let her get away with whatever she wants. I know it and I hate it but I taught her to treat me badly.

Russ, divorced father of a fourteen-year-old daughter

Floater Dads

Floater Dads enjoy the same freedom Floater kids do; they move easily from one group to another without arousing resentment and are genuinely liked for who they are.

A lot of fathers fall into this category, which includes men who have for the most part matured emotionally to the point where they truly float, but here's the catch: Like Floater Moms, Floater Dads don't speak out when the Entitled are being difficult. They're savvy enough about social hierarchies that they reason, "Hey, there's no point in acting like a teenager again. Let the other guy huff and puff and blow himself out." As I'll discuss later in the book, this means that the Floater's child is often left holding the bag—butting up against the Entitled kids and whatever their Entitled parents have wrought in the classroom, on the playing field, or in the lunchroom.

Reformed Dad

Like his female counterpart, Reformed Dad was stuck for a while in a role he first assumed when he was a teenager. He could have stayed one of the Entitled, Stuck and Silenced, or a Wannabe, but instead he's grown into a genuinely cool guy. He's realized the cost of continuing to be in one of these other roles and had the courage to change. He can laugh at himself while at the same time feeling strongly about his core beliefs. He's learned to have authentic relationships with other men. He doesn't solely depend on his wife to create and maintain his social life. It's not unusual for this man to have women friends independent of his wife's women friends.

The Left Out

Invisible Dads

Invisible Dads are the grown-up versions of the Invisible boys in Boy World. They're good, well-meaning parents who try to attend all the school functions and never say a word. If anything, they're even quieter than the Invisible Moms. They can't identify with the other parents asking question after question of the principal or speaking up at Back-to-School Night.

Outcast Dads

Outcast Dads, like Outcast Moms, don't live in the "right" neighborhood or go to the "right" church. The biggest difference in the Outcast category between moms and dads is that in most communities single moms are easily put in this role, while being single never makes a dad an Outcast. On the contrary, people will admire him.

When Dads Get Mad: Fathers in Conflict

One of the most crucial lessons men take from Boy World into their adulthood and fathering is the way they express their anger. Dads from every walk of life have shared with me their resistance to confronting another man who's being cruel, although they all feel a responsibility to intervene when a confrontation becomes physical. When men see someone being humiliated by another man (as we'll examine in greater detail in Chapter 8, "Field of Nightmares"), they often convince themselves to dismiss it, reasoning that nothing they do or say could improve the situation. Boy World mandates that you adhere to a strict code of conduct when you see another guy being mean or degrading. You have one of two choices, to step in physically or to do nothing, as Boy World doesn't teach boys how to talk through the problem.

As men grow up to become fathers, coaches, teachers, or principals, they take this code of conduct with them. Usually it seems as if they've gotten beyond Boy World—until there's a conflict, and then its rules come back in full force. And, just because a bully never targeted you for direct degradation doesn't mean you escaped the lesson. The bully used his victim to show you and everyone else his power. Men who were harassed by bullies when they were teens or who got fed up having to babysit their bullying friends and pull them off people with a "Let it alone, man, it's not worth it" will do anything to avoid similar situations as adults.

So boys and dads are primed to dismiss problems, telling themselves that "it's not a big deal," when the truth is that the problems *are* a big deal but our culture teaches boys and men that they're too difficult to do anything about. As one father put it, "As a man, you have two choices when you're angry at another man. You can get in his face or you can blow him off." When boys watch the men in their lives avoid standing up to a bully, avert their gaze, or laugh or shrug it off while saying, "That's just the way he is," they learn that being a man often means saying nothing in the face of cruelty. If dads believe that their only choices are to challenge the bully or blow him off, why wouldn't they take the easier route? It is one of our culture's greatest ironies that it values physical courage as an essential masculine characteristic yet teaches men to be cowards when the confrontation can't be solved through physical means.

> *If a guy is an obstinate bully at forty-five, you think, "Why am I going to bother if he's forty-five and still acting this way?" You ignore and appease him so he can be satisfied that he got his way. If you confront him, he's going to focus all of his hostility on you and no one is coming to come to your rescue.*   Sam, father of teenagers

So dads are less likely than moms to challenge the power structure in Perfect Parent World. Most fathers appreciate that the *Lord of the Flies* mentality that rules Boy World can easily show up again among men—and it doesn't take a lot for some men to exert their power in much the same way. Moreover, whether they realize it or not, men get a clear benefit when they buy in to Perfect Parent World in the form of respect, power, and privilege in their community.

If you're a man reading this, I want you to remember an experience from your youth when someone humiliated you or you watched someone else being humiliated. Did someone come to the rescue? What did you learn about boys and men in that moment? What lessons from that experience have you carried into your interactions with people today? How do they influence the father you are today?

Where you fit on the Dad Totem Pole will further influence how you handle conflict, whether it involves overt bullying or not. Kingpin Dads facing off will butt heads until one of them wins. Sidekicks or Wannabes will suck up to the Kingpin Dad and end up agreeing with him. Everyone else will blow off the Kingpin but let him get away with his bullying behavior.

When a Floater or Reformed Dad has a bad experience with another dad, he may wonder why that guy is the way he is, or even complain to his friends about the incident—once. But he won't rehash every word and nuance of the conversation over and over again the way even a Floater Mom is prone to do. He's not likely to feel that his entire ability to parent has been called into question because of the encounter. Floater and Reformed Dads are much better at cutting their losses and saying to themselves, "That experience was terrible and now I'm going to let it go," just as boys do.

Once these dads actually engage in a conflict, they're usually able to talk things through more effectively than two warring moms. Dads expect to have this conversation once, after which it's done. Moms are more likely to hold grudges and expect to be in the same battle with the parent again. Dads are able to do this not because they're inherently more rational and mature but because they're more likely to believe each other's apologies. In Boy World, a guy is less likely to use an apology as a tactic for manipulation, as girls do in Girl World, and that lesson carries over into adulthood. (I'll discuss this issue in greater depth in Chapter 6.)

But no matter where a dad fits on the totem pole, most resist or refuse to talk to angry mothers, and when they do, it's a cop-out. There's no other way to say it. Just as I used to tell girls when I taught self-defense that you can cry and fight at the same time, Dads can listen to angry women and still have a conversation with them. When they don't, it's because they've carried over the lessons from Boy World that being emotional means being out of control and that it's okay to dismiss an emotional woman.

There are so many well-meaning dads who cut and run when they have to have difficult conversations with moms. Men often pass off the problem to their wives, particularly if it's a social issue, either because they've been socialized to avoid conflict with women or because they consider family issues to be "women's issues"—or both. Kids learn two things from this: First, dads can't be role models when it comes to handling interpersonal relationships, and second, social issues aren't as serious because women are handling them. After all, they're not important enough for a man to be involved.

There are dads who fight me on this. They claim that men just aren't "relationship-oriented," that this is a feminine quality. I don't believe it. Maybe men don't want to chat on the phone with each other every day (and neither do I, by the way) but that doesn't mean they don't want strong relationships with their family and friends.

Some dads tell me that the problem with children today is that fathers don't enjoy the same respect or authority they had a generation ago. We need to recognize that losing the traditional authoritarian father role doesn't have to mean losing your authority; in fact, I believe it allows men to be truly respected. Men need to learn to move beyond this false dichotomy—you're either a my-way-or-the-highway dad or you're a feminized wimp—and speak up in a way that is respectful of themselves and their co-parents. I love the comment below because it shows how an engaged father can assert himself in the best interest of his child:

> When my son entered ninth grade I said to him, "We have four more years with you and I just want to let you know that before you leave my house I will kill you myself if you turn out to be a mindless, selfish, dependent male. You will know how to do your laundry and the rudiments of cooking and cleaning." I haven't gotten around to teaching him how to sew—because at least he needs to know how to sew a button—but he has to be self-sufficient. It's more important to me that he's resourceful than have resources.
>
> Tom, father of a high school student

STAY-AT-HOME DADS

If we want to look at how men are grappling with new roles, we need to consider stay-at-home dads. Do fathers feel the same tension mothers do over the decision to work inside or outside the home? What do working dads really think about stay-at-home dads? The title of a December 2004 article in the *New York Times* pretty much says it all: "Housewives, Try This for Desperation: Stay-at-Home Fathers Face Isolation and a Lingering Stigma" by Jennifer Medina. According to the article, there are only 1.4 million stay-at-home dads versus 8.4 million stay-at-home moms, and societal acceptance seems to lag equally with the numbers. The fathers in the article reported snide comments from their former co-workers, uneasy looks from moms and nannies at the playground, and a decided imbalance in the kind of play date making that stay-at-home moms take for granted. The most telling quote came from Gregg Rood, a father who'd stayed home to care for his daughters for two years: "It takes one's manhood, chews it up, spits it out and does it again. You really need a strong marriage and confidence."

I talked to a lot of dads who have spent at least some time as stay-at-home dads. They were very articulate about what the experience has meant to them and how it has affected other men's reactions to them. I asked dads from both sides of the stay-at-home divide what they thought.

> When men say [to stay-at-home dads], "You're so lucky," they usually don't mean it. Some dads really respect it, some are really patronizing: "Isn't that good of you, little man."
>
> Randy, stay-at-home father

> "How's the commute?" Is there really nothing else male acquaintances can talk about? Guys always want to know what I "do for a living" and about my "job situation." Men don't usually know how to talk to me.   Gordon, stay-at-home father

I think most stay-at-home dads would laugh as hard as most stay-at-home moms at the idea of calling child care "time off" and "relaxing." It's clear that many fathers who work outside the home do appreciate that child care is hard work:

> I do respect men who stay at home to take care of the kids. I have the utmost appreciation for my wife that she's with our kids

eight hours a day. However, I would rather tar the roof on a hot
summer day.   Matthew, father who works outside the home

As more fathers make the decision to stay at home or have wives who earn enough income that it makes more sense for them to be the primary child care provider, I think we'll see more challenges to the cultural constructs of Boy World and the Dad Totem Pole.

HOME DEPOT DEMOGRAPHICS: PERSONALITY PROFILES FOR DADS

Just as I did for moms, I've developed personality profiles for dads based on my observations and feedback from fathers all over the country.

Lock-Her-in-a-Closet Dad

This dad thinks he can control his daughter's every movement and has the power to veto her friends and boyfriends. He also thinks that teaching her to "just say no" will keep her away from drugs, alcohol, and sex. (It won't.) The daughters of these fathers often become champion sneaks. If the fathers do succeed in keeping them locked up tight until they leave home, the daughters can get in serious trouble because they haven't learned the skills or resources to help themselves. I'm singling out daughters because this dad usually has a completely different attitude toward his sons—and his children are well aware of the double standard. His daughter will have a strict curfew while his son either won't have one or won't get in trouble for breaking it. He's a Kingpin.

Hip Dad

Just like Hip Mom, he's so desperate to be liked by the kids that he not only allows the partying, he might even aid and abet it: "Okay, kids, since I know you are going to drink, party over here!" Then he goes upstairs, closes his door, and turns on the TV, blissfully unaware of whatever's going on downstairs. The next day a parent (usually a mother) calls to scream, "Did you have *any idea* that kids were having sex at your house last night and a kid had to go to the hospital with alcohol poisoning?" In response he sputters, "What did you want me to do, police every move they make?" He's a Sidekick or a Wannabe.

Maverick Dad

He doesn't buy in to the dictates of Perfect Parent World and is confident and interested enough to take a leadership role in his child's life (beyond athletic coaching). He can be a member of the PTA and he's comfortable working with women—even if he's the only man. Moms love him and most dads think he's okay—maybe a little weird for being so into the school and maybe a little annoying because he makes them look bad. He's a Floater or Reformed.

Sideline-Star Dad

He brings the pizza, buys the jackets for the team, and cheers big-time along the sidelines. Sometimes he embarrasses the other parents with his all-out enthusiasm, but he's so positive they forgive him. He's a Floater or Reformed.

Throbbing-Vein Dad

He's the Sideline-Star Dad's evil twin. He cheers and yells way too much at the games. The other parents love it that he buys the uniforms, volunteers to be in charge of raising the money, or runs the grill at the concession stand. But then his involvement spills over into becoming abusive on the sidelines, which he dismisses as "getting caught up in the moment." He's the one yelling, "You're worthless!" or "You're such an idiot!" at the hapless fourteen-year-old refereeing the soccer game for the under-elevens. He's a Kingpin or a Sidekick.

Closed-Book Dad

Like his female counterpart, Closed-Book Dad thinks that the family's problems are no one else's business. He equates privacy with never acknowledging weakness. Other parents know not to ask him anything too personal. He's a Kingpin or a Banker.

No-Excuses Dad

He demands the best from his kids. He tells them to get back up no matter how many times they've been knocked down. Although teaching your kids to persevere is wonderful, he fails to teach them that sometimes they need to ask for help—because he sees it as a sign of weakness. When his kids get in trouble, they might feel ashamed that they're not strong enough to overcome their problems on their own. He's a Kingpin or a Banker.

Silent Presence

He stands on the sidelines, silently beaming encouragement to all the players. He will cheer when it's appropriate, but he'll do it for everybody, because he knows the other kids on the team and is as genuinely interested in their welfare as he is in his own kid's. He respects the fifty-foot rule, keeping his distance from his child so the kid won't feel embarrassed. He might be shy but he's a great friend and an even better dad. He's a Floater, Invisible, or Reformed.

BULLETINS FROM THE FRONT

When I interviewed fathers for this book, the rooms crackled with the same kind of electricity I felt when I first started working with sixth-grade girls. I heard the same giggles and excitement from the dads: Was I really asking their opinion? They could tell me what they really thought? Was the door closed?

The vast majority of dads with whom I spoke believe one thing: Being a good father isn't just about financially providing for their family. It also means being emotionally connected to their children and spending time with them. As a result, many feel torn between work and family but don't think they can or should admit it. Many expressed very strong feelings about not being the remote, controlling fathers they had. But even in the most progressive families, it was very difficult for me to find a father who was as involved in the logistics of his children's school or social lives as the mother. (It was equally difficult to find a mother who would give up her jurisdiction over these two areas.) It was also hard to find fathers who thought they could take time off from their work or other obligations to take care of their children—even if their employers had policies to support them. So I asked the questions you see below, which might appear superficial but on closer examination reveal the challenges moms and dads still face if they want to be equal caregivers to their children. Here are some of their responses.

WHEN YOU ANSWER THE PHONE AND IT'S AN ANGRY OR UPSET MOTHER, WHAT DO YOU DO?

I want to get off the phone as quickly and politely as possible. Why? Because they're going to yell and it'll take forty-five minutes. I mean, it's not that I don't want to be involved [squirming in his seat] *but I don't want to be involved* [laughing]. *I don't want to get yelled at.*

It's a no-brainer—I let my wife take the calls. I know I'll be happy now if I let my wife take the call. It's concrete, immediate gratification compared to the potential goal that I'll be a better parent in the future.

I always take those phone calls. Sure, I get calls relating to the kids and saying, "Is your wife there?" I used to get hostile but I've learned to say I'm pretty familiar with the issue and then force them to talk to me.

WHY DON'T FATHERS GO TO MORE SCHOOL FUNCTIONS?

Because our wives ask us to go and then we get there and my wife huddles up with all her friends and catches up. Fifteen minutes later she'll look around. "Is my husband here? Where is he?" Meanwhile I'm standing there feeling awkward and then I have to talk to the guys about sports—you know, the fallback guy things you talk about. So why would I want to go?

It's really hard for dads when an issue comes up that we're supposed to know about. I feel like I'm coming in from left field. The moms know all about it and I don't.

WHY DON'T FATHERS PLAN MORE LOGISTICS?

I can take kids to games, but I'm not authorized to make spend-the-night arrangements because I don't ask the right questions. I think there's a fifteen-to-one ratio of what moms think is the right amount of questions to ask and what I think I should ask. As soon as I get off the phone, I'm barraged with questions, so why should I even try if there's no way I'm going to get it right?

Because she tells me to do it, then she gets on my case about it. So I tell her, "Look, just back off. I'm gonna do it my way, so just leave me alone or I'm not gonna do it." So she ends up taking over.

WHY DO MOST FATHERS HAVE TO BE COERCED INTO READING BOOKS ON CHILD CARE?

I was tricked into reading one because there was a football on the cover, but it was really good.

The only time I read part of a parenting book was when I was stuck on an airplane and there was nothing else to read. But last year when we got our new puppy, I rushed right out and bought a book on the breed and read it cover to cover.

I don't read them because it's a reaction to the completely obsessive way people have children.

WHY DO SOME DADS LOVE TO MAKE LUNCH FOR THEIR KIDS?

Making lunch is a big deal not only because it's a good thing to do but it's a sign of love. I make their lunches every day and I make sure they're really good—healthy but really good. One day my daughter came home and told me that she didn't have enough but Johnny's mommy had packed enough, so Johnny gave her some of his. It broke my heart! I've gone to the supermarket at 5 a.m. to buy just the right things for them so they would be ready by 7:15 a.m. when they leave for school. [Laughing] Love makes you insane.

My mom went back to medical school, so my father would make my school lunches. He wasn't very affectionate or nurturing but he did make me great lunches. Honestly, I would have so much food I would feed other children. Actually, I had to feed them because so many kids had horrible lunches. My wife is one of those people who had terrible lunches so I don't trust her to make the lunches because she had bad role models. So there are a lot of reasons why lunch is so important to me.

Obviously, whether you're a mother or a father has a profound effect on your parenting, but that's certainly not the only influence on how you perceive your "choices" in Perfect Parent World. In the next chapter, I'll dissect the other factors that color our view when we interact with other parents and how other parents interact with us.

Turning the Lens on Ourselves

Understanding the Filters
Through Which We View the World

I've referred to culture throughout this book as though there were only one way to define it. Of course that's not true—it's way more interesting than that. We see our culture through a series of personal filters such as our race, socioeconomic background, and religion. It's not as if these filters are separate from the culture; it's just that every person has a slightly different way of responding to the culture based on them. In this chapter, I want to take a look at a few of these filters so we can see how they often invisibly guide our assumptions, actions, and reactions in our parenting.

Although there are hundreds of ways that people filter their experiences, I've focused on a few that I see often come into play with parents. These are the hot-button issues I hear about most as I speak across the country: marital status, race, class, religion, generation. The filters I describe in the pages that follow affect you whether or not you have personal experience with them, so I'm asking you to read all the sections even if you don't think they're relevant to you. For example, you may be married and think the section on single and divorced parents doesn't apply to you because you're neither single nor divorced. However, you interact with people who are. All these filters are powerful influences because in large part they dictate what we think we can and can't say to one another.

Before we start we have to address three issues. First, while it's human nature to seek shortcuts to understanding others, there isn't a single, simple root explanation for the myriad complexities of human behavior.

For example, when people ask me my astrological sign, whatever my answer is will fit into their preconceived opinions of me. The same is true if people ask your birth order (as I write this I know many people will be angry that I am comparing birth order with astrology). My point is that most of us tend to fall back on that one "aha" that explains other people.

Second, let's also admit that almost all of us love to practice talk-show psychology. Recall the last time you thought someone did something horrible — especially if this horrible behavior was directed at you. As you stared at the ceiling in your bed that night, ruminating about how much you hated this person, perhaps you said to yourself: "Well, the reason he's so horrible is because he had an abusive dad who emotionally abandoned him and he was never taught to express his anger in an appropriate way — that's why he feels so threatened by me. You know, I really feel sorry for him." Then you fell asleep reassured of your own emotional maturity. We have to admit that we often analyze the people we're angry with not to understand them but to rationalize why we're better (read: more sane, enlightened, mature) than they. Unfortunately, we rarely apply the same level of analysis to ourselves. That's precisely what I'm asking you to do in this chapter.

Third, we like to think of ourselves as enlightened, unencumbered by stereotypes. If we do admit we have stereotypes at all, we almost never realize how those stereotypes are influencing our behavior in the moment. In order to stop blindly reinforcing stereotypes, we need to focus on how they're subtly invoked in our everyday interactions and can sabotage our ability to live together as a community. At the least, we have an obligation to be more aware of their subtle influences on our own and others' interactions and therefore be better equipped to treat people unlike ourselves with dignity.

MARITAL STATUS

I've found that many married parents assume that a single mother will have full custody of the kids and that if she doesn't, there's probably something wrong with her. They assume that a single father is more likely to be an every-other-weekend Disney dad than a hands-on parent with full knowledge of the children's schedules — and they'll therefore be more likely to touch base with the mother for school events, play dates, and the like, effectively freezing out the father.

I've spoken with divorced parents who shared custody with or gave full custody of their children to their exes because they saw it as in the kids' best interest—and then felt attacked by parents who told them they "hadn't fought hard enough for their kids." Many worry that married parents assume single parents can't be as good parents, and therefore behave more defensively when conflicts arise. Single mothers have shared with me the pain of losing their friends after the divorce, particularly if their financial situation worsens as a result. Many of them feel under suspicion by married mothers who automatically assume they're trolling for a new mate—to the point where some single mothers have a policy to avoid one-on-one conversations with married dads. Clearly, these unspoken assumptions can profoundly impact single parents' ability to have strong, supportive relationships with other adults in their children's lives. But if you're married, you may need to question your assumptions about single parents or consider how they affect a single parent's behavior toward you.

RACE/ETHNICITY

I've worked with parents of many different ethnicities and backgrounds and know that most parents will do anything to avoid talking to each other about these subjects. To come to a better understanding of parenting in an interracial world, we need to think about what questions we have about other races but are afraid to ask. What does this have to do with parenting? Our assumptions about people based on their race impact our ability to interact with them as parents. You could send your child to a school comprising only one race and it would still matter. Why? First, because most white kids think that racism doesn't exist anymore—it's something that happened in the South a long time ago, and then there was the Martin Luther King Jr. Day, and now we have Black History Month. So we need to teach them that racism is still with us and that we have a responsibility to stop it. Second, your children are or will be interacting with people of different races and you don't want them being and acting foolish and ignorant.

Why White People Are Annoying

I, a white woman, would like to offer up a generalization of my own: One of the most irritating yet understandable things that white people do is treat race and racism as if they don't exist. I believe this happens for two reasons. First, your race privilege (the status, respect, and opportunities you're afforded in our society because you're white) blinds you to the fact that you're privileged in the first place. It's the air you breathe, so basic to your existence that you don't notice it's there—except if it's taken away from you.

Let me give you a concrete example. If you're a white parent of a teenage son who drives, have you ever sat down with him and told him what he should and shouldn't do when pulled over by a police officer? Probably not. In contrast, every black parent with whom I've spoken—no matter their socioeconomic status—carries the fear that the police will assume the worst about his or her child and act accordingly. In fact, it's common for black organizations to sponsor programs called "Driving While Black" for their sons and daughters for just this reason. Black parents teach their sons to immediately place their hands on the steering wheel so the police won't assume they have a gun. Every time their sons go out, these parents fear that the very people who are supposed to protect their children could hurt them. And while some black parents have the education and means to address a bad experience with the police after the fact, they know they have no control over it in the moment.

The other reason white people are annoying is because they're so worried that if they talk about race, they'll say something wrong and come across as racist. This stops them from asking the questions and getting the answers that would make them more confident about entering into those conversations. Because they're afraid, they say nothing and often come across as ignorant, insensitive, or deceptive. Basically, they reinforce the stereotype that white people are all closet racists.

I assume that [black people] think I'm thinking down on them. So then I try to be too nice to prove that I don't think that, but then they notice that, too. Amanda, mother of teen

One of my [white] friends is married to a black man and they have two children. We got a great new teacher who was also a black man. Before she met him she was asking about him, but no one, including me, could say that he was black. When she asked what he was like, I always said, "He's tall, he's charming." My PC-o-meter just wouldn't let me say he was black. So she goes to school looking for this new teacher and she comes back pretty irritated: "Why didn't you tell me he was black?" I just get so uncomfortable. It's ridiculous.

Rhonda, mother of teens

In general, my experience with people of all different races is that they want to be asked questions directly and they welcome conversations about race. So if you find yourself having a conversation with a person who's a different race or ethnicity and you find yourself stammering because you're uncomfortable, just say so. There's also nothing wrong with admitting that you're worried about sounding ridiculous or even racist. If the other person gets angry, just say, "I'm sorry that I said something to offend you. I don't know what I did and I want to do better, so could you please tell me what I did wrong?" You have a right to ask questions and you have a right to be treated civilly.

Equal-Opportunity Racism

If you're black, Latino, Asian, or any other race or ethnicity besides white, of course you have the right to be frustrated when you have those awkward conversations with white people. Chances are good that you've been thinking and talking about race and racism throughout your life — it's your field of expertise. I know it's not your job to explain race to all the white people in your life, but if you want them to understand the world you're living in, then you can't walk away secure in your frustration or knowledge — read: assumptions — of white people.

Certainly white people aren't the only ones with prejudices. I grew up learning racial stereotypes in the black community from my black grade school friends. It was from them that I learned that the darker your skin, the worse it was considered to be, and that softer and "whiter" hair was better than nappier hair. As an adult who has worked with girls of all different races and ethnicities, it's clear to me that people within a race can be the harshest critics of people within their own group. I believe strongly that every one of us needs to reflect on whether unrecognized, internalized racism is guiding our behavior. Although children of minorities are educated about white racism, they almost never receive education about internalized racism—so it becomes shameful and taboo to talk about.

BLACK MOTHERS SPEAK OUT

Because "racial incidents" can blow up so quickly in our communities, I sat down with my friend and colleague Shanterra McBride and a small group of black women to talk about the most common racial differences that we see leading to problems with other parents and educators. Below are my questions, the women's answers, and my commentary.

WHAT EXPERIENCES STICK OUT RAISING A BLACK CHILD?

In the winter, my son will take off his coat when he goes into a store so no one can accuse him of stealing. He doesn't even think twice about it—it's automatic.

WHAT'S GOING ON?

Imagine having other people automatically assume your children are dishonest and of bad character from the time they're able to walk. You'd be so hardwired to protect your child that you wouldn't be able to do anything else. So if you're ever in a confrontation with a black parent and you can't understand why he or she is fighting you so hard, keep in mind that this parent has spent the child's lifetime feeling like it's necessary to defend the child's character. It still doesn't excuse bad behavior—yours or the other parent's—but you need to know that this history could very well be driving the other person's behavior.

WHY DO BLACK PEOPLE GET SO ANGRY OR INCREDULOUS AT WHITE PEOPLE WHEN IT COMES TO DIFFERENCES IN DISCIPLINING CHILDREN?

Once I was in the grocery store, I think my child was about three. She was throwing a tantrum and I was trying to get her under control. A white woman, without even looking at me, asks my daughter if she's okay. What about asking me if I'm okay? I'm stressed out trying to deal with this situation and she's accusing me of attempting to hurt my child. I think East Asians and Asians are the same way as us with their kids. They expect things to be handled and their children to be under control when they're out in public.

I babysat in college and I couldn't believe some of the things the white parents would tell me. For example, when they would tell me what the child would have for dinner they'd say, "If you can get her to eat her broccoli that'd be great, but if she fights you on it, don't worry about it." If that happened in my family [laughing], I wouldn't be eating.

What's Going On

We all know that parents can be incredibly critical about how other people discipline their children. In general, my experience is that many white parents do assume that black parents are harsh disciplinarians. And black parents, along with pretty much any other nonwhite parent to whom I've spoken, think white parents are too lenient with their kids. This may not seem like an issue that would make parents distrust each other, but it does—from play dates to high school parties. To understand why, please read on.

WHY DON'T BLACK MOTHERS TRUST WHITE MOTHERS?

We are wary of white parents. Because white people are too lenient with their kids. They don't have control over their kids.

White people are in denial about their kids and what's out there. If I don't know you, why would I let my kid come over to your house?

White parents are much more likely to have those out-of-control parties where everybody is drinking and the parents aren't there, because their kids aren't scared of them.

WHAT'S GOING ON?

When you say, "I don't know you," as the woman quoted above does, you should literally mean that you haven't made up your mind about another person's parenting skills because you have no evidence either way. However, I've heard parents say "I don't know you" to justify their suspicions and distrustful attitude toward white parents.

The assumptions we make about who is a good parent can blind us to who really is a good influence for our children and who really isn't, and can stop us from reaching out to each other for help. For example, if a black mother feels like she should be in control of her child and her child gets into trouble for drinking, eating disorders, or other risky behavior, she can be very reluctant to get help from other black parents because these kind of problems "don't happen" to them—they happen to white parents. Likewise, it might be harder for her to ask for help from white parents because she might feel that her struggle will confirm the white parents' assumptions about blacks. These are problems all parents in a community have to navigate together and support each other through.

WHY DO BLACK PEOPLE SEE A RACIAL PROBLEM WHEN IT'S NOT THERE?

I just had a meeting with the director of the Learning Center, who told me that maybe this school wasn't the place for my daughter. I know there are white kids who aren't doing as well as my daughter and they aren't being asked to leave. Then she called me "hon" and that was it. It's on now.

WHAT'S GOING ON?

This mother's experience shows the dynamic in which a white person thinks he or she is discussing a problem with no racial undertones and the black person sees that the problem is all about race and a way to justify racial discrimination. The mother met with a teacher who told her that maybe this wasn't the right school for her daughter. What this mother heard was this teacher doesn't want black students, in particular her daughter, in the school. Compounding the problem, she thinks this teacher wants to deny her child a good education—the one thing minorities and immigrants believe is the one way to ensure equitable opportunities for their children. This teacher is threatening her child's future, so if the mother must resort to acting like the stereotype of the intimidating black woman, then so be it. What's so unfortunate about this situation is that negative racial stereotypes are reinforced without the white person knowing what she's doing is contributing to the problem.

RELIGION

Before writing this book, I knew that parents of different religions wanted to ask each other questions but were often too afraid to do so because of the same dynamic that closes down communication about race. A mother came up to me after a parent assembly and asked if she could talk to me privately. It was obvious that she was very nervous:

> My daughter has been invited to fifteen bat mitzvahs this year. I'm not Jewish and I don't want to offend anyone, but I really don't understand what's going on here. All of the presents seem to cost about $100. We can't afford that—I'd be spending $1,500 on these presents. Is that really necessary? Is this normal? And when we're invited as a family, sometimes the events go really late. I have a ten-year-old son and the last one we went to, they started a video about this girl at 11:30 p.m. I didn't want to be rude, but we had to get home.

This mother had legitimate questions: Did she really have to spend so much money on presents? Would it be okay to decline an invitation? Could she leave before the end of the event, exhausted kids in tow, without offending the hosts? However, she was terrified to ask anybody because she was afraid she'd look anti-Semitic.

Just as some parents of color use people's fear of appearing racist to get what they want, parents can manipulate fears of appearing antireligious. One school administrator got into a heated battle with some Jewish parents when he criticized them for giving out themed sweatshirts — "I went to Tiffany's bat mitzvah!" — at their daughter's celebration. Naturally, the attendees all wore their sweatshirts the next Monday, broadcasting who had been invited and who hadn't. When the principal called the parents to tell them he discouraged this kind of behavior, he was told, "You can't tell us what to do because the Holocaust was a horrible experience and we need to celebrate these kinds of occasions in any way that we see fit." I'll go into more detail about problems like this in Chapter 10, but suffice it to say that no one should be able to use the fact that their group has been persecuted to justify or excuse their own individual hurtful behavior.

Fortunately, stories like these are in the minority of what parents shared with me. But it's these stories that get circulated and reinforce stereotypes in part because the specific behavior in question is never challenged. If we truly want to stop negative stereotyping, then we have to be strong enough to challenge the individual behavior that seems to confirm the stereotypes in the first place.

However, what I've been astonished by is the bullying between parents within the same religious community and the great sense of pain so many parents feel as a result. People of the same religion often assume that they'll share the same values. When they don't, it feels like a bitter betrayal. This kind of conflict will most likely occur between families who attend the same church, synagogue, or mosque or who send their children to a religious school. Why does the conflict feel so devastating? They've sent their children to religious school or live in faith-based communities because they want a sanctuary from a culture they perceive to be bad for their kids. When this sanctuary reflects the culture by backing up the bully, refusing to address the problem, or alienating the family in pain, they feel that the one place they relied on for safety betrayed them.

From a Christian parent:

I view my church as a sanctuary. We're in a church family so that automatically puts us on a level of trust with our "brothers and sisters." We share the same faith, so how different can we be? Well, I've never read The Art of War, *but these ladies [in the church] know a thing or two about conflict resolution—kill the enemy, destroy the troublemaker.*

           Janice, high school mom

From a Mormon parent:

The girls who had bullied my daughter were from the same church. Their fathers were some of our church leaders. When they found out about the problems our daughter was having with their girls, they totally dismissed it. We had to change churches and put my daughter in a different school. We were totally ostracized.

           Rebecca, middle school mom

From a Jewish parent:

I was so proud to send my child to a Jewish school. Then, as it grew, its values changed. The wealthiest parents had more influence. Our little school became this place that was against all my Jewish values of inclusion and generosity of spirit. There was nothing I could do. I felt so helpless.

           Barbara, middle school mom

If you're ever in this situation, here are some things to remember. No matter what religious community you belong to, your community is vulnerable to the situations like the ones described above. In order for religious communities to get themselves out of these messes, they have to use their religious values to give structure to the process of self-reflection and awareness. Bullies in any community depend upon your silence and your reluctance to air the community's dirty laundry. It's their insurance policy. More so than any other type of community, religious communities can fall prey to the belief that their values and religious foundation make them immune to the rest of the world's problems. As a religious person, you owe it to yourself and your faith to act according to its values.

SOCIOECONOMIC STATUS

*I always clean when my child's rich friends come over. Sometimes I
even bake cookies.*   Cheryl, middle school mom

*When I pull up to someone's house and it's one of those big fancy
houses, I'm so intimidated. I mean, I know this kid. He hangs out at
my house all the time. It just gives me this horrible feeling in my
stomach.*   Noreen, middle school mom

*I was talking about my problems with my kids' private school when
the woman I was talking to gave me a look that said in no uncertain
terms, "Not everyone has this choice." I felt two inches tall because of
course this mother wants nothing less for her children than I want for
mine.*   Karenna, middle school mom

Most of the parents I address identify themselves as middle-class, whether
they live in a three-bedroom house with one car and have all their kids in
public school, or they live in a sprawling McMansion with their teenagers'
cars—gifts for their sixteenth birthdays—with their private-school bumper
stickers parked outside. How can these families think they're in the same
economic class? Obviously they're not, but no one (especially the people
who live in the really big houses) wants to admit it openly—we prefer to
pretend it's normal. We're experiencing a kind of "luxury creep": many
parents consider the latest flat-screen TV or several kinds of private lessons for the kids not as luxuries but as just keeping up, even if they have
to take on mountains of debt to do it.

The real pitched battles I see aren't between the haves and have-nots;
they're between the have-mores and have-plenty-mores. Even in the
wealthiest communities, no matter how much you have, there's always
something newer or better to own. It's not what you have that indicates
your social status; it's your ability to demonstrate that you have *more* than
your peers.

This dynamic gets played out among parents in plenty of trivial ways,
such as who can buy the teacher the most expensive present, donate the
most for new team equipment, drive the kids around the most "because

this new model is so much safer," host the class party "because the kids will enjoy the pool," deliver the most elaborate care package to sleep-away camp, and so forth. It becomes toxic when this "status leakage" results in wealthier parents demanding (and getting) more power and influence in the school and community, and in kids absorbing (and demonstrating) the message that displays of materialism are more important than values.

In addition, issues of class can stop parents from having good relationships with one another.

> When my child was five, he had a play date with another child in his class. He had a great time and the parents were very friendly with me. But when their child came over for a play date at our house, that was it. The way they acted toward me, they may as well have said, "You're the white trash of our town and we're not, so our child won't be playing with your child." They never asked to do anything with us again.
>
> Laura, elementary school mom

> A few years ago I received a large amount of money. We moved into a nicer house and we had friends who just couldn't handle it. They told us, "We don't feel comfortable anymore coming over to your house for dinner." We tried but they just wouldn't.
>
> Jack, middle school dad

Class differences between parents can make it much harder for us to talk to each other. We feel that we can't be messy around each other. We can't make mistakes. As our children get older and maintain their friendships (even when we no longer have any contact with their parents) and make their own messes, we may have trouble admitting the kids are having problems and reaching out to each other for help.

Let's return to the first quote above and discuss a situation I see often. When the kids become adolescents they spend a lot of time at each other's houses. Say the wealthier child's parents go out of town for the weekend and he has a raging party. The other parents find out about the party but are conflicted about what and how to tell the host kid's parents. They're worried that these parents will deny it or blame it on another child (one whose parents have considerably less money and social power). And maybe, in spite of their best efforts not to be smug, they can't help but feel a little vindicated that *their* kid doesn't throw raging parties whenever he has an unsupervised moment. And what if the less well-off kid throws the raging party? The wealthier parents often go ballistic on the lower-class parents because they can. We have to set our prejudices aside so that we can be there when our kids inevitably get themselves into trouble.

Issues of class don't affect only parents. Increasingly, teachers can't live near the schools they teach in because they can't afford the housing. This is true not just for the really expensive private schools but also for public schools in many major metropolitan areas. This isn't a minor issue; the implicit message teachers get is that while they're good enough to work from 7 a.m. to 7 p.m. in the community, they're not good enough to live in it. If you reside in a community like this one, advocate on behalf of the teachers in your community so that they can afford not only to teach in your community but to be a member of your community. You want your kids running into their teachers in the coffee shop or when they walk down the street.

GENERATION GAPS

No matter how and when they were raised, today's parents are likely to have a set of common beliefs. They believe that parenting is harder than in earlier generations, that children are having a harder time than children in the past, and that there's one right answer for any child-rearing problem. They think that if they read enough parenting books, they'll find the one right book that will make them the perfect parents. As a consequence of the first two beliefs, they develop a herd mentality, allowing group-think to dictate their outlook on any given child-rearing issue.

Beyond these commonalities, your style of parenting and the way you judge the parenting of others are profoundly affected by your age. Most of the parents of teens today are from the baby boom generation, born between the end of World War II and 1960, or Generation X, born between 1960 and 1975. What is the filter parents bring because of the generation they belong to?

Boomer Bust?

First let's look at the baby boomers. Many of us, including boomers themselves, are convinced that everyone in this generation grew up antiestab-
lishment, antiwar, and in favor of free love, women's liberation, and civil
rights, and that everyone from this generation has a strong sense of self
and a deep commitment to social issues. What has amazed me when
working with boomer parents is that they simultaneously assume that they
are the worst and best parents. Could they be right? Are boomers particularly terrible parents? Allow me to make some generalizations about this
generation's parenting challenges based on my work with them:

- As much as these parents talk a good game about not wanting to be
  popular with their kids, they really, really do.
- When they aren't able to enforce rules with their kids, they whine
  or demand that the schools do it for them.
- Boomer parents will get any technology for their kids because they
  can't say no and they don't want to be left behind ("All the other
  parents are giving their kids one, so I have to, too").
- They're often overwhelmed by technology, which can cause
  them to throw up their hands and forget that they should demand
  ethical behavior from children. For example, I watched a school
  administrator respond after the fact to an annual spring vicious
  high school hazing masquerading as a powder-puff football game:
  "You know kids with their cell phones and text messaging. There
  was no way for us to know where they were going to meet. It was
  out of our hands." It never occurred to him that the principal
  could have addressed the students before. "I don't know exactly
  when or where it will take place but if it does, anyone involved
  will be immediately suspended and letters will be sent to all the
  seniors' colleges."
- They have trouble upholding authority with their children because
  they don't respect authority even now. They don't like to set cur-
  fews. They grew up seeing themselves as fighting adult authority in
  any form—especially that of parents, teachers, and school adminis-

trators (even if the parents themselves are now in a professional position of more power than the school person). As they grew up and became parents, this attitude has come back to bite them on the backside, and they can be ridiculously conflicted.

My husband wanted to teach our two-year-old to question authority. I felt like I needed to explain the reasons for everything to the same two-year-old so he would understand that I wasn't being as unreasonably authoritarian as my own father had been. So of course my son believed for a few years that rules had to pass the test of his own logic before he was obliged to obey them. I finally grew up enough to relieve him of that notion.

Barbara, elementary school mom

Generation X

Boomers have been called the "Me Generation." We Gen Xers have been gifted with our own unflattering stereotypes. We're apathetic slackers, ungrateful, and lazy; we don't vote, don't care, couldn't be bothered. How do we stack up as parents? Here's what I've observed from working with Gen X parents:

- We don't think of ourselves as a group like the baby boomer generation. We have vague recollections of people calling us Generation X, but it always felt more like a marketing ploy.
- We revere the information we get from the Internet and turn to it first. We'll read five thousand unsubstantiated articles on the Web, come up with our own conclusions, and then assume that our belief is the one truth. We'll then use what we've learned to challenge people with genuine expertise on the subject.
- Our dependence on the Internet is exacerbated because we're raising our children without our own parents nearby, so we don't get the everyday benefit of their experience and common sense.
- We assume that every technical advance is a birthright and we want it faster and more powerful. So while a boomer parent might

give a second grader a cell phone only because all the other kids in her class have one, Gen Xers would never question getting the phone in the first place.

- Free love? Please. We never thought of sex as free love. We grew up with AIDS, STDs, and assemblies on date rape. We had sex anyway, but we never had the luxury of not having to worry about the consequences.

- We knew our parents did drugs; we even knew where they kept the drugs if they were still using them. We even stole them if our parents forgot they had them or were too embarrassed to admit it. We had no prescriptions of our own, unlike today's generation, who can take their own meds or sell them to their peers.

Of course, we all know parents who don't fit these generalizations, but it's easy to see how these differing outlooks can promote mistaken assumptions when conflicts arise. Compounding this, of course, is that people have multiple filters. Listen to one mother who describes this clearly.

> *As a black, single mother living in a middle-class neighborhood, I do assume that people will think I had my children when I was young and out of wedlock. That's why when I got divorced there was no way I was going back to my maiden name. I also assume my neighbors wonder how is it that I can afford to live in this neighborhood. And even though I was born into a pretty poor family and I have worked for years in a high-tech company, I still worry that our neighbors wonder. I won't speak for all black women in my situation but I think many women in my situation feel the same way.*

Obviously, like anyone, this woman brings a lot of filters to her conversations, but so would a white man whom everyone thinks is always in a position of privilege. What I hoped I have shown in this chapter is that everyone brings these filters to their interactions with others, just as people bring theirs in their interactions with you. In order to have the most genuine and respectful relationships with others as possible, I do think you have to be as self-aware as possible about your own filters. And while there's no way to know for certain about someone else's, just keeping in mind that they exist will enable you to understand more clearly where the other parent is coming from.

Becoming aware of your filters is the first step toward cleaning them. That sharper perception is a crucial part of becoming a more effective communicator. In the next two chapters, I'll discuss two other important factors: decoding what other parents say and confronting them respectfully.

Cracking the Code

Communication 101

For the last five years, your seventh-grade daughter, Mary, has been close friends with Lindsay. You and your spouse are friends with Lindsay's parents. The four of you have gone out to the movies and had each other over for dinner. You wouldn't tell them your darkest secrets, but you consider Lindsay's folks good people.

Now it's the night before her history test, and Mary is studying in her room—well, not exactly. She does have her history book propped open, but she's actually instant-messaging all of her close friends to try to find out why Lindsay has dumped her for a new group of friends. But you don't know this. All you know is that it looks like Mary is blowing off her history test to IM with her friends. You walk past her door, stare at the back of her head, and sigh loudly. She keeps sending messages. You tell her to stop chatting and start studying. She sighs in return, glares at you, and turns back to her textbook. The next day, as she's walking to her history class, she runs into Lindsay and her new friends, gets up her courage, and asks, "Lindsay, are you mad at me?" Lindsay looks at her, right hip out, hands on hips, and says no in a manner that clearly communicates that *of course* she's mad at her and that Mary's question is further proof of how pathetic Mary is for even asking. As Mary walks away she hears Lindsay say, "I can't *believe* I was ever friends with her." Mary takes her history test—but all she can think is, "What did I do? What can I do to make Lindsay like me again?"

A few hours later, Mary comes home from school, plops down on the couch, and watches TV. That's where you find her when you come in—exhausted from working all day, grocery shopping, and then making a mad crosstown dash to pick up your son from soccer practice. Your blood begins to boil. "How did you do in school today?" you ask, trying not to betray your annoyance. You get a one-word answer: "Fine." You try again: "How was your history test?" Mary looks at you as if you are the cause of global warming, worldwide extinction of pandas, and ripping her favorite jeans and says, "You just don't understand what's going on in my life!" Then she stomps upstairs to her room, slamming the door behind her.

Demonstrating great emotional maturity, you put your grocery bags down and go to her room. As she tells you what's going on, your first reaction is that you hate Lindsay and want terrible, painful things to happen to her. But you also have a horrible feeling in the pit of your stomach. Why would Lindsay be so mean? Why would she reject your daughter? Is your child a social misfit? And what, if anything, should you do about it?

In the first four chapters of this book, I've focused on how we can better understand ourselves as parents. Now I want to discuss how we take that understanding into our interactions and conflicts with others. Often, the trouble begins when your child has a problem with another child. Such conflicts can all too easily become your own—and those of every other parent whose children are involved. How you navigate these situations is crucial.

One of the reasons why conflicts can be so tricky is because Perfect Parent World has its own language; what we say is often very different from what we mean. If you want to model good conflict resolution skills for your child, the first step is improving your communication skills. That entails cracking the code of what others are saying (I call this "fixing our receivers"), appreciating the feelings beneath the words, and expressing your own feelings honestly and clearly ("fixing our transmitters"). In this chapter, I'll focus on helping you fix your receivers and transmitters so that you can crack the code of what parents are saying, listen more effectively, and respond more clearly.

Let's return to the saga of Mary and Lindsay. Since most children's conflicts occur when parents aren't around, your first step should be to help your child prepare to speak to the other child. I explained this process in great detail in *Queen Bees & Wannabes;* let me offer a summary here. (You'll find other examples of how to help your child handle conflict throughout this book, and I'll show you how to adapt this method for adults in the next chapter.)

In almost all situations, your child should plan to speak to the child one-on-one, since anyone is likely to be less defensive when they're not surrounded by their peers. To help your child prepare, have her talk through (with you or another adult you approve of) and write down what she didn't like that the other person did, what she wants to happen instead, and whether she wants to continue the friendship with that person (if they are friends). Your child's goal isn't becoming best friends forever or vanquishing her enemy. Rather, she will have succeeded if she can do any of the following: take the bad feelings she has in the pit of her stomach and put them into words, strategize about where she might have the conversation with the other girl, and ultimately explain to her why her behavior wasn't acceptable. Any part that your child does is a success.

So you sit down with Mary and strategize about what she can say to Lindsay to help the situation. The next day Mary talks to Lindsay and although Lindsay doesn't apologize, she does say she'll stop "whatever Mary thinks she's doing that's so bad."

The trouble is that Lindsay's behavior doesn't get better—it gets worse. Although Mary always mutes her cell phone in school as she's supposed to, she sees the phone light up as she's sitting in math class and surreptitiously flips it open to read, "Everyone thinks you're pathetic. Want to know who this is? You'll never know." Later that day Lindsay and her new friends walk by Mary and whisper and laugh to themselves.

Now you're at a crossroads. Mary and Lindsay's conflict is about to become your own. You screw up your courage and call Lindsay's parents. Her dad, Robert, answers the phone and after listening for about five seconds says, "I think the girls should work it out by themselves, don't you? But let me get Kathy." Kathy gets on the phone and is equally unhelpful. "I think the girls just need to work it out and go their own ways for a little while. You know girls. They'll be best friends again next week." You hang up, feeling completely blown off, and you're not sure you even understand why. After all, Robert and Kathy have a point. In an ideal world, shouldn't the girls work it out themselves? You don't want to micromanage the girls' friendships or be one of those overinvolved parents whom everybody barely tolerates. But you also can't believe that Robert and Kathy are so heartless. You have a kid who's crying herself to sleep at night and doesn't want to go to school—you have to do something.

Now let's walk through the phone conversation with Robert and Kathy so as to decode the messages they sent you and better understand why you found it so unsatisfying.

The first red flag was "Let me get Kathy"—Robert's strategic pass-off of the phone to his wife. As you'll recall from Chapter 3, this is usually dad-speak for "This isn't my jurisdiction, this is women's work, and now I'll run away." By passing the phone to Kathy, Robert signaled that your problem wasn't worth his attention. He'd hand off that phone even if Kathy were getting dinner on the table, folding laundry, helping with homework, and juggling flaming bowling balls all at the same time.

"Let's let the kids work it out" is the second red flag. It says, "I'm not listening to you." After all, the kids tried and weren't able to work it out, as you explained. The problem was big enough in your eyes that you were willing to clear a major hurdle to address it: calling another parent. Parents who receive these phone calls often forget how hard it was for the other parent to call in the first place.

Moreover, there are two other messages hidden in Kathy's comments: a judgment of your parenting abilities and a suggestion that the problem between the two girls lies with Mary. When Kathy dismisses your concerns and tells you that the girls need to work it out for themselves, she's also saying, "*We're* enlightened; *we* don't need to micromanage our daughter's life because *we* have faith that the kids can work it out. *Our* kid can handle it—why can't yours? Has it occurred to you that your daughter could be doing just fine, but you're such an overanxious parent that you can't see it?" Frankly, the people most likely to have this reaction are the parents whose kids are being mean, not the parents of the kids who are bearing the brunt of the meanness.

Once you've cracked the code of what another parent is saying, you can begin to figure out how to talk with him or her more effectively. In this situation, you need to let Robert and Kathy know that however differently they might view the situation, your daughter's pain and your concerns are real. So take a few calming breaths and pick up the phone again:

YOU: *Hi, Kathy. Is this a good time to talk? We've known each other a long time, and I want you to realize that I wouldn't have called you in the first place if I didn't think we had a problem the girls need our help on.*

KATHY: *Look, I just don't believe in butting into the girls' business. I really think this will blow over. Or maybe the girls just need to go their separate ways for a while.*

YOU: *That may be, but right now Mary is really hurt. Mary has talked to Lindsay and things aren't getting better. I'd like you and me to sit down and talk over some ways the girls can handle this so that everyone feels treated with respect, whether or not they go their separate ways.*

KATHY: *Is that really necessary? It sounds as though we're planning a summit meeting!*

YOU: *I do think it's a good idea. If my daughter has done something to Lindsay that she needs to take responsibility for, I want her to hear it—even if it's difficult for her to hear. But I also want Lindsay's hurtful behavior toward Mary to stop.*

KATHY: *Fine, I guess that makes sense. When do you want to get together?*

LANDMINE!

Please delete the word *inappropriate* from your vocabulary, as in "It was inappropriate for your child to speak to my child in that manner." While you might be right, the person with whom you're talking is likely to become extremely irritated and defensive when he hears the word—whether he's twelve or forty-two. Instead explain exactly what you're seeing or what the person is doing that you define (in your mind) as inappropriate.

WHAT WE REALLY MEAN WHEN WE SAY . . .

Of course, there are many codes to be broken in Perfect Parent World. Below are statements that I've heard from parents; I'm sure you've heard them too. Although they all look reasonable at first and even second glance, they're often code for powerful value judgments that can make other parents feel deeply inadequate. Naturally, we don't always speak in code; often we're able to say what we mean plainly. Nor do we speak in code only when we want to send a negative message. Sometimes we do it because we want to soften a harsh statement or invite a more open discussion. However, my focus here is on the encoded messages we send when we're intentionally or unintentionally trying to make ourselves feel like we're better than other parents, and on the ones we receive that make us feel like we're worse than other parents.

"My biggest priority is my kids"

Cracking the Code "I have a better relationship with my children than other parents do because I spend more time with them and am willing to sacrifice more for them."

For Parents on the Transmitting End *Of course* your biggest investment is your kids. Having given birth to two children myself, I can't imagine putting so much effort into having them in the first place and then not doing any follow-up. When I hear parents say this, I think it comes across as asserting a kind of moral superiority over others. Specifically, they're saying three things: First, they spend more time than other people do with their children. Second, they believe that the amount of time they spend with their children is in direct proportion to the quality of their relationship with their kids. Third, they think that the more after-school activities they schlep their kids to, the more they've demonstrated their self-sacrifice, which they equate with being better parents.

If you've heard yourself say these words or if you've made these assumptions, I hope you'll reconsider them. You might think you know how much time other parents spend with their children, but unless you're stalking them, you don't really know. Also, it doesn't necessarily follow that the more time you spend with your kids, the better the relationship you'll have. You only have to look at the child who can't be away from his mom for five minutes without having a panic attack to know that. Lastly, there is no medal for the parent who sacrifices all of his or her time schlepping the kids from one activity to another.

For Parents on the Receiving End What are you supposed to say when someone says this to you—maybe "Really, I admire that so much. I tried making them my top priority, but frankly my kids come right after going to the gym and watching TV"? Recognize that statements like "My biggest priority is my kids" can be power plays intended to put you on notice that the other parent is taking you on under the guise of a higher calling: the welfare of his or her own kids. Don't feel that you have to prove yourself as a parent. You aren't in a contest.

"I'm my child's best advocate— I'm acting in the best interests of my child"

Cracking the Code "I'm the only person who can be trusted to do right by my child. I have to keep close tabs on everyone else to be sure my child isn't undermined, unfairly treated, or denied resources or opportunities that are rightfully his."

For Parents on the Transmitting End The code phrases "biggest priority" and "best interests"—often used with the best of intentions—can also be used to justify some of the nastiest parental behavior. If you tell yourself that you're acting in the best interests of your child, it's only a short step to the assumption that anyone who disagrees with your opinion is acting *against* the best interests of your child—which makes that person a threat that needs to be eliminated (see the next section, on protecting your child). And while you think you know your child better than any teacher or other adult because, after all, you *are* the parent, I need to ask you to adjust your thinking a little. It is true that you know your child best— within the context of your relationship with your child. Other people know your child in different contexts and what they know isn't necessarily less valuable than what you know—especially when what is at issue is how your child functions outside of your immediate jurisdiction, such as at school, on the playing field, or during extracurricular activities.

It can be very hard to accept that you don't know your child best in another context; it might feel almost like admitting that you're a bad parent. The next time you hear yourself saying, "I know my child, and he would never do that"—after all, you know your little Kelly doesn't lie, so the other three kids and their six parents *must* be wrong about that altercation during lacrosse practice—consider the possibility that you *don't* know everything about Kelly.

> *My mom never would have believed the way I was at school. At home I was sociable, agreeable, a nice boy. At school I was uncoachable and unteachable.* Chris, high school student

For Parents on the Receiving End

> *People are always telling me that I should "fight for" my kid. That I'm my "child's best advocate." But does that mean I have to fight for getting her into every dance class and every other activity, and if I don't, I'm a terrible parent? That I shouldn't send her to a public school? Does it mean that I shouldn't trust anyone else to advocate for her or do right by my kid? There's no way to think this through clearly.* Joanne, mother of two girls, ages eight and eleven

Actually, this mother *is* thinking clearly. She's feeling confused because her common sense goes against the prevailing wisdom of Perfect Parent World, which says that in order to be a good parent, she needs to fight constantly for her child, and that if she doesn't buy into the prevailing ideas as to the "right" schools and the "right" activities for her child, she's abdicating her moral duty as a parent. Many parents experience the same confusion.

"My job as a parent is to protect my kids"

Cracking the Code "I love the feeling of being the mama or papa bear and I'm going to apply that life philosophy not only when my child is in physical danger, but anytime my child feels frustrated, unjustly punished, or like a failure."

For Parents on the Transmitting End Of course we want to protect our kids. Most parents are hardwired to be a mama or papa bear when their child is threatened. I've had parents tell me, "I'd kill for my kids" or "If you mess with my kids, you mess with me, and I'll do anything it takes to protect them." Let's examine these statements more closely. Protect them from what? Most parents aren't keeping man-eating tigers away from their progeny. These parents' fierce love for their children can become a justification for protecting them from failure, disappointment, or punishment.

It can be really hard to spot yourself behaving this way. I believe demanding a grade change falls into the category of protecting your child from frustration or failure—as does complaining about him or her not making a team or not getting a part (or getting the *wrong* part) in the school play, or petitioning a coach for more playing time.

One of our hardest tasks as parents is to stand by and watch our kids experience frustration and failure, but it's one of our most important tasks as well. Protecting your child from disappointment creates an incompetent child. It stops her from developing the skills necessary to overcome life's natural challenges. It's by facing—and sometimes being defeated by—these challenges and through the lessons we learn from our disappointments that we forge our character, our beliefs, and our ability to be in meaningful relationships with others. If you don't learn how to struggle, then you leave as soon as it gets hard. You leave a job, you leave a relationship. Parents who overprotect their children also send them the implicit message that they aren't capable of handling these challenges, which in turn teaches children to be helpless.

Have you ever heard yourself or someone else say:

"Where's the evidence of my child's . . ." (as the first response to hearing a report of your child's misbehavior)
"I think the punishment is too severe. This is the first time Sally has done something like this." (if convinced that your child did misbehave and/or if there's a preponderance of evidence)
"I think everyone is taking this a little too seriously. The kids were just joking around."
"You know girls. This is just the way they are. Girls will be girls."
"You know boys. This is just the way they are. Boys will be boys."

No matter who's speaking—it could be a parent, teacher, principal, or coach—statements like these send the same message: The behavior in question is normal (that is, acceptable), so why should the child suffer consequences or be punished? In addition, the speaker can dismiss the other person's perspective and abdicate the responsibility of providing boundaries for children.

Allowing your child to struggle isn't simply a matter of instilling good character. Overprotecting your child can be truly *dangerous* because your child is likely to push and push to find out when he'll actually be held accountable. (Remember the minister's son I quoted in the Introduction.) This process can get him into heaps of trouble.

It's appropriate to protect your child when his mental or physical health and safety are at risk. When your child has tried to the best of his ability to confront a problem and continues to be dismissed or mistreated, it makes sense to step in. But much more often your job is to comfort him—to kiss his boo-boos when he's little and to validate and affirm his experience and his pain when he gets older (and kiss his boo-boos if he'll let you). You'll encourage him to face fears and difficulties by showing him that you have confidence he can do it. You won't walk away; you'll watch, not breathing, until he gets through. Your job is to be there every step of the way as he does it on his own.

Here's what I tell parents to put the fear of God into them: If you raise incompetent children, they'll live with you forever and they won't be able to take care of you when you're old. Is that what you want?

For Parents on the Receiving End When other parents make these kinds of statements to you, be wary of them. Although they aren't usually self-aware enough to realize it, they're telling you that they can't be trusted to hold their child accountable for bad behavior, and they can easily see your child as the problem.

"My child needs a cell phone so that if anything goes wrong she can get in touch with me"

Cracking the Code "The world is a dangerous place. If I don't know where my child is all the time, bad things will happen to her and I won't be able to do anything about it. If I do know where she is, I can save her."

For Parents on the Transmitting End Before I tell you why I don't approve of kids having cell phones, I'll admit there are some benefits. Parents have told me that grandparents call their grandchildren directly, which helps establish independent relationships between them. If your child is lost or late, she can call you. Okay—that's about it. I just don't think children need a cell phone before the age of fourteen. (I do think it's a different story for the high school years, when logistics usually become more challenging—especially if your child is driving—but that still doesn't get you off the hook from reading this section.)

Please don't feel guilty or defensive because I'm telling you not to give your child a cell phone and your eight-year-old already has one. When I talk about cell phones in my presentations, almost every parent in the room looks down at the floor. Maybe your child nagged you to death to get one, but I bet another reason you felt compelled to buy her a cell is because Perfect Parent World seems to require it. After all, good parents know where their children are 24/7, don't they? Cell phones are an easy way to feel that your child is safe. But *is* she safe?

I empathize with parents who feel that they should use any tools available to make their kids safer. But I'm not persuaded that equipping them with cell phones actually does that. I think cell phones simply reinforce the idea that the world is a very frightening place. If our churches allow priests to prey on our children, if our neighbors can be pedophiles, if our kids can be snatched away without warning and even the presence of the store video camera can't stop it, we feel an overwhelming sense of danger and feel out of control, consumed with anxiety. As psychologist David Anderegg, author of *Worried All the Time: Overparenting in the Age of Anxiety and How to Stop It*, writes, "Excessive worrying causes suffering; suffering that is both unnecessary and very real . . . People who are overwhelmed with anxiety often make bad decisions or fall for simple solutions because simple solutions promise an end to overwhelming anxiety." As parents, we have to realize that the same anxiety that compels us to take every precaution for our children is likely to leave us feeling that they're *still* not safe enough.

So why are cell phones so problematic?

1. They give us a false sense of security. Cell phones, ironically, can make it *harder* to know where your child is. In fact, teens couldn't have dreamed up a better way to confuse their parents about their location. If you were like me as a teen, you used the following strategy to fool your parents. You wanted to go to your girlfriend or boyfriend's house, but you knew there was no way your mom or dad would let you. So you lied and told them you were hanging out with a friend. Then you had your friend lie for you when your parent called their house. Your friend said, "Uh . . . she can't come to the phone, she's in the bathroom right now." Then your friend called you at your boyfriend or girlfriend's house so you could call your parents right back and lie. Basically the existing technology limited your ability to conceal your location. With a cell phone, your child's ability to conceal his or her location is virtually limitless. He or she can call you from anywhere and pretend to be wherever he or she's supposed to be.

2. They stop you from being a gatekeeper. When you were growing up, you phoned your friends at home. When their parents answered, you spoke to them: "Hi, Mrs. McBride, is Tony there?" Most likely, Mrs. McBride would ask you a couple of questions about your parents or your basketball team before putting Tony on the phone. The point is that you often had to go through an adult to talk to your friend. You established and maintained a relationship with that parent and vice versa. Cell phones make that much more difficult. If we're going to have communities where people look out for each other, then parents need to feel protective of their children's friends, and their children's friends need to feel that these parents are watching over them.

You also want not just your child but his or her friends to have a healthy sense of fear and paranoia about you, because you want them respecting you and believing that you won't hesitate to step in as a parent by proxy if need be. When the kids bypass you by speaking to each other directly on their cells, that relationship doesn't get built.

It's not just your child's friends who need to go through you. One counselor with a five-year-old son described how her husband struck up a conversation about kids with another guy at the gym. The other fellow mentioned that he had two daughters who babysat. He then gave the husband the daughters' cell phone numbers rather than the family's home phone. The two men were strangers to each other, so why did the father of the two babysitters give out such a private piece of information rather than asking the husband to connect with the family first through their home phone?

3. Cell phones teach your child to be helpless and irresponsible. A parent told me this story after one of my presentations. I couldn't possibly make this stuff up.

> *I was hanging outside my house when the boy who lives four houses down rode by on his motor scooter and then one of the wheels broke. I watched him as he whipped out his cell phone, called his mom at home, and told her to come over and fix the scooter. I am not joking when I say that I watched this woman get into her car and drive four houses down to help this kid.*
>
> Betty, middle school mom

I hear these stories all the time. One of your child's most important tasks during adolescence is to become self-sufficient. How will that happen if you're micromanaging your child via cell phone?

I recently conducted a faculty training at which a faculty member described going on a seventh-grade canoeing trip where every student had a cell phone. I immediately visualized a kid falling out of the canoe and flailing around while desperately calling Mom on the cell to find out how to get back into the canoe (or drowning while trying to keep his cell phone and iPod dry). What would you want your child to do in that situation? Spend his time calling you so you can explain to him how to get back into the canoe? Or would you rather he concentrate on figuring it out himself? If a kid needs adult help on such a trip, isn't it best for him to reach out to nearby adults—who, by the way, all have cell phones? By equipping their children with cells, parents are inadvertently teaching their kids that as soon as they get into trouble, they have to run to their parents—the only adults who can or will help them.

4. Cell phones are status symbols. Cell phones are like jeans or any other material good that signifies status in Girl World or Boy World. Kids compete over who has the latest one with the most features, coolest ring tone, etc. Some parents are eager to contribute to that perception of high status by buying their child the latest model. I see cell phones as a sign that you can't say no to your child. I don't care how much your child begs or pleads. You survived without one; your child will as well.

5. Cell phones are devastatingly effective tools for bullies. Let's go back to the story at the beginning of the chapter. One of the ways Mary was attacked was by text messaging on her cell phone. Kids forward messages and humiliating photographs (superimposing a person's face on another person's body is a favorite) via cell phone all the time. Cyberbullying—bullying via modern technologies such as e-mail, blogging, live journals, instant messaging, cell phone text messaging, and camera phones—is an epidemic. Don't give your child the chance to contribute to it or become a victim of it. At the very least, if you must get a cell phone for your child, limit its use by blocking text messaging and photo capabilities. (For more information on how to talk to your kids about cyberbullying, check out www.empowerprogram.org for a pamphlet on the subject written by the Empower Program in association with Unicel, a mobile phone company, and Rachel Simmons, author of *Odd Girl Out.*)

If You're a Parent on the Receiving End When another parent tells you, "You don't understand, my kid *needs* a cell phone," it can be code for "I know where my kid is and that he's safe—but you're clueless about your kid. Who's the better parent?" If you're still tempted to buy your child a cell phone, ask yourself why. Are you letting your child take the necessary steps toward independence? Have you scheduled so many activities that your kid needs a GPS device embedded in his neck for you to find him? If your child is still in middle school and already has a cell phone but you want to take it away, what is going to be your greatest obstacle in achieving your goal? If your answer is that you don't want your child to be angry with you, admitting that takes tremendous courage. Now use that courage to give you the strength to take the cell phone away.

"I want to give my kids every opportunity I didn't have"

Cracking the Code "I'm going to make sure that nothing stands in the way of my child getting the best—not even my child. If I give her every opportunity, she'll have more chances to excel—and outshine the other children."

For Parents on the Transmitting End Any good parent wants his or her child to learn new things and have the opportunity to excel. But this very natural desire has a dark side, especially in Entitled parents. If in your desire to see your child excel you push her to compare herself with and compete against other children, you stand a good chance of making her incredibly anxious. You risk turning the activities your child enjoys into jobs or into a barometer of your love—and that's a surefire way to make her resent you when she's an adult.

The other problem with thinking you have to give your child every opportunity is that it can make you feel like a failure if your child doesn't take advantage of each one, or believe that people who deny your child these opportunities are hurting your child's future. This can lead to torturous indecision: Should Mark take French, Spanish, or German? Which will help most in later life? Which will impress other parents or college admissions officers? It can also make you crazily, absolutely decisive: Your child will take all three, and he'll catch up on sleep later, maybe in his next life—the one that comes after Yale. The two of you scurry to activities from dawn to dusk.

This mind-set has had some unintended consequences in the academic arena. Fifteen years ago, studies came out that documented girls' reluctance to study math and science. Admirably, many schools and parents encouraged girls to enter these fields. At the same time, parents came to believe that their daughters would stand out in the college admissions process if they excelled in math or science. This led to a flood of parents demanding that their daughters be put into AP calculus, chemistry, or physics even when they didn't have the grades or aptitude to handle the classes, and sometimes even if they had no interest in the subject. I'm all for challenging kids, but ask yourself whether you're out to plump up a high school transcript or help your child pursue a genuine academic passion. Listen to the head of an upper school describe her dilemma:

> *Every fall it's the same thing: Parents demanding that their girls get into the AP classes. They say to me all the time, "My child will not get into college if she doesn't get into the advanced classes. Therefore it is in the best interest of my child to take these classes." Meanwhile,*

the math department believed that they served the best interest of the student by matching her skill level with the appropriate class. In those meetings the kids would often mimic their parents only to later go to us and tell us they didn't want to be in the class but were too afraid to go against their parents. Naomi, high school principal

I often hear parents harp on "opportunity" when they're frantic to get their kids into "all the best classes" so they can get into the "best schools," which they assume will give their children the best chance at a successful life. Parents who believe their kids must take advanced classes to get into college don't mean that literally; of course you can get into college without taking AP classes. These parents are really talking about getting into a college that's acceptable in Perfect Parent World. This kind of pressure is so insidious and invidious that I'm giving it a whole chapter—Chapter 12.

If you're "giving your child every opportunity" in extracurricular activities, be careful that *he's* the one who loves and takes pride in the activities, not you. One mother remarked about her son, "He's such a good cello player. He hates practicing, but he could get a scholarship and it would be a shame if he gave it up." Yes, in some ways it could be, but maybe not.

When our daughter was young, she was matched with the oboe by the school's music teacher. But even though she was good at it, it was clear from early on that she really didn't enjoy it. For the last two years, she's been begging us to allow her to stop. My husband is in a few amateur bands and he always dreamed of playing with her one day. We both hoped that her ability would enable her to receive a scholarship to college. And I didn't think we were being good parents if we let her quit something that she was good at. Just recently we came to the decision to allow her to stop. But we're grieving about it. My daughter is also an artist, but she always downplayed her art and dismissed her ability because no one cared about art. Last night she told me, "I have my charcoals and I'm happy." It is still so hard—that scholarship could have really come in handy—but I have to admit that she is much happier. Cora, high school mom

These weren't ego-driven parents living their lives through the accomplishments of their children. Both receive great satisfaction from their work and are wonderful members of their community. If they can be caught up in this rat race, anyone can.

Does this hit a nerve? Take a hard look: When a teacher or coach denied your child, was your reaction based on the issues above? Do your child's activities reflect what he or she really loves to do, or what you wished you'd had a chance to do when you were a teenager? Don't forget that even if a child gives up something he's good at, he'll have learned a great deal from the process and most likely will have developed skills that will last a lifetime. It's not all or nothing. Children learn from quitting; they learn to admit when they have too much on their plate and that they can decide what they really love and why.

For Parents on the Receiving End If you hear other parents talking about all the extras they give their kids, it's easy to feel inadequate. Maybe you didn't even know about the PSAT tutor who's already all booked up. When Maysie wanted to quit piano after two years, you said okay; she hated to practice, so why pay the money? And you didn't push her to join any of the after-school clubs; she just likes to come home after school, do her homework, and paint. You get a sinking feeling when another parent describes how "completely exhausted" she is ferrying her kids around all the time. Shouldn't you be an exhausted parent, too? Isn't that part of the job description?

No, it isn't. Here's the truth: You aren't a failure if you don't push your child to pursue every opportunity, and neither is your child. Your job is to cultivate your child's interests but to let her take the lead in pursuing them. When you feel the pressure to keep up with the Joneses, pull back and remind yourself that your child's path is unique.

"I hear that Aretha got a 5 on her AP Physics test— how nice for you"

Cracking the Code "I envy your child and wish my child were equally talented/high-achieving" or "You must have given your child an unfair advantage."

For Parents on the Transmitting End We can be genuinely happy that other kids do well. But let's admit that it's hard to see all the other kids parading up on stage to collect their trophies and certificates on Awards Day while our child stays slumped in his seat. We may need to remind ourselves that we are *not* our kids' achievements and that we can be good parents even without the external validation bestowed on Awards Day. If we become obsessed with awards and tributes, we risk giving our children the message that they're not worthy without them.

We've also got to be careful not to assume that other kids get awards because their parents have somehow cheated the system. This kind of scorekeeping only feeds the social hierarchy of Perfect Parent World and keeps us from reaching out to one another when our kids get in trouble.

For Parents on the Receiving End Of course we love it when others congratulate us on our children's achievements, but none of us wants to look like we're bragging. And there really are parents who are proud of their children's accomplishments without needing to advertise them on a billboard.

Some parents are so uncomfortable talking about their children's achievements that they'll only discuss them with their closest friends. This can lead to some rather strange conversational gambits, as when two parents are sitting together observing their children, perhaps at a basketball game or class play. Parent X will compliment Parent Y's child; Parent Y often responds by putting her own child down ("Yeah, but she's doing so terribly in science" or "She has no friends") and then complimenting Parent X's child ("Thanks, but your daughter's the real whiz kid"). I always chuckle when I hear this; it's funny to hear adults sounding like adolescent girls ("Oh, no, I look like a total cow, my thighs are enormous; you look completely gorgeous"). Being humble is a great thing, but if parents consistently downplay their children's achievements, kids can grow up thinking that whatever they do isn't good enough.

On the other hand, if you brag about your child all the time and think everything he does is amazing, neither you nor your child will be able to distinguish between when he's doing well and when he needs to improve. I think the competitiveness of American culture can be confusing; the superstar archetype is so predominant that many parents dance between the two poles of bragging and silence.

"It's so competitive today"

Cracking the Code "I'm justified in doing whatever it takes to help my kid."

For Parents on the Transmitting End According to psychologist David Anderegg, parents today have exaggerated fears about the competitive world facing their kids. He explains that we use our fear of increasingly scarce resources and opportunities as an excuse to give our kids more of those "opportunities we never had."

Parents trying to give their children a leg up have an amazing ability to rationalize writing their kids' college admissions essays, papier-mâchéing their dioramas, and "editing" their kids' English papers (and then responding angrily when teachers don't give their children the grade they "deserve"). Parents tell me that they're so worried that their kids will be squeezed out of the good colleges that they can't afford to let them get B's. And what do the kids learn? That the world is a zero-sum game, one they can't navigate alone. And that unless they get into the most desirable college, whether it's an Ivy League school, their parents' alma mater, or the school all their friends think is ultra-cool, they've wasted their time and effort.

For Parents on the Receiving End This is another situation where it's difficult not to get sucked into feeling hypercompetitive. If you can't resist the urge, you'll be drawn into that arms race that turns every parent gathering into a heated discussion of teen leadership camps, AP courses, and lobbying for the best teachers. You can feel sympathetic for the parents who feel they have no choice but to play this game, but you don't have to join them.

"I don't know what I did to deserve such a good kid"

Cracking the Code "Through a combination of DNA and good parenting, my child is better than most other kids. I've really dodged a bullet."

For Parents on the Transmitting and Receiving Ends When parents end up with a kid who speaks in complete sentences, says "please" and "thank you," and isn't shooting drugs, pregnant, or keeling over from an eating disorder, many feel like they've won Olympic gold. Why are they so relieved? Because movies, TV talk shows, and nighttime dramas are filled with story lines portraying teenagers as immoral, superficial, violent, hedonistic party animals who can't get enough sex, drugs, and alcohol. First, there are many teens who don't abuse alcohol and drugs and aren't having sex. Second, and not surprisingly, most of the parents I talk to assume that there are legions of "bad kids" out there, and they're frantic lest their progeny fall into their clutches. Over the last dozen years, I've worked with every kind of kid under the sun, including violent offenders—kids other kids are scared of—and I've come across only a handful who truly deserve the label "bad kid." The danger in accepting the notion of a world swarming with bad kids is that you're "othering" other kids—putting them lower on the social ladder than your own, labeling them "less than"—and this encourages your child to do the same.

Or maybe you're just grateful that your child turned out okay *despite* the myriad ways you think you've messed up as a parent. Again, why so much anxiety? Because the expectations of Perfect Parent World are that if you just work hard enough at it, you could be the terrific parent you're supposed to be. Search under "parenting" on Amazon.com, and you'll find more than fifty-three thousand books (including this one) inviting you to improve your job skills.

After a recent presentation, a woman approached me to ask for advice about how to talk to her five-year-old daughter about how babies are made. About halfway through my answer, she burst into tears and said, "I'm just so worried about messing up!" She felt that any misstep on her part would doom her daughter to . . . I'm not sure what. Her daughter having sex by fourteen? Being pregnant by fifteen?

True confessions time: If I have one single moment each week when I think I've parented well, that's a good week. I hope you never assume that people who advise other people how to parent are perfect parents themselves. We struggle with exactly the same problems as everyone else. As I write this, I'm very aware that my husband and I have a parent-teacher conference in two weeks and I'm praying that it will go well.

The truth is that the only way you're going to seriously mess up your children is if you consistently humiliate them and make them feel ashamed of themselves. (I mean ashamed of their whole being, not of doing something unkind or unethical.) Children are resilient. You will make mistakes. This doesn't make you a terrible parent—it makes you a parent just like everybody else. If your children see that you're doing your best to live according to your values, that you have the courage to admit your mistakes and learn from them, that you do everything in your power to create a safe, consistent, and loving home for them, you're golden. So what if you make a few mistakes along the way?

Whether you think your kid is good *because* of your efforts or *in spite* of them, are you looking at other people's children in a black-and-white way? Think back on the times you've said "I have such a good kid." What was happening that caused you to feel like you needed to say it? Are you keeping your kid away from the "bad kids"? And what makes those kids bad—bad grades? Bad habits? Bad haircuts? Are these judgments fair?

"My child and I have an open relationship— she tells me everything"

Cracking the Code "I'm a good parent because I know everything that's going on in my kid's life."

For Parents on the Transmitting End Parents who claim they have an "open" relationship with their child—which they generally define as one with honest communication in which everything is transparent—usually think this is the same thing as a great relationship. Many assume that the more they know about their kid, the better. I disagree. Showing appropriate respect for your child's privacy, personal boundaries, and choices is one of the most important things you need to do in order to parent a teen. It helps keep you from projecting your thoughts and beliefs onto your child, and makes your child more likely to come to you for help because she won't be as anxious about you freaking out and taking over.

Parents often get caught up in thinking they need to know the specifics of a situation in order to instill their values. Not true. Let's suppose your child is about to walk out the door to a party. It's very powerful to say, "Come here and sit down for a moment. Whatever you end up doing tonight, this is how I expect you to behave: If you see someone, including yourself, being taken advantage of or coerced into doing something you know isn't right, I expect you to uphold this family's values and step in to stop it—friends or not. I can't control everything you do or every decision you make, but you know what this family stands for: treating every person with dignity. So I trust you to go out and act honorably." Note that none of the impact of this discussion rests on your insisting on knowing every last detail before and after the party. (You will, of course, have already checked out the situation vis-à-vis adults in attendance, etc.; please see Chapter 11.)

Many parents don't appreciate the degree to which kids are likely to lie to protect what they see as their right to privacy. While I know there are kids who are completely honest with their parents, you simply can't assume that your child will always be truthful.

I'm also taken aback by the number of parents who encourage their kids to be frank with them about their sexual experiences under the guise of "open and honest communication." I do *not* mean that parents should shirk their responsibility to communicate clearly and forthrightly their values about sex and the basics of sex education. I do think it's violating a necessary personal boundary to inquire about the details of a child's sex life. As one dad said, "I'm stunned by how much fathers know about their sons' sexual exploits. They're living their lives through their sons and how much sex they're getting." Remember the "Act Like a Mom" and "Act Like a Dad" boxes. Having a child who fits into the "Act Like a Boy" box validates those fathers because it makes this dad feel that both are in the box.

Another problem with the supposed benefits of an "open relationship" is that parents don't set appropriate boundaries around their *own* private lives. They believe that they're not being honest and open with their kids unless they share every detail of their drug- and alcohol-fueled past, relationships, last night's fight, etc. As I'll discuss in Part Two, it's essential to keep these boundaries in place as you communicate your values about these situations.

For Parents on the Receiving End If a parent stresses what a great relationship she has with her kid, she could be trying to hint to you that her daughter has told her something about your child that she feels you should be aware of but she doesn't know how to bring it up. If you suspect this, you may need to create the opening yourself: "It's great that Laura tells you so much. If she ever tells you anything about my Megan, I hope you know you could share it with me."

TUNING YOUR RECEIVER: BECOMING A BETTER LISTENER

The first step in effective communication is figuring out what the other person is trying to say. As I discussed in Chapter 4, your reaction to others is based largely on personal filters such as gender, socioeconomic status, and the like. Your position in Perfect Parent World also influences how you listen. A Sidekick or a Floater's opinion has more authority in Perfect Parent World than that of a Wannabe or an Outsider—and you'll usually make these assessments without even being aware that you're making them. This weighting of opinion isn't necessarily bad. In fact, it's to our benefit when we use our social intelligence to understand other people's motivations. But as I've said before, it's wrong to devalue someone's opinion (including our own) based on social position.

Becoming a better listener can help you overcome your biases. There are a slew of self-help books offering guidance on how to do this. Most of them offer advice based on the concepts pioneered by Thomas Gordon, Ph.D. Dr. Gordon was one of the earliest proponents of "I" language and "reflective listening." Using "I" language means stating how you feel about another's actions in terms of how it affects you: "When you were late, I felt anxious and concerned" rather than "You're always late because you're inconsiderate and you knew how important it was to get to the meeting on time."

While I agree with the logic behind these listening strategies, I don't think they are often implemented effectively. I was raised by a mother who really believed in "I" statements. Her motivations were entirely good, but nothing annoyed me more than her constant affirming communications. If there was a glass on the edge of the table that she thought might spill or break, my mother would say, "I feel really uncomfortable because that glass is so close to the table edge." Or if I was angry with her, her response always began with "I hear you that you are very angry with me." Unfortunately, her affirmations always infuriated me because they never made me feel like she was taking ownership for what she had done that had made me angry in the first place. I felt managed; it often seemed that she was above the fight and merely placating me so I would settle down (when it fact it achieved the opposite reaction). On the flip side, when she was more straightforward, I might disagree with her decisions, but I felt like she was really telling me what she was feeling. One of her most effective ways to shut down one of my endless arguments/negotiations was to say "I know it sounds hypocritical, but that's what I think." You can't argue with that. I know. I've tried.

I think one of the reasons why women like to use the "I"-statement strategy is that it helps them avoid coming across as overly emotional. But I see two problems with this. One is that it enables them to deny their anger—to themselves and to whomever they're angry at. "I'm not angry with you, I'm just really frustrated" is a favorite strategy. Women have a right to their anger and they have a right to express their feelings without being dismissed. The other problem, which affects women and men, is that a less-than-deft use of "I" statements can come off as incredibly patronizing—which further enrages the addressee. (And not coincidentally, "I" language as schools teach it is often ridiculed by adolescent boys and girls. When two boys bully a girl by creating a composite photo that makes it looks as if she's giving someone oral sex, then send it via picture phone to all their friends, her saying "My feelings were really hurt when you made it look like I gave Scott a blow job" doesn't really cut it.)

So the goal of reflective listening is critically important to managing conflict with each other. The point of "I" talk and other such communication devices is to foster empathy and develop the sense that you really understand what the other person means. Without empathy, you can reflect someone's statement perfectly and still miss the whole point of what he or she was saying.

One of my favorite definitions of listening comes from Drs. Redford and Virginia Williams, authors of *LifeSkills*: "You're not really listening unless you're prepared to be changed by what you've heard." This means that when you hear something, particularly something you don't want to hear, take the time to absorb it rather than instantly mount a defense against it. Here are some techniques I use to help me listen:

- *Don't interrupt.* If possible, let the other person get to the end of her sentence or paragraph. If you jump in too soon, you're sending the message that what she's saying doesn't merit your full attention or reflection.
- *Assume the other person isn't insane, stupid, or vindictive.* Sounds

obvious, but when we feel we or someone we love is being attacked, it's easy to assume the speaker has horrible motives.

- *Find the speaker's emotional truth.* Whether or not the speaker can
  articulate it, he's almost certainly speaking from an emotional truth
  that's every bit as valid as your emotional truth.

- *Insist on civility.* If the speaker is starting to lose it, or if you think
  you're on the verge yourself, call a time-out for the conversation. "I
  really want to hear what you've got to say, but if we can't be respectful, we'll have to continue the conversation another time."

- *Be aware that your tone is very important.* As I've explained above,
  when you reflect it's very easy to come off as controlling or managing the other person.

- *Ask, don't tell.* You're the expert on your thoughts and feelings; the
  other person is the expert on his or hers. If you catch yourself saying something like "You think that . . ." or "You're just upset because . . . ," you've leaped to an assumption. Pull back and check
  in with the other person: "I want to make sure I've got this right.
  Are you saying that . . . ?"

- *Know that it matters.* You may think it's the most trivial, stupid discussion in the world, but if another person took the trouble to seek
  you out to talk about it, it's important to him or her—reason
  enough to respect the issue and take it seriously.

And remember Robert and Kathy? That was a real experience, and
what happened over the next few years clearly demonstrates why it's so
important for parents not to allow conflicts between their children to sabotage their ability to work together when necessary. Mary and Lindsay became friends again in high school but the parents stopped talking to each
other. When Lindsay began drinking, smoking, and dating a senior boy,
she also stopped talking to her parents (but spent more time at Mary's
house and frequently talked to Mary's mother). One Saturday night Lindsay had a huge fight with her mother (her dad refused to get involved because he was tired of them fighting so much). She called her boyfriend to
pick her up, put some clothes in a bag, and a few minutes later got into
his car and drove away. Her parents had no idea where she was going or
when she would return. The adult who had the best chance of knowing

where Lindsay would be was Mary's mother, but Lindsay's parents didn't know that.

This is why it's worth the effort to crack the code of other parents' communication: We need to support our kids together. Now that you've tuned up your transmitter and receiver, you're ready to explore confrontation in Perfect Parent World in even greater detail. We'll take that up in the next chapter.

Into the Muck

Confrontation 101

Now it's time to get into the muck. Sooner or later, we'll have a misstep with another parent's child, or we'll object to how someone interacts with our child. And when it comes to our kids, we're not very forgiving of other people's mistakes or poor judgment. Whether it was the principal who embarrassed your child at a school assembly, the soccer coach who lost his temper when your son botched an easy play, or the mom who didn't invite your child to her child's birthday party, you probably didn't feel especially kind and civil toward that person. In these situations many parents feel a dangerous sense of moral authority that in their view entitles them to talk down to, scream at, or question the integrity of the "offender" since they're doing it for a noble cause—the welfare of their kids. It's easy for the person on the receiving end of this treatment to respond poorly, whether that means bullying back or mounting an incoherent defense—which the aggrieved parent will then seize on as further evidence of the person's incompetence or deceptiveness.

It's essential to learn how to confront others fairly. After all, our children are watching us. If we don't treat others with dignity when we're angry or we're silent when someone bullies us, we squander our chance to show our values in action and we leave our children with the idea that we act according to those values only when it's easy. Our character is demonstrated precisely in those moments when we're so angry that we want to spit nails, not when we're getting along with one another.

In this chapter, I'll do my best to give you good advice on how to handle these situations. What do I mean by "these situations"? I mean the kind where you begin to doubt other people's goodwill. When all the adults act like they're twelve. When the combatants gossip, turning people against each other—children, parents, teachers, principals, coaches. When you can't sleep at night or you're so angry that you know beyond a shadow of a doubt that other people are being intentionally malicious. When it's all you think about and all you talk about.

THE DEATH THREAT

I'm going to share an experience related to me by a middle school counselor that demonstrates how easy it is for a common fight between girls to escalate into a conflict between adults where people's integrity, competence, and sanity are questioned. Situations like this are very common; I've heard variations on this theme throughout the country.

> It was my first year as a school counselor and there were two sixth-grade girls who were best friends/worst enemies. One of the girls, the Sidekick, became jealous of the other and told their friends that she "hated the girl so much that she could kill her." Of course it got back to the girl and she told her mom. The mother chose to believe that this comment was a true death threat. She called me and the other counselor to report it and demanded that we kick the other girl out of school. We listened and promised to get back to her. We interviewed both girls and they agreed that there was no threat behind the statement. The target insisted that she wasn't fearful of the threat being carried out. Her mother didn't agree. She insisted that her daughter was trying to please us and therefore lying to us. She reported that her daughter was up at night crying.
>
> We also had a meeting with the other girl's parents, who were very appropriately concerned. The girls talked, the jealous girl apologized, and the girls reconciled and became good friends again.
>
> Shortly after, the Queen Bee mother asked to see me. Initially, she seemed so calm that I assumed she wanted an update, and so I closed my door. I later regretted that because I didn't have witnesses, although the other counselor and a secretary could hear her screaming, attacking my credibility as a counselor and adding that there was

no way I could understand because I didn't have children. I just let her go at it and tried to stay professional, but after she left, I broke down and cried.

When we refused to kick the other girl out of school, the mother told people in the community that her daughter had received a death threat and the school had done nothing about it. She called me at home and threatened to sue me and the school. Unfortunately, the father didn't help. He called me at home on one occasion and attempted to remain calm and seemed to have an attitude that he was going to try and resolve the situation. However, the minute we began making strides, the mother began yelling and interrupting (she was listening on the other line) and Dad immediately ceased to talk. Finally, the family withdrew both their children from the school.

Let's investigate this anatomy of a non-murder. Who are the people involved and what are their motivations? The key events are as follows:

- Two sixth-grade girls who are friends had a conflict. One told their friends that she hated the other girl so much she could kill her. Girls, like many of us, are prone to uttering extreme statements in order to make their point.
- This statement was perceived by the target's mother as a genuine threat to her daughter's life.
- The school counselors spoke to the aggressor and the target and determined that there was no genuine physical threat.
- The school counselors met with the aggressor's parents and punished the student as they saw appropriate.
- The target's mother became so angry at the situation that she challenged the competence of the school administration, threatened to sue the counselor and the school, and told her community that the school was irresponsible. She eventually withdrew her children from the school.

These facts describe what happened but don't take into account the attitudes of the parties involved or the social context in which these events occurred:

- Both girls had considerable social power. According to the counselors and teachers at the school, the target was the Queen Bee of the class and the aggressor was her Sidekick.
- The target's mother didn't trust the school counselor's competence to assess the threat. Her actions indicate that she believed she was the only one who could.
- The target's mother essentially gave the school an ultimatum: The only acceptable response to the "threat" on her child's life was for the other girl to be expelled.
- All the adults in this situation believed that they were acting in the best interests of the child.
- The children reconciled quickly but the adults never did.

Why did the situation unfold the way it did? To quote political consultant James Carville, "There's the truth, the whole truth, and nothing but the truth—which one do you want?" It's crucial to realize that with any conflict, each participant acts out of his or her own perception of the truth. Here's what I see as each side's version of the truth, based on working with many parents in similar situations.

The target's mother believed that her daughter's life was threatened and that everything her child told her was true. She was protecting her child and exercising her right and responsibility to do whatever was necessary to keep her safe. She believed that if school officials didn't meet her demands, they were doing nothing. When she told her community about this experience, she did so because she genuinely believed that she was obligated to tell people the "truth," both to protect her daughter and to safeguard other children from a similar experience.

I have met a lot of mothers who act as this mother did. Why do they do it? It's not that this woman was a Queen Bee mom (although she was reported to be)—it's way deeper than that. I believe women like this mother see their mothering as a measure of their overall competence in their own eyes and in the eyes of their community. Moreover, this woman, as many women have, had left a job that gave her respect and recognition in order to raise her children. Her mothering was now the sole arena where she could demand respect. Small wonder she lashed out against the

counselor—she was fighting to regain her sense of power and competence as much as she was fighting to protect her daughter.

First, the codes I discussed in Chapter 5 are alive and well here. The
idea that she knew her child the best and that she was the only true advocate for her child made her see the counselor as the enemy the moment
the counselor disagreed with her (which then justified being the Mama
Bear).

And where was the dad? The dad's phone call to the counselor was the
typical response of a Caveman dad who doesn't want to get involved in
"mother's issues," tries to make everyone get along when the conflict has
gotten out of hand, and then runs away when he is challenged by the
mother.

The parents of the Sidekick who threatened the Queen Bee heard the
counselor out, absorbed the difficult truth that their daughter had misbe-
haved, and properly insisted that their daughter apologize. When the girls
became friends again, they thought the whole drama had blown over.
They were unaware that the other family was trying to get their daughter
expelled. If they had found out about it, things probably would have es-
calated even more.

The school administrators felt they acted correctly. Yet their expertise
and knowledge of both girls were dismissed. They felt pushed into a defensive posture by the target's mother, whose intimidating vehemence
and efforts to mobilize other families against the school made it difficult
for them to maintain all parties' confidentiality (which they had to do for
moral and professional reasons) while they knew their own reputation
was being trashed.

While all this ugliness was going on with the adults, the two girls found
themselves in the center of a swirling drama. Children in these situations
are often torn. First and foremost, they usually want the problem to go
away. Second, they want to please the people in front of them, whoever
that may be—from parents and teachers to counselors and friends. This
means that they can say and believe wildly contradictory things from moment to moment, which makes them dangerous. Third, they may not be
entirely displeased at being the center of attention.

Keep in mind that the target's mother reported that her daughter was
crying at night in fear of her life but that she wouldn't admit it to her

friends or teachers because she wanted to please them. This might very well have been true. It might also have been true that the girl cried because she was exhausted and anxious at the end of the day.

Remember also that the girl who was being threatened was identified as a Queen Bee and the girl who threatened her was her Sidekick. Girls like that generally don't like adults getting involved unless they feel they can control them. When the target's mother stepped in, it made her Queen Bee daughter look weak and out of control. That meant that the Queen Bee had two choices. Her first option: She could back her mother 100 percent, which meant she had to publicly agree that her life was threatened, which was risky because most girls would doubt it. (If there was a consensus among the girls that she was making too much of it, she might be tempted to exaggerate or lie to substantiate her claim; if that happened, her mother would most likely believe her and see anyone who doubted her daughter's words as a threat to her daughter's and her family's integrity.) The Queen Bee's second option: She could do the opposite and make friends with the girl again. It was far simpler to tell her friends, "Sorry—you all know how weird my mom can be. She's *completely* out of control." Don't *you* remember apologizing to your friends for your parents' lame behavior? And frankly, a lot of girls in that situation do a little of both: cry to their mothers at home and then complain about their mothers to their friends and teachers.

Almost any situation can escalate into a conflict as large as the one I just described, so you need to know how to think through conflicts when you're so angry you can't see straight and/or when you're on the receiving end. Too many parents have only a few reactions at their disposal. Some are all plot and no action, letting other parents run roughshod over them. Some ignite World War III. And, of course, some parents hide.

HIDING BEHIND THE FERN: WHY WE DON'T CONFRONT

My daughter Jill has been having an escalating skirmish with another girl at school. One day this girl told her, "My mom says to say she thinks you're being really mean." Jill was devastated. I saw the mother at parent pickup, and I knew the mature thing would be to go up to her, check in with her about the situation, and talk it out. But this woman has a formidable reputation for defensiveness. So in-stead I hid behind a fern so she wouldn't see me.

                                        Elizabeth, mother of a sixth grader

If you're like me, you've probably had your share of "fern moments." You find yourself in a situation where you know you should talk to the other adult. Instead, you hide when the "enemy" is nigh. You realize you're being ridiculous—haven't you watched enough *Oprah* to overcome this? Perhaps you have friends who make a policy of avoidance, embracing their Inner Wimp. You've confronted that person in your head a million times. You know you're fully capable of having this conversation. So why don't you just do it?

Here are some of the rationalizations I've heard from parents about why they don't confront:

1. "I can only change myself; I can't change someone else."
2. "Others have tried and failed; it's useless for me to try."
3. "It will only make the situation worse."
4. "It'll be social suicide for my kid if I interfere."
5. "I'm making a mountain out of a molehill."
6. "Parenting is private. It's not my business."
7. "I'm turning the other cheek; it's how I was raised."
8. "I'm not going to stoop to the other person's level."

My son was on a baseball team that played a team that had a coach that tried to intimidate the other coaches and umpires. It was painful being another adult at one of those games. But it wasn't the other adults' place to get involved, so we would just sit through the experience.   Tom, high school dad

My daughter was left in the dust by a friend. We [the mothers] decided that it was between the kids. I really thought the kid was wrong. But you can't tell another parent that.   Rosa, middle school mom

Let's take a closer look at these rationalizations. It's true that you can be responsible only for your own behavior, but "I can't change anyone else" can easily become an excuse to never confront anyone. Moreover, just because others have tried and failed to reason with someone doesn't mean you won't succeed if you make an effective case.

When you assume someone won't change, you ignore your responsibility to your child and the school community. Why do I say community? Machiavelli wrote in *The Prince* that "whoever controls the public space controls the populace." If someone is saying something malicious in a public space—a school hallway, athletic field, grocery store, auditorium—he's doing so because he believes he has the right to say those things and that he won't be held accountable. Unchecked, that mistaken belief affects the entire community.

Telling yourself that you want to let the kids handle it, that you want to avoid causing your child's "social suicide," or that you're making a big deal out of nothing may sometimes be valid. But don't make the mistake of thinking that getting involved is an all-or-nothing proposition—"all" meaning that you fight your child's battles and "nothing" meaning that your child works it out without any adult guidance. *It's never all or nothing.* Even when kids are working things out for themselves, at least one adult should be behind each child helping her articulate the problem and figure out how to handle herself in the confrontation in a way that's consistent with the family's ethical guidelines.

If you've considered becoming involved, it's probably because you recognize that the kids aren't playing on a level field, or because they've already tried and failed to work it out themselves. Getting involved at this stage can mean emphasizing the importance of seeing the other person's perspective. (It's always good to say to your child, "I'm not taking away what happened to you, but what do you think the other person would say if I asked what happened and why?") If your child begs you not to get involved because it spells social suicide, what does that mean to your child? Often this phrase makes parents so fearful about their child's sudden social isolation that they can't think through the rest of the conversation. Would confrontation really mean social suicide, or only a social injury from which the child could recover? What are the costs of not speaking out?

LANDMINE!

If your response to a potential conflict is to say you should "turn the other cheek" or "kill them with kindness" because you don't want to "stoop to someone else's level," ask yourself what is really behind your response. Parents often use these phrases to run away from conflict or to assert their moral superiority over the person with whom they're angry.

Redefining a Successful Confrontation

Just like our children, it's easy to get hung up on the notion that a confrontation is successful only if we get what we want, if we convince the other person to agree with us, or if we're all best friends afterward (or if not best friends, the othe person suffers terrible public humiliation as punishment for what he or she did to us). Because we rarely see this anywhere but TV sitcoms, it's easy to tell ourselves that there's no point in trying. Instead, I'd like to redefine the goals of a confrontation:

1. You articulate to yourself what's happening that you don't like.

2. You establish boundaries with the other person, saying, "This is my limit, and here's why I think you crossed it." Then you explain what you want instead.

3. No matter how much you're tempted to act out, you remind yourself to behave according to your values and, in doing so, to model for your kids a clear, respectful way to communicate when there's conflict.

You can't control what happens after you confront someone, but you can always control these three aspects of the confrontation. So what would be the common obstacles to achieving these three goals?

Anger Mismanagement

The "Act Like a Woman" box and "Act Like a Man" box can give us great insights into the ways men and women feel they're allowed to express their anger. Conventional wisdom says that when boys are angry, they get into a fistfight and two seconds later it's over and all is forgiven, but that when girls are angry, they whisper behind each other's backs and it's never over. It's important to understand why these stereotypes so often hold true and how boys and girls (and therefore men and women) interpret and express anger.

Essentially, there are four unwritten rules that I see guiding most girls' anger.

1. They sit on it forever, never tell the other person they're mad, and then turn their anger against themselves.

2. They sit on it almost forever, finally get their nerve up, and then timidly ask for the abuse to stop, only to have the other person dismiss them or laugh it off by saying one, if not all, of the following:

- "You can't take a joke. You're so uptight."
- "You're being so emotional and oversensitive."
- "I'm just being sarcastic—you know that's the way I am."

3. They sit on their anger until something sets them off (typically something that looks inconsequential to everyone else) and then they explode—in tears or screaming or both—whereupon the other person dismisses them in one of the ways described above.

4. They adopt a "You have no idea who you're dealing with and I will take you down" stance. They may physically fight the other person (with or without weapons) or set out to destroy that person socially or psychologically.

Most girls' anger goes underground at an early age because they quickly learn that if they express anger forthrightly they'll be punished; the other person either won't take them seriously—mocking or ignoring them—or will break off the relationship. Hence the "but she'll get mad at me" excuse that girls so often use to justify why they don't express anger.

The girls who fight (psychologically and/or physically) usually do it to assert their power publicly. But when they're angry at people with whom they want to maintain a relationship, they'll tolerate being trampled on so as not to risk the relationship.

I see mothers express their anger in the same four ways, only with a lot more rationalizing. Repressing anger—or exploding—is one of the primary legacies many women carry with them into adulthood, and it's the hardest coping skill to unlearn. Strong friendships are built on negotiating and working through conflict. But if women won't admit when they're angry, they can't develop truly strong friendships or intimate relationships. I think this is one of the reasons so many women tell me they don't really like the other women they hang out with when to an observer they look like the best of friends. They're too scared to get into the muck of a conflict with a friend, so the friendship never gets the chance to become stronger at the broken places.

The fear of confronting others with our anger often makes us bow out of confrontations altogether. I spoke with one mother who complained about the Queen Bee Mom who held sway over the school her kids attended. She told me, "It was sickening how the other women who had known her a long time would just let her treat other people badly because they couldn't risk their own social standing." I disagree with this woman's assessment. I think this woman, like the other women, isn't confronting the Queen Bee Mom because she's scared. These women don't think they're capable of expressing anger effectively and therefore assume they won't be taken seriously. If you catch yourself making excuses such as "I know she'll never change, so there's no reason to try," examine your motivations more closely. Even when they do try, women typically use code phrases when they're angry: "That was interesting . . ." "I thought it was strange when you . . ." We have a hard time even raising the issue of our anger, let alone expressing it more directly. Listen to this woman discuss her relationship with her friend after they had a huge fight:

> *We both want what's best for our kids. When our kids hurt, we hurt. We have not shown anger to each other but sadness about the situation. We gave each other lots of meaningful hugs last night. We talked last night for an hour about the situation! We love to talk!*

This woman had given me a blow-by-blow account of how her friend's behavior hurt her deeply. I don't believe for one second that she wasn't angry at her friend. But she was so uncomfortable with being angry that she dismissed her own feelings. And when we don't admit our angry feelings to ourselves, what's left? Mistrust. We learn not to trust other women not because they're dishonest but because we're trained not to say what we really mean (because we have to be friends afterward). We never work through our mutual mistrust and emerge in a better place.

Boys and men don't have it any easier; they just have it different. Our culture doesn't teach boys that their first and best option is to talk or negotiate when they're angry at each other. What are the most common ways boys express anger? I see the following:

1. They blow it off: "It's not a big deal. Don't worry about it."

2. They laugh it off. Laughing is a way of tricking themselves into thinking that whatever they're experiencing or observing is funny—nothing they have to do or say anything about.

3. They rely on other boys to help them contain or manage their anger. Thus it's not uncommon for one boy to babysit an aggressive friend who he worries will do "stupid stuff." He excuses his friend's behavior by saying things like "You can't push him like that. He just loses it."

4. They verbally or physically attack.

Boys grow up into men who can, as one father put it, either "kick someone's ass or blow it off." What does this look like in Perfect Parent World? If you're a mother reading this, have you ever had the experience where smoke rose from your head as you fumed at the father of your children because he walked away from a conflict with a parent, teacher, or coach when you thought he should have intervened? The culture of masculinity can be paralyzing.

Let's suppose you could peek a few decades into the future. Your child is now an adult. How would you feel if you caught her hiding behind a fern instead of confronting her problems head-on? It's okay to be afraid, but don't let that stop you. Learn the right skills, then teach them to your child so he or she will be able to present a case well, whether it's in the hallway at school or in a college or job interview. It's time to get out from behind that fern, and don't let others silence you or take advantage of your fear of speaking out.

The Skills You Need

Your Friendship Bill of Rights

I'm going to ask you to do the same thing I ask my students to do. Take a quiet moment during the day. Sit down with a big cup of coffee or tea, put some music on, and get out a piece of paper and a pen. Now ask yourself the following question: "What are the three most important things I need in a friendship?" Write them down. Feel free to add more if you like. This is your Friendship Bill of Rights. (You may think it's silly, but do it anyway.)

For example, if you said you have to have respect, honesty, and empathy in a relationship, take a moment and visualize what those look like to you. Those three standards are your unbreakables. If you're going to be in a relationship with anyone, respect, honesty, and empathy will be the bedrock of that relationship.

Now write down the names of the people you feel closest to. Go down the list one by one and ask yourself: "What are the first three words that describe my relationship with this person?" Compare the words that describe your relationships with the qualities you listed on your Friendship Bill of Rights. Do these relationships reflect what you say you must have in a friendship?

Of course, you must hold yourself to these same standards. Do you act consistently according to your standards, or at least try to? When is it hardest for you to act according to your own standards?

Now for the hardest question: If you're in a relationship with someone who doesn't match your standards, why are you in that relationship? What you are getting out of it and what are you sacrificing? Is it worth the cost? Do your children see you in relationships like this? What are they learning from watching you in those relationships?

Let me tell you what you'll find on my Friendship Bill of Rights: comfort, honesty, a sense of humor, and generosity. What does comfort look like to me? It means that when I'm with a real friend, I can feel like a fool, make mistakes, or be embarrassed about something I did, and my friend will empathize and say he or she is sorry I had that experience. What does honesty look like to me? My friend can challenge me or disagree with me but communicate how he or she feels in a way that doesn't make me feel put down. Likewise, I can tell a real friend when he or she is doing something I disagree with and we can talk about it. I know I won't find out later from some-one else that my friend was actually really angry at me; if that's the case, he or she will tell me. What does a sense of humor look like to me? We can laugh—especially at seemingly inappropriate times. Got a deep, dark problem with one of your family members that's worrying you to death? That's a great time for a horrible joke between friends over a glass of wine. What does generosity look like to me? If my friends can't do something, they'll say so, but if they can, they'll do it and not think of it as a burden.

The critical part of this process is to articulate to yourself exactly what qualities are important to you in the people with whom you want to sur-round yourself and whether you can give back to them what you require of them.

Going through this exercise can be unsettling. If you're reading this and realizing that you have relationships that don't match your standards, know that you are not alone. And try not to beat yourself up about it. It's easy not to be aware of this until you literally put it down on paper.

If you're a parent, you have a responsibility to do the best you can to be-have with dignity and to demand that others treat you with equal dignity so that you serve as a strong role model for your children. I'd like you to keep asking yourself: "What does it tell my child if I'm in relationships with people that are contrary to what I say I need in a genuine friendship?"

Think of the people in your life who do fit your standards. They are your support system. If you don't have anyone who fits them, then it's time to start making friends again—this time by choosing what's best for you. (This is one of the benefits of not being fifteen anymore.)

Widening Your Net

Use this same exercise to help you establish criteria for your extended support system. Your child's educators and coaches are a vital part of this support. Consider criteria such as:

- Ability to listen to children
- Ability to encourage a love of learning and intellectual curiosity (I believe that a teacher has to have these qualities in order to impart them)

- Fearlessness in taking intellectual risks
- Focus on critical thinking
- Openness to constructive criticism
- Open-mindedness
- A love of working with children and watching them learn and develop (a concrete sign of this love is that the teacher moves around the room from student to student while teaching and isn't stuck to the board)
- Ability to see parents as colleagues (which also means that the teacher won't allow him- or herself to be intimidated by bullying parents)

Stop, Explain, Affirm and Acknowledge, and Lock In/Lock Out

Once you have your support system, you need the skills to get through the muck. I'm going to give you a strategy that you can apply in any situation. It's the one on which I base my curricula, my teacher trainings, and my own life. (In fact, when I don't use it in my marriage, my husband quickly reminds me.) It's called SEAL.

SEAL stands for:

- *Stop:* Stop, take a breath, look, and listen to the other person.
- *Explain:* Explain what happened that you don't like and what you want instead.
- *Affirm and acknowledge:* Affirm everyone's right to be treated with dignity and acknowledge any wrongdoing on your part.
- *Lock in/Lock out:* Lock in the friendship or lock it out.

Some of you may read this and think, "Oh, no, not another cheesy conflict resolution strategy." Fair enough. But I've been using and teaching SEAL for more than eight years, and I've found that it's a highly effective, easy-to-remember way to handle conflict with respect and clarity. SEAL can help those of us who sometimes rage at others to communicate anger in a way that people can tolerate. It can convince those of us who don't feel our voice matters that we have the right to speak out.

The goal of SEAL is to get both parties engaged in the process. It's not to be best friends forever or to vanquish the enemy. Ideally, you'll listen to each other, understand what each of you has done, hold yourselves accountable, and feel affirmed and acknowledged by the other side. Obviously we don't live in an ideal world, and the person you confront might hop off script; so might you. But that doesn't mean you don't try. Your goal is to fully articulate to yourself when your personal standards of treatment are being violated, think strategically about how and when to confront, and then proceed with the face-to-face confrontation. *If you do any of these things, you should consider yourself successful.* We don't all have to be best friends to make the world a better, more forgiving place.

I'd like to offer a real-life example to show you how SEAL works. Here's a story from a father who had an encounter with some mothers who were disrespecting his fourteen-year-old daughter:

> *I was at school to pick up my daughter from a soccer game. As I was walking to the field, I overheard two mothers talking to each other about how they couldn't believe what my daughter was wearing and calling her a slut. I got so angry but I didn't say anything because, frankly, part of me thought they were right. Just before that, we'd gone to a swimming pool and she was wearing a tiny bathing suit and I talked to her about it. It was horrible seeing all these men look at her. But she blew me off. I hate to say it, but part of me was embarrassed for her but I also felt bad that I didn't stand up for her.*

I spoke with this father at some length. He's divorced and has visitation rights, but when his daughter says she'd rather hang out with her friends than stay at his house for the weekend, he acquiesces. (I've seen this pattern of capitulation with a lot of divorced dads.) Because he had a father who constantly blew up without notice, the last thing this man wants to be is an angry, out-of-control dad. In addition, as a noncustodial parent who "doesn't put in the time" with his daughter, he believes he can't say what he needs or feels concerning her. Basically, he doesn't think he has the right to have people treat him according to his standards, nor does he think he has the right to get angry about it. His teenage daughter recognizes that she has the power to dominate him and takes full advantage of it. (That doesn't mean that she's a bad kid—she's a teen and she'll do it until someone puts the brakes on her behavior.) No wonder this man was speechless when he overheard these women badmouthing his daughter! I see this man as a warm-hearted, intelligent, self-reflective person; he also works with children. So if *he* reacts to those women by saying nothing, remember that we can all have moments where we don't take the right action.

Here's how this father could use SEAL to confront these two women. First, he needs to articulate the problem to himself. This means being aware of the filter through which he's seeing the situation: his feelings as a divorced father limit his ability to speak out. He needs to remember that he has to fight for his relationship with his daughter, even if that means she's furious with him about making her spend time with him instead of her friends. He needs to acknowledge that while he's upset about his daughter's appearance and developing sexuality, those women are still disrespecting her. He needs to communicate his anger in a manner that is respectful of both himself and others. Later, he needs to assess his discomfort about his daughter's appearance, why she may be dressing that way, and how he's going to talk to her about it. But for now he has a more urgent matter.

Now comes the issue of timing. When you're in the moment, you have one decision to make: Should you confront now or later? If you're so worked up that you don't trust yourself to get through the conversation without blowing up or speaking inarticulately, put it on hold. Get to a quiet place and write down what you saw and heard that you didn't like. Talk it out with someone in your support system and listen to his or her honest feedback. Think through the four steps of SEAL. If you feel it's reasonable to confront the person, then think of a time and place that will give the other person a chance to listen thoughtfully. You might want to practice what you want to say in the mirror, role-play it with a close friend, or visualize it.

The next step is to get up the courage to confront this person in real life. Remember, baby steps, and every one of them counts. Here's how SEAL would work for this father:

Stop: Dad breathes until his heart rate slows down and he feels calm. Are there a lot of other people around? If there are, can he tell by their body language whether they heard? Is his daughter around? Did she hear? The answers to these questions are critical. If he has an audience, he needs to be aware that the mothers might be more defensive in the face of witnesses, and that his embarrassment in the face of an audience might make it harder for him to speak his mind. If his daughter is nearby and hasn't heard, he might want to draw the women aside so as to spare her the embarrassment of overhearing their crude assessment of her. If she did hear, she's already angry and mortified; the father should model how to handle his equally strong emotions. In his situation, the two mothers were standing right in front of him and no one else was around. If he can be calm, I would encourage him to talk to those mothers in the moment.

Explain: We've all had the experience of leaving an unpleasant encounter only to dream up the snappy comeback that would have come in handy five minutes earlier. It's easy to lose your words in moments of stress, so before you say anything out loud, review in your head exactly what happened that you didn't like and—just as important—what you want instead. In this situation, the father explains to himself that no matter how he feels about his daughter's attire, that's a private discussion; no one has the right to disrespect her, and doing so in public is especially harmful to her. He can't permit it, and these women need to appreciate why.

Affirm and Acknowledge: Affirming someone is about connecting with him or her, finding the common ground between you before you make clear the divide. For example: "We both have kids on the team [or in the same class]." "I've known your kids for a long time; you have great kids." "Our kids work together; I hope you'd feel you could talk to me too if something like this came up again. If you have a problem, I certainly understand that these things aren't one-sided; please feel comfortable telling me about your daughter." You then explain what you see as the problem.

There are at least two ways the person receiving this information can take it. He or she can be gracious ("I appreciate what you're telling me") or defensive ("I think you're making a big deal out of nothing").

Again, the goal isn't to have an I'm OK, you're OK moment. It's to say, "I have the right to my opinion and you have the right to your opinion. We can differ on the facts, but I can't question how you feel and you can't question how I feel."

In the father's case, he should point out that all of them have kids on the same team and share a desire for their daughters to be treated respectfully.

If necessary, this is the place where you can admit any wrongdoing on your part. Because this dad overheard these mothers and had no relationship with them beforehand, he's off the hook.

Lock In/Lock Out: Depending on how important the relationship is to you, you have a decision to make: Do you want to lock in the relationship or lock it out? If you want to continue the relationship, you lock it in by affirming it again: "You're such a good parent," "I understand where you're coming from," "Thanks for hearing me out."

When should you lock it out? First, decide whether this is an issue between parents, between kids, or both. If the situation involves both kids and adults, discuss with your child how he or she feels about maintaining the friendship. Before you take any action with another adult, determine whether the kids involved are comfortable with their solution. If this is a one-time thing, you probably don't need to lock out the other adult. If the recent actions indicate a pattern, locking out is a more reasonable choice.

In most cases, I'd give the other person a chance to redeem him- or herself before ending the relationship. By this I mean that you've clearly explained to the other person why his or her behavior or words are a problem, communicated where your boundaries are, and explained what you'll do if it happens again (in other words, lay out the consequences). I generally operate on a three-strikes-and-you're-out philosophy.

> *Strike one* (the first time): "Hey, that's not okay; let me explain why."
> *Strike two* (the second time): "I need you to understand that this is affecting our relationship." It's important to articulate precisely how you feel as a result of the trespass; "I don't like it" is too vague. And watch your tone. You're stating what you have to have in order to continue the relationship.
> *Strike three* (the third time): "We've talked about this before, but it's happening again. I'm upset that I'm not [or my child isn't] being respected. I value our friendship/relationship, but I don't want to continue it right now. It's too hard." Adults as well as children have the right to say, "Let's be civil, but let's not be friends."

In this situation, the dad has no relationship with the mothers, so it's not a big deal for him to lock them out. Of course, he might also decide that he wants to be gracious and be able to exchange pleasantries the next time they run into each other, at which point the moms might dive behind the ferns.

Describing the four steps of SEAL in such detail might make them sound complicated. Perhaps you're afraid that I'm asking you to make a long, drawn-out speech. In fact, the best SEAL talks are to the point. Here's what the father's SEAL conversation would look like. First our dad stops, takes a deep breath, and collects himself. Then he begins:

> *Excuse me, I'm sorry I don't know your names, but I need to tell you that I just overheard you calling a girl on the team a slut and criticizing what she was wearing.* [Explain] *I don't think we should speak like that about any girl, but it was especially painful for me to hear because I'm her father. As parents yourselves, I'm sure you can imagine what that felt like for me to hear. We all have daughters on the team, and we all want them treated respectfully.* [Affirm and acknowledge] *So I'm asking you to stop talking like that about my daughter or any girl. Thank you for listening.* [Lock In] *It was really hard to say and I hope that if you ever need to tell me anything, you'll be able to come to me.*

If the mothers are rude to him, the father should say that he welcomes speaking to them further but only when they can talk to him in a civil, respectful manner. Then I hope this father walks away and gives his daughter a big hug. She'll wonder why and maybe brush him off, but so what? He'll know that he stepped up for her and all girls.

The Power of Apologies

This kid has been horrible to my son all year. Making fun of him, getting other kids to gang up on him. His parents don't take it seriously. I'm so angry at them I don't know what to do with myself when I see them. But what makes me the angriest is that their son never apologizes and neither do they.   Marion, mother of a middle school boy

Legions of parents seem to hold grudges against other parents because they didn't get an apology, either to themselves or to their child, when they thought they should have. Yet these same parents rarely ask for the apology they so desperately want because they've convinced themselves it'll only make the problem worse. In fact, I think one of the key reasons parents persuade themselves that a conflict is "between the kids" is that the adults are scared to death of confronting each other. So now that we've gone over how to speak your truth when you feel someone has wronged you and/or your child, let's take a look at what you should do when you or your child has wronged someone else—especially because this is a prime time to apologize. Remember, you may strongly disagree with the other person's assessment of what happened, but if he or she tells you that you did something hurtful, it doesn't matter that you see it a different way—*you need to apologize.*

It's a safe bet that if you confront someone, he or she will:

1. Have a different perspective
2. Be equally annoyed by something you did

In any confrontation, you have to be prepared to hear something unpleasant and be ready to acknowledge wrongdoing on your part. If you reach the end of the discussion and realize you've done something wrong, your communication isn't complete until you apologize.

What do I mean by "apologize"? An apology is a public statement of remorse and an affirmation of the dignity of the person who has been wronged. A sincere apology is transformative for both the person apologizing and the person receiving the apology. Here's how I define an apology.

- You take the right tone: "I'm sorry" needs to be and sound genuinely apologetic.
- You state clearly what you did wrong (for example, "I didn't take your concerns about the drinking incident seriously").
- You focus solely on what *you* did wrong, without mentioning any wrongdoing, real or perceived, on the other person's part (for example, if you say, "I'm sorry about what I said; I just got so mad after you attacked my credibility that I lost my temper," you're actually smuggling in an accusation).

- You don't sneak in any last-minute put-downs ("I'm sorry you were hurt that I left you off the committee, but you seemed so uninterested that I didn't think you'd care").
- You're genuinely contrite and take full responsibility for what you've done ("I'm so sorry that my thoughtlessness caused you so much distress").
- Your apology doesn't double as a request or plea to receive something that will benefit you ("I'm so sorry I made a fuss about the party; I certainly hope you'll consider inviting Becca now").
- You apologize without the expectation of a return apology; if you do get one, consider it a happy bonus.
- You express the sincere desire to make amends in a specific way ("I'm going to call the other parents I spoke to about this and tell them I was wrong" or "Please tell me what I can do to make it up to you").

If you're the wronged party and an apology is important to you, your communication isn't complete until you ask for the apology in a civilized manner.

- Don't threaten the person with ultimatums.
- Clearly state what you believe is the other party's offense.
- Ask for the apology ("I'd like you to apologize for what you said").
- State what you consider appropriate amends ("It would mean a lot to me if your child apologized to my child").
- Affirm the relationship ("Thanks for hearing me out").

Remember, you're not making this request with the assumption that you'll get the apology—that's icing on the cake. You're making the request in order to express yourself clearly and to ask to be treated with dignity.

"I'm Sorry": Male vs. Female

Do apologies mean something different to men and women? I think in many cases they do. I recently worked with a teacher who'd had a baffling experience with a mother of a student. The woman's son had gotten into a conflict with a girl in his class. Both children were guilty. The girl apologized to this woman's son, but the son's mother was still furious. In her view, the apology was a ruse, the girl's way of ducking further punishment. The school was puzzled; why was this woman still so angry after the girl had told her son she was sorry?

Remember that girl in your middle school who would cry when she apologized as a way to get people to feel sorry for her? Or how you asked for an apology in an effort to get people to treat you better only to have them turn on you so that *you* ended up apologizing to *them* simply because you had challenged their right to treat you badly?

Women also can apologize without meaning it—we say, "You can't talk on the phone right now? Oh, I'm so sorry I interrupted you!" and then we keep talking. Some of us apologize constantly as a way to put down what we do. We cook for a full day and then apologize for how bad the meal turned out. Other women do it as a tactic to get away with bad behavior, for example, when a Queen Bee Mom apologizes to you by saying "Well, I'm sorry you took it that way," which really means you're pathetic and what she did wasn't so bad. We may even have used this strategy ourselves, with or without accompanying waterworks. Last but not least, some women have heard too many empty apologies from men who continued to behave hurtfully. Is it any wonder women don't trust apologies?

I think women need to admit that we're pretty terrible at apologizing and forgiving each other—and that we'll never reach our individual and group potential so long as it continues. We apologize when we don't mean it. We apologize when we're still mad. We end the conversation still feeling resentful and unsettled. We say we forgive people when we don't and hold on to the grudge as though we never got an apology in the first place. We apologize when we aren't really sorry and use our apologies to get sympathy.

Apologizing is about recognizing the other person as an equal to whom you've done harm. If you're not prepared to issue a sincere apology when warranted, you won't succeed in granting him or her that equality.

Men have it a little easier when it comes to apologies. When I teach boys, it's often hard to get them to a place where they can genuinely apologize to one another, but when they do, the apologies are usually heartfelt, and there's a sense that the air has been cleared. Grudges are dropped, and the boys do forgive each other. However, a boy often apologizes to a girl to keep her from being upset or to placate her so that she'll do what he wants or let him do what he wants. Either way, these apologies rarely lead to changed behavior. My observations of men have been the same.

YOUR CHECKLIST

You can apply the principles of SEAL to almost any confrontation, but there are some common stumbling blocks you'll want to consider as you prepare for an encounter.

Timing Is Everything

If you've decided not to confront someone in the moment, here are some hints for choosing a better time:

- Call between 8 and 9 p.m. Avoid the dinner hour, when your call will be as welcome as a telemarketer's.
- Don't call after 9 p.m. Other parents are probably supervising homework, helping their children get ready for bed, or taking a hard-earned moment to unwind.
- Check in with the other person — "Is this a good time to talk?" — *before* you launch into the conversation. Many people are so nervous and/or angry that they barrel ahead without asking. Your goal is to be heard; if you catch the other person at a bad time, he or she will be on the defensive and less able to listen productively. If it's not a good time to talk, you can decide on a mutually convenient time when you can talk.
- That said, you should appreciate that the more time there is between the incident that concerns you and the time you decide to discuss it with another adult, the more opportunity there is for the "spin cycle" to do its work. Any socially intelligent child, male or female, knows that if he or she is about to get into trouble, it's critical to get to the parents first to put his or her own spin on it and do

damage control. So hold on to your critical thinking skills and remember that every situation has many "truths."

- Don't call teachers, counselors, or other school administrators at their homes at any hour unless they've specifically given you permission to do so, and then only as a last resort.

Location, Location, Location

It's helpful to meet in neutral territory—perhaps a quiet coffee shop. Your choice of location sends a message: "We're equals, and I want us to have each other's undivided attention." If you're meeting with a school administrator, arrange a convenient time to meet at his or her office.

Stay on Script

Which means there ought to be one. If you're meeting with someone, bring a log noting when the incidents that concern you occurred. Write down a list of questions to ask and points you want to make in advance of the meeting. This will help you resist the temptation to go flying off with accusations you can't support.

When you create a paper trail, your goal is to create an accurate account of what happened and when, and to keep records of all communications. Please be aware that when you send e-mails, you have no control over where they'll be forwarded. Let me give you the same advice I give girls who want to sign a petition, whether it's about a girl they dislike, a

---

LANDMINE!

If you bring a pad of paper to a meeting like this, other people may get a tad defensive. Take the initiative and assure them that you are writing down what they say because you want to make sure that you understand their point of view and don't want to forget anything they say. Of course, you're also keeping a record of what happened.

teacher they hate, or even a gripe about the cafeteria food: Please assume that the petition will end up in the hands of the very people you most want to keep it from. Don't sign your name to anything that isn't clear and respectful or that would embarrass you if you saw it on the front page of your local paper.

A FINAL BAGGAGE CHECK BEFORE YOU BOARD YOUR FLIGHT

As a parent, I know that nothing pushes your buttons more than what you see as an attack, insult, or unfair act visited on your child. I hope I've convinced you that you can and should approach others to air your concerns and request change. There are, however, times when a confrontation may not truly be in the best interests of your child. Before you take action, ask yourself these questions:

- If your child has already worked the conflict out to his or her satisfaction, do you still need to get involved? Why?
- Do you feel your pride or reputation as a good parent is under siege? Why?
- If you catch yourself sharing your grievances with people in social situations, such as on the bleachers while watching a game or in the grocery line, ask yourself why you're telling them.

As you can tell, deciding whether to get involved in a conflict is perhaps the most important decision you'll make. In Part Two of this book we'll look at the stressful situations parents experience most often and zero in on how you can cope with them.

Part Two

The Principal Will See You Now

How to Deal with Teachers, Counselors, and Principals

Parent-Teacher Night was fabulous. Your sixth-grade son's teachers seemed terrific and the principal gave an inspiring speech. You pull into the driveway feeling optimistic about the new school year. Inside, you decide to check in with your kid and tell him how great the evening was. He's at his computer, probably getting a jump on that English essay. He's such a good kid; he's always been that kind of student. But wait—what's that on the screen? Oh, my God, is that—?

It is. And it's worse than you thought. You review the computer's browser history and find more than forty other pornography sites. "Where did you find these?" you demand of your sweet twelve-year-old. He confesses that he's been swapping pornographic links with other sixth-grade boys.

I'm not making this up; it happened to two parents whose son went to a wonderful middle school. How did the parents handle the sixth-grade porn ring? How would you? And what did the school do?

Yes, the school. Perhaps you're thinking that this is a private matter—that since it happened at home, it should have been resolved at home. I disagree, and I'm glad these parents felt the same way. Children have experiences outside of school that affect them at school as well as the school community. *The Internet always falls into this category*—it obliterates physical boundaries between home and school, which is exactly why parents and schools have to work together.

The following morning the parents of the twelve-year-old boy called the school to report what they'd discovered. A counselor explained to me how the school responded:

> The next day the head of the school, the health teacher, the counselor (me), the head of the middle school, and the computer specialist met with all the sixth-grade boys. We knew that some of the boys wouldn't know about it but we also knew it was only a matter of time. The head of the school said, "It has come to our attention that some of you are involved in sharing pornography on the computer. This isn't a disciplinary issue—no one's getting in trouble. But we're concerned because we don't want pornography to be a part of our school community. It contradicts our school's mission of respect."
>
> The health teacher talked in general about healthy sexuality. We defined pornography for them and explained that what they were seeing on the computer was not reflective of healthy adult relationships. The computer specialist told them that Internet pornography is a multibillion-dollar industry that will do anything to pull kids in. We finished by saying that we knew this would be embarrassing to discuss with their parents but we expected them to talk to their parents that evening. As soon as the assembly was over, we contacted all the parents by e-mail or phone to tell them what had happened, our response, and our expectation that their children come home and talk to them.
>
> The last thing we did was have our computer specialist post to the school Web site step-by-step directions allowing parents to track the Web sites their children visit. We didn't have one complaint from a parent. Only thank-yous.

As a result of their swift, intelligent response, the school administrators and teachers were well prepared to handle other concerns that arose:

1. A mother whose son wasn't involved in the porn ring called the counselor wondering if the boy's lack of involvement "was a problem because he wasn't doing the things the other boys were doing." The counselor was able to explain to the parents the pitfalls of wanting a child to fit into the "Act Like a Man" box.

2. The school recognized that the porn ring had become a way for the boys to prove their masculinity. In that context, the school could more

clearly understand why so many of the boys became involved so quickly. It wasn't that they were sex-crazed twelve-year-olds; they might have been curious, but they were driven to participate as a way to prove they fit into the "Act Like a Man" box.

3. The school then held assemblies for all grades. An eighth-grade girl admitted that she'd given her personal information to someone over the Internet, but she hadn't been worried before the assembly since "he didn't live nearby, he lived in England." The counselor was able to explain to her and all the other students the danger of sharing personal information on the Internet.

What I love about this story is that it shows that even in messy situations, good things can happen when adults are able to get over their discomfort and put children's best interests first. This was a situation in which parents could easily have blamed one another ("My son was only brought into this because of your son—who never gets the supervision he needs because you're not around," etc.). The parents who first found out could have been so embarrassed that they never told the school. Because the parents had the courage to call the school, the sixth-grade boys learned a concrete example of what the adults in their lives stood for, and an eighth-grade girl was saved from a potentially dangerous situation.

I wish that every school would be so enlightened and that every problem between kids, schools, and parents could be resolved so effectively. Although you'll never be able to control the responses of teachers and school administrators, this chapter will teach you how to conduct yourself in your interactions with them, whether your child is innocent, guilty, or anywhere in between. I'm out to help you answer the big questions: When and how much should you get involved with your child's problems at school?

CHECK YOUR BAGGAGE

- What was your fondest memory of a teacher, counselor, or principal when you were in school? What was your worst memory of a teacher, counselor, or principal when you were in school?

- How do you think those experiences impact your interactions with adults in your child's school now?
- What role did you most relate to in Chapter 2 or 3? How do you think that affects your interactions with others at your child's school?
- What filters do you have that influence the way you conduct yourself in your child's school?

Difficult Truths

An ongoing challenge of parenting is that your child can be an unreliable narrator—he or she might give you wrong information, not tell you at all, or do anything in between. (As a general rule, daughters are more likely to tell you when something's wrong. Boys tend to suffer in silence.) Even if you have one of those kids who takes forty-eight hours to recount a twenty-four-hour day, you're still getting your information secondhand. It's helpful to keep a few things in mind when your child reports a conflict at school:

- Remember that your child can be one person at home and someone completely different at school. (I don't necessarily mean better at home and worse at school; I mean different.)
- Unless you're stalking your child, you won't be present when a problem arises, so you won't know exactly what happened. Your child will always spin the story. This doesn't mean he or she's lying; that's just human nature.
- If you're stalking your child at school under the guise of dropping by or taking advantage of the school's new open-lunch policy, this is a problem—and don't rationalize it by saying you just want to be an involved parent.
- There are *always* two sides to a story. If you go in with guns blazing and later find out that your child was responsible for any part of the problem, you'll lose credibility, get embarrassed and defensive, and find your point of view more likely to be dismissed.
- When someone tells you a horrible story about how a child was

mistreated and how the school "did nothing," there's a good chance that the school personnel thought they did everything they could.

- Heads of schools and counselors are in an impossible situation. Their actions might look arbitrary and unfair because they have to protect someone's confidentiality. Outsiders might make assumptions about these decisions that school personnel aren't allowed to refute; these assumptions then become "fact" in the community.
- Educators hate delivering bad news as much as parents hate hearing it. Thus teachers and other school personnel may dance around a painful truth even as they believe they're being clear, while you as a parent will be so eager to hear good news that you'll ignore ten signals that your child is in trouble. That's how two parties can walk out of the same meeting with totally opposite interpretations of what happened: "Oh, I told them the bad news; they took it surprisingly well." "Oh, she said that James is doing great and they're looking forward to him coming back next year."

When should you get involved with your child's problem? Here's my suggested hierarchy of parental involvement:

Level one: Your child confronts the educator.
Level two: You and your child confront the educator.
Level three: You confront the educator.
Level four: You confront the educator's direct supervisor.

When a parent comes to see me, the school has a population of one: their kid.   Sam, head of upper school

Working Effectively with Teachers

Problem: Your Child Receives an Unfair Grade

"Dad, my teacher totally hates me. I totally failed my history test. I studied everything she told me to and she put things on the test that weren't even supposed to be there. She's such a terrible teacher, it's totally unfair."

Your child is devastated. He studied really hard for that test and got a B–. (Don't get me started on how many parents—and kids—consider a B– a "failing grade.") You look over the paper. You can't help thinking that the teacher was really picky; doesn't she know how hard your child worked? The snowball of parental anxiety begins to roll, then picks up momentum: This test was important to his overall grade. If he doesn't do well in this class, it'll pull his GPA down. Then he won't be eligible to take honors courses next year—meaning he'll be surrounded by average (read: stupid) students with the worst teachers. Then he won't get into the best colleges and his life will be ruined forever. . . .

Get yourself off that runaway freight train, and get your child off, too. A bad test grade doesn't have nearly as much effect on your child's future as does teaching him how to cope with it effectively. I'd like to challenge you to go beyond your initial reaction to your child's bad grade and figure out *why* you're reacting as you do. Then help your child analyze his reaction and figure out what kind of response he might want to make.

Step One: Prepare, Using SEAL to Give Structure to the Process

Stop: Turn off the TV and other distractions and have your child bring the assignment and all related material to a room where he feels comfortable. Give him a few minutes alone to calm down and review the material. Then come back to the room (knock first) and ask him why he thinks he wasn't graded fairly. You're asking him to present his position as he would if he met with his teacher.

"I don't know" and "Because she hates me" are unacceptable answers. Your child has to give you a thorough answer, because if he can't do it with you, how will he convince his teacher? After you look at his work, it may be clear to you why he received the poor grade; explain that to him in a way that allows him to take responsibility without feeling incompetent ("Michael, I know you're really mad at your teacher and I hate seeing you frustrated, but I have to be straight with you and tell you that I can see why she gave you that grade"). Then explain specifically why you think his efforts fell short. If he gets frustrated and wants to walk away, that's okay, but set up a time when you can continue the conversation. Your goal is to get him to appreciate where he went off course so that he can do it differently next time.

But what if you think your child is right?

Explain: Have him write down specifically what he's upset about and why. Review what he's written to make sure he's getting his point across, but don't change it all around—it's not your letter. Then have him practice out loud with you or someone else of his choosing what he wants to say. Finally, strategize about the best time for him to speak to that teacher.

Affirm and Acknowledge: Have your child practice affirming why the meeting is important to him and acknowledging where he might have gone off track.

> Wrong: "I really need to get a good grade in this class."
> Right: "It's really important to me that I learn as much as I can, and I want to do better. I thought I gave answers that show that I understood the material, but maybe I wasn't detailed enough. Could we please discuss it?"

Please do not stress out if your kid doesn't say the speech perfectly. If he or she gets any part of it right, he's doing well.

Step Two: Your Child Talks to the Teacher
If your child makes a good case, the teacher ideally will adjust the grade, or at the very least explain her reasoning for it. At this point, give your child the option to use the "L" in SEAL—in other words, lock in the

LANDMINE!

Under no circumstances should your child (or you, for that matter) speak to the teacher in the middle of class, two minutes before the next class, or when there are ten other kids trying to talk to the teacher. Make sure he knows that he needs to make an appointment to meet with the teacher at a mutually convenient time.

relationship ("Thanks for hearing me out, Ms. Clarke. I understand what you mean and I'll try to do better next time"). Tone and attitude matter; teachers know the difference between sucking up, sarcasm, and respect. Your child's definition of success might be that he gets his grade raised. Your definition of success should be whether your child communicated clearly and was treated fairly. Remember what I said about not protecting your child from disappointments and frustrations? If the teacher stands by her grade, then I generally think that decision should be respected. To my mind, you should consider getting involved in only three cases:

1. Your child's work is consistently being marked poorly because of unclear criteria. You confirm this by looking at your child's notes about the assignment or the teacher's written explanation of it and comparing that to the child's execution of the assignment.

2. Your child has tried to do better and he's not improving.

3. Your child feels disrespected by the teacher, which you will determine by asking him for specific examples, writing them down, and verifying them with your child. Remember that kids are prone to exaggeration, especially when the teacher's hard ("You don't understand, she just really hates me!"). The disrespect I'm talking about here isn't name-calling; I'll address that below. Here I'm referring to your child's sense that his concerns weren't being taken seriously. Ask if the teacher said anything positive when your child spoke to her. Did he feel that she listened to him? Did the teacher look him in the eye when he spoke? Did she offer to review the material with him? If you've determined that your child isn't being treated fairly, move on to Step Three.

Step Three: You Talk to the Teacher

A parent had a meeting with me because he felt that his child didn't receive a high enough grade on a project. He told me he'd gone to a very prestigious university and admitted that he'd helped his kid on the project. He wanted to know how this teacher graded because it seemed very subjective. Well, the teacher had given very clear written criteria—but the child had forgotten to bring them home.

Eldon, high school principal

LANDMINE!

I've had parents come in and tell me right off the bat that they're going to sue me. From that moment, not only do I know that they aren't willing to work with me, but they don't even understand the problem.   Norm, high school principal

I hope most parents would be horrified to hear their child threaten their teacher by saying, "If you don't do X, my father is going to sue you." But many teachers have had this experience. So please sit down with your child and make clear that threatening the teacher or giving her ultimatums is disrespectful and inappropriate. It's also counterproductive because there's no better way to get a teacher to hate your child.

Make an appointment for a meeting with the teacher.

Wrong: "Ms. Clarke, you gave my son a bad grade and we need to talk about this right now."
Right: "Ms. Clarke? Hi, this is Michael's dad. I'm sure you're really busy right now, but I'd like to set up a meeting where Michael and I can talk with you about Michael's last test score. When would be a convenient time for you? After school on Monday? Great. Thanks so much."

Keep in mind that when the Ms. Clarkes of the world get phone calls like this, they might sound a little defensive no matter how polite and respectful you are because their previous experiences talking to parents about grades and test scores have probably ended in challenges to their professionalism.

Now prepare your child for the meeting. Start by deciding who should say what. Plan for your child to begin the meeting and lead it as much as he can; you're there as support and backup.

Wrong: "My child's test score was completely unacceptable and I expect something to be done about it."

Right: Your child says something like, "While I respect that as my teacher you decide my grade, it was really hard for me to get up the courage to talk to you. I felt like all you thought I was there for was to get a better grade. I did want a better grade, but I also wanted you to tell me why I didn't get one so I could learn for next time. I walked away feeling like I was disrespected and now I'm worried that you're mad at me." (Your child should then give specific examples of what the teacher said or did that made him feel disrespected.)

At this point, check in with the teacher to confirm that her interpretation of events matches your child's: "Is that a fair description of what happened when Michael spoke to you?" What you want is for the teacher to describe her point of view and apologize if indeed she's been unfair. What if the very way she responds to your question confirms your suspicions?

YOU: *Michael, could you do me a favor and leave the room for a minute?* (Wait until your child has left, sit down, and look the teacher in the eyes respectfully—remember, she tolerates working with thirteen-year-olds every day for eight hours, and she deserves your respect if for no other reason than that.) *Ms. Clarke, it's important to me that my child learns to respect his teacher and her decisions. However, I asked to meet with you because, as you know, Michael was very disappointed in his grade. We talked about it and went over your criteria, and then he talked to you about it. While I respect that his grade is your decision, I need to share with you that he came back from the meeting feeling disrespected and I feel that this disrespect is continuing in our meeting right now.* (Give specific examples.)

Then ask for what you want in a respectful way, without assuming that you're going to get it: "It would be very helpful if you could acknowledge to Michael that you didn't really hear what he was telling you and that you understand what he was trying to say." (Please note: *acknowledge* is a less incendiary word than *apologize*.) Chances are that if you've approach the situation respectfully, the teacher will meet you at least halfway.

What should you do if your meeting with the teacher leads you to believe that your child has exaggerated his claims?

TEACHER: *I told Michael that I was disappointed in him because he's bright and clearly didn't study the material I specified in the handout, which I gave out last week.*

YOU: *I want him to be held accountable for that. I want him to learn not just about the test, but how he conducts himself. What are your suggestions for how we work together on this?*

Don't go over the teacher's head. I mean it. Going over the teacher's head should be an absolute last resort. When you hear yourself say, "I'm going over to that school right now" or "I'm picking up the phone and getting to the bottom of this," stop. Ask yourself, "Is someone going to die in the next five minutes?" If yes, move. If your answer is no, then collect the facts, which you can do only by going to the sources: your child and the teacher. On the whole, parents are far too comfortable going straight to the principal.

Problem: Your Child Is Assigned a Group Project and Ends Up Doing All the Work

Group work teaches children to work collaboratively—clearly an invaluable skill in their professional and personal lives. The teacher announces a major project that counts for a huge portion of the final grade. He assigns three students to each group, ideally choosing kids whose strengths complement one another. In practice, this sometimes means that one kid will do all the work—this time it's your daughter.

First things first: Take a deep breath and recall that almost every kid believes that she's doing more than her fair share of work. Ask your daughter to give you specifics. Let's suppose you think she *is* doing all the work. You have some version of the following conversation:

YOU: *Honey, you just need to tell those kids to do their fair share.*

YOUR DAUGHTER: *Mom, you just don't get it. Sherrie's super-popular and she says she's doing everything she's supposed to be doing, and Tina just started asking me to go ice skating with her friends on Fridays. I don't want to mess things up. There's no way I'm asking them to do anything.*

YOU: *Well, then, I'm just going to call your teacher and set everybody straight.*

YOUR DAUGHTER: *No! You can't do that! Everyone will hate me! Promise me you won't do anything! I'm sorry I said anything.*

Now you're really annoyed. How will the teacher know who did what? Why should your daughter have to do all the work just so her grade won't suffer? How does the teacher expect the kids to be able to work out a fair division of labor? Your daughter's too shy to stand up for herself, or maybe she's tried but the other kids have blown her off and now she doesn't think she can do anything. Should you be calling the other parents? The teacher? And what can you do now that your daughter's hysterical about the idea that you'll get involved?

When your child shares a problem with you and then tries to make you promise to *say* nothing, that doesn't mean you should *do* nothing. Your child wants you to be a sounding board. She wants sympathy and help thinking through what to do. At the same time, she might fear that if she tells you, you'll freak out and make the situation worse. Don't fall into the trap of making that promise. Instead, say something like this:

YOU: *I'm so sorry you're doing all the work in your group. That isn't fair. I understand why you wouldn't want me to say anything, but I can't make that promise—but that doesn't mean I'm going to freak out and force you to do things you don't want to do.* (Go get a cup of coffee while you wait for the pleading and begging to stop.) *We're going to work on figuring this out together. You've just told me that the kids in your group are taking advantage of you. As your parent, it's my job to work with you to figure out these kind of problems. I respect your opinion, and I won't do something without your knowledge, but my job is also to make sure you're strong enough to handle difficult situations— including facing the people who make you miserable.*

Have your child write down who did what work in the group and when. Ask her how she thinks the project is affected by the unequal division of labor. Then have a discussion about why it's hard for her to stand her ground. Why is not confronting someone who's taking advantage of her more important than being in a working relationship where everyone pulls his or her weight? Decide with your child what she wants the next step to be. She has three choices: (1) she can do nothing and accept the situation, (2) she can speak to the group, (3) she can speak to the teacher. It's her decision, but she has to pick one of these options.

Obviously you want to encourage her to speak to her peers or her teacher. If your child can coherently explain to you why she's being treated unfairly, then she's able to articulate her case to others. However, her peers' social power could silence her. Ask her: What's the worst thing that could happen? ("We fail and they all hate me.") What's the best? ("We get an A and they all love me.") What would be an acceptable outcome? ("We're not best friends, but we get the job done.") Have her role-play the conversation. Strategize where and when she'll talk to the group. Remember, if after all your discussions and preparation she decides not to say anything to the group, she's still learned at least two invaluable lessons: that you're a good resource and that she has it in her power to clarify her motivations and options. This puts her one step closer to standing her ground.

If your daughter decides she'd rather speak to the teacher, follow the same procedure: Have her write down what she wants to say, practice it, and strategize about where and when. Have her also practice how she'll request an appointment with the teacher.

And what if she decides not to speak to either the group or the teacher? Is it okay for you to step in then? There are always ways for your kid to have a voice. First try saying, "As your parent, it's my job to advocate for you if you truly feel you can't do it yourself. You did a great job preparing, but I understand that you're not ready. Let's wait twenty-four hours." Sometimes a child will sleep on it and feel ready to speak up the next day.

If your child still doesn't feel ready, you can say, "I totally respect that. I'm not going to fight your fights for you. I propose that I contact the teacher. You tell me what you'd want to say if you could say it yourself." Your child's primary fear is that you're going to say something crazy and make things worse, so reassure her: "You're part of this. I'm going to use your words and be your conduit." Your goal here is to find that middle ground of involvement where it's primarily your child's voice, not yours, that gets heard. Then when you call the teacher to set up your appointment, please request that the teacher respect your child's privacy and not report that she's complaining. Instead, tell the teacher that you would like to verify if this is actually occurring by having the teacher request information from each member of the group that should reflect his or her contribution and involvement thus far. That way it doesn't come down to your kid ratting out the other students.

Problem: Your Child Has Told the Teacher That He's Being Called Bad Names by Other Kids, but the Teacher Blows Him Off or Says He Can't Do Anything About It

Your son has tried to tell the teacher that he's being insulted by some other kids, but the teacher's response is, "Well, I didn't see it so I can't do anything about it" or "I've tried to talk to them and they're just not getting it." Your son tells you but begs you not to do anything; he's worried that the teacher will get angry and the kids will make his life even worse. What should you do?

First, understand that teachers aren't the only educators who do this. There are plenty of school administrators and principals who abdicate their responsibility by saying that they can't take action because they haven't personally witnessed the offending behavior. This reaction drives me crazy because it sets an unrealistically high standard of proof for action and fosters the attitude that harassment is acceptable so long as you don't get caught. This is one of those situations when doing nothing isn't an acceptable option. Harassment has created a hostile educational environment for your child that hinders his ability to learn. So the options are: (1) your child speaks to the teacher again, (2) your child speaks with the teacher again with you by his side, or (3) you talk to the teacher.

As I said before, everybody deserves one chance to make things right. If the teacher doesn't fix the situation within a few days after you or your child has brought the problem to her attention, then I suggest you go to the teacher's supervisor, most likely the principal. Make an appointment for a mutually convenient time, and follow SEAL. Be very clear about what steps the school plans to take next and when you can expect a progress report. Get a specific timetable for action.

LANDMINE!

If your child continually reports that other children are mean to him, please don't tell him "Just ignore it" or "Just be nice back." These strategies don't work in Boy and Girl World. Use SEAL instead.

Problem: The Teacher Has Called Your Child a Name

Unfortunately, there are teachers who insult or plainly humiliate students, such as making a shy, nervous kid reread the same word after he's stumbled over it or telling bullies that they should be nicer to a kid with learning disabilities because "you know he's special." This is the kind of behavior that cannot be ignored.

If your child comes home complaining that the teacher insulted her, your first step is to confirm it: "Did he use that exact word?" If the teacher has indeed insulted or humiliated your child, this is the rare situation where I think you have to handle it. Tell your child, "I'm going to speak to your teacher. I don't think this is your fight to fight." Make an appointment with the teacher and use SEAL. Be very clear with the teacher about what your child reported to you. If the teacher denies it (which then challenges your child's integrity), repeat the insult in question: "I just want to be clear: You never told my daughter that she was stupid? Why do you think my child reported this to me?" Take notes during the meeting because you want to make sure there's no further misunderstanding. If the teacher confirms the insult, request that he or she apologize to your child. Tell your child afterward, "If this teacher ever does this again to you or any other child, I want to know. And we'll take it step by step."

Should you tell the principal? I think that depends on the situation. If your child reports that the teacher continues to insult or humiliate kids, definitely make an appointment and speak with his or her supervisor: "There's a pattern of behavior from the teacher that's keeping my child from learning." Let your meeting with the teacher guide your action; your child may have been unluckily in the line of fire during a particularly monstrous day and the teacher's bad act may be a one-time occurrence.

Problem: The Teacher Is Being Mean to Someone Else's Child

Your child reports that the teacher is being disrespectful toward another child in his class, calling him stupid, humiliating him, etc. Should you handle this any differently from the way you'd handle it if your child were involved? Do you call the kid's parents? The teacher? Coach your child on what advice to give the kid to stand up for himself?

Your child can still be affected by something even if it doesn't happen to him or her directly because it creates a hostile environment in the classroom. Frankly, we should all care about our children's welfare. If you know the other child's parents and think they'd handle it well, let them know what your child reported. If you don't think the parents will handle it well, consider calling the teacher yourself. I think it's very powerful to take action when it's not your child. If you're concerned that the teacher will exact revenge on your child, call the supervisor, protecting the identity of the accuser: "It was reported to me that this occurred in the classroom. I know that you want a school that insists on respect. Please understand that my concern is so strong about reprisal against my child that I'm asking you to keep the source confidential."

> *It's too much to ask kids in elementary school to stand up for themselves or for another kid to the biggest authority figure in the room—the teacher. Parents should call the principal and tell them. As the principal, I want that phone call. Maybe I have a sarcastic teacher who does this regularly to all the kids. I need to know.*
>
> Albert, high school principal

WHAT DO TEACHERS WANT PARENTS TO KNOW?

When parents call me and say, "I just want to collaborate with you," they really mean they want me to do everything their way.

Alene, teacher

I hate it when parents say, "Just so you know," to give me background information they think will be helpful to working with their child—and then they go on to trash another kid in the class.

Nancy, teacher and coach

Imagine it's 8 a.m. on Christmas morning and you're opening presents with your family and the phone rings. It's a parent of one of your students asking how to work the new computer he just bought for his kids.

Aaron, teacher

It's so ridiculous watching parents bring the various things that their kids forget to bring to school: lunch, athletic shoes, their homework. And they call their parents and the parents drop everything and bring it on over. Sometimes more than once a day!

Lindy, head of lower school

Parents: The next time your child calls with this kind of request, express your sorrow and then say, "Forget it!" I think it's fair to bail your kid out once a semester, but more than that and you're being played. Say no and let your children get their own shoes or go hungry at lunch. A mom I know charges a fare for "Mom's Taxi Service" to bail her kids out; the money goes to a charity they all agree on.

I was bullied in high school and I vowed that I would not allow that in my classroom. It was hard at first to teach the boys who reminded me of the boys who bullied me when I was in school, but as an adult now I realize that I have to be fair to them, too. Every child in my class has the right to learn.

Emory, teacher

Counselors

Counselors have a job that's poorly defined yet cruelly exacting in its requirements: nothing less than complete understanding of the developmental issues and abilities of preadolescents and adolescents. In practice, this means everything from helping a preteen survive a vicious lunchroom snubbing to convincing checked-out parents that their daughter is cutting herself with a razor blade. Counselors need to be infinitely creative and flexible when helping kids solve problems; kids have to find them "relatable" (or they won't talk to them); they have to mesh with the other members of the educational team, especially teachers; and they have to do it all with a fully stocked jar of candy on their desk, an endless supply of tissues, and a finely honed sense of humor. Good counselors laugh at themselves—sometimes through tears—as they help students and parents through difficult problems. They must manage their own emotions and reactions in extremely contentious situations where they can easily be scapegoated. In return for all this, they're paid poorly and often not given adequate resources or training. I'm amazed at how many exceptional counselors there are or that anyone is willing to take on the job in the first place.

> *[The job is] very emotionally draining. Teachers and parents don't get it. The kids get it. I'm dealing with potential suicide, abuse, and I'm keeping it together while kids are sobbing because I can't fall apart. [Kids say,] "I don't want to live anymore" and they're twelve.*
>
> Paul, guidance counselor

If they work in private schools, counselors are aware that they owe their paychecks to parents' tuition. If they work in public schools, they're aware that their salaries are vulnerable to politics and budget cuts. All of these factors can make it that much harder for them to defend themselves, and bullying parents can smell their insecurity a mile away. Everyone who is in a counseling position does it because they like the feeling of helping others—myself included. It's great for the ego. But for some, that need gets in the way of doing a good job. Bad counselors usually suffer from poor boundaries, inability to maintain confidentiality, difficulty thinking on their feet, and oversensitivity (for example, they might be offended if a student seeks help from someone else at school).

Over the years I've had the pleasure of working with a lot of excellent counselors. The unfortunate reality is that the nature of the job leaves no room for mediocrity. Good ones save lives. They know when to bring in other school personnel or outside help. The bad ones lecture instead of listen, and convince your child that adults are the last people to go to for help—leaving your child vulnerable and isolated.

The big problem for even the best counselors is that in order to become as good as they need to be, they have to survive on-the-job training in extremely difficult situations, such as dealing with kids' potential suicide and all manner of abuse—and they're bound to make mistakes. It's painful and they never forget it.

During training sessions one of the recurring questions counselors ask me is how to request respectful treatment from angry parents. One young woman asked me what to do when a parent says "F--- you!" during a parent-teacher meeting! After I picked myself up off the floor I told her, "When a parent says that to you, say, 'Please leave the office to get yourself together. I won't continue if you're going to speak to me this way. My door is always open if you're civil.'" Likewise, as a parent you have the right to be treated respectfully by educators and counselors.

Problem: Your Kid Went to Discuss a Problem, Only to Have the Counselor Blow Him Off with a Brochure

Let's face it, you'll be lucky if you ever hear about this from your child. More likely you'll find the brochure crumpled at the bottom of your child's backpack. After you've recovered from your case of the vapors, you'll realize that it's actually a *good* thing that your child has sought out a trusted adult. Remember, good parents recognize that there are other adults who can and should be sources of guidance in their child's life. You don't have to be Yoda all the time.

The first step is to ask your kid about it. "I found a brochure about bullying in your backpack. You want to talk to me about it?" Whatever her answer, ask her if she's getting all the necessary information and help from the counselor. "I'm here for you to talk about this, but I also realize that maybe there's someone else you want to talk to. I respect your privacy and that I don't have to be the person you talk to, but I would like to know who the person is." Your child may feel comfortable enough to tell you that the counselor hasn't taken her concerns seriously.

The next step is to coach your child on how to speak to the counselor to get more help. If he or she doesn't feel ready to do that, make an appointment with the counselor to discuss the issue. Your goal in this meeting isn't to violate your child's confidential relationship with the counselor but to assess that person's competency in handling your child's concern: "I'm sure you're very busy, but Maggie didn't get enough information when she spoke to you. Do you have any other resources you can recommend? Can you make time to talk with her again?"

Finally, reassure your child that she did the right thing by speaking to the counselor and remind her that you're there for her: "There are going to be times you think you can't come to me with a problem, but you always can; try me. If you can't, I want to be sure you have another adult you trust and can confide in." Brainstorm with your child which other adults she feels she could go to: a relative, a member of the clergy, a close friend's mother or father? Make sure that support system is in place.

Problem: The Counselor Breaks Your Child's Confidentiality

Let's say your daughter is going to a counselor and she breaks your child's confidentiality. There are three ways counselors can make this mistake, and all three are easy to do. First, they can tell your child's teachers. After all, teachers often want to know what's going on with their students, and they sometimes take offense when the counselors refuse to tell them anything. Counselors have been known to cave under that pressure. Second, in trying to untangle a conflict between students, counselors might inadvertently reveal privileged information when the group is all together (remember, students can be very tricky). Third, they can tell a parent information that was not intended to be shared.

> *I tell my students that I won't tell parents, friends, teachers unless they say it's okay. I'm not allowed to break confidentiality unless you're being hurt at home or you are in danger because you are going to hurt yourself.*   Damian, guidance counselor

Breaking confidentiality is a very serious violation of your child's rights. If a counselor breaks this golden rule, I do think you have an obligation to inform his or her supervisor. Tell the counselor that you'll be reporting the incident.

WHAT COUNSELORS WANT PARENTS TO KNOW

I would like the parent to give me any information that might affect the child in school (recent death or illness, family changes, emotional changes, friend issues, parents' job or schedule changes). The more information the parent can share, the better.   Morris, middle school counselor

One kid I'm working with is depressed. His dad comes in and tells me, "He's just shy; why does everyone put a label on it? My brother was shy as a kid and he's a lawyer now." Now the child is having neurological problems. He has no affect and desperately needs help.

Tamar, middle school counselor

Some of my students have cognitive difficulties. . . . Some of these kids' automatic response is to push a kid when the other kid gets too close or gets in his way. It's really hard because those kids often get branded as bad kids and they're not. So the other kids' parents come to see me and say things like, "I've heard terrible things about that kid," "I don't want my kid in that kid's room." And I can't tell these parents that the problem is deeper than that kid being a bully because I have to respect my students' privacy.   Steve, middle school counselor

I hate it when parents say:
- *"He's in your building; you fix it."*
- *"He was never like this before." (My response is, "Well, he wasn't thirteen before.")*
- *"It's the other kids."*
- *"I've taken away all his stuff and he's still terrible."*
- *"You're not helping me. My kid's having a problem and no one's seeing it and no one is doing anything about it." (My response: "I'm trying, I'm trying!")*   Mark, middle school counselor

The Principal Will See You Now

The vast majority of principals I've worked with are intensely committed to their jobs and love their students. Here are the qualities I particularly cherish in a good principal. He or she (I've used *he* in these examples to simplify):

- Knows every part of the school like the back of his hand because he's put in honest shoe leather time, walking the corridors, getting the kids in and out of cars and buses, and popping into lunch and recess. He knows most of their names and greets them in the morning.
- Accepts responsibility when the school makes a mistake.
- Has extra clothes in the office for students' emergencies.
- Backs up the teachers, who know that they'll be held responsible for wrongdoing but also that they'll be listened to and that their professional expertise will be respected.
- Treats everyone with equal respect, from coaches and parents to teachers and the lunchroom staff.
- Holds his own with powerful and/or bullying parents.
- If male, prone to wearing ties with pictures of children, animals, or cartoons.

I want to share with you an experience I had that demonstrated a great principal in action. Brad Crozier, principal of Happy Hollow Elementary School (yes, that's the school name), asked me to visit his school while I was in his district giving a presentation. As we walked into the school's administrative offices he was faced with three sixth-grade boys sitting in chairs ringing the room, looking down at the ground with tearstained faces, elbows on the knees of their torn and wet pants. Brad apologized to me that we would have to postpone our meeting, got dry clothes out of his closet, and escorted the boys into his office. When the boys came out ten minutes later you could tell that peace and justice had been restored.

No one wants to invite a guest to talk about bullying prevention in his school only to have her walk in to see three boys sent to his office for a fight. But his priority, as it should be, was to those kids, not to me. First he made sure their physical needs were taken care of. Once they were in dry clothes they met in his office. Only after he felt that the situation was taken care of did our meeting resume. As we talked and walked around the school, he simultaneously said hello to every student that walked by. Need I add that he wore a tie with cartoon children on it?

On the other hand, I've had to work with a handful of bad principals. These folks always strike me as more politicians than educators. When you walk out of a meeting with them, you're never sure what really happened—except that whatever you wanted to get accomplished didn't. They're unable to take responsibility for their mistakes, eager to scapegoat others. Their teachers never know whether they'll be supported, although they're certain that if it's politically expedient, they'll be sacrificed. They blow off the parents who don't impress them. The only time they leave their power base—their office—is for administrative functions, to attend the athletic events for which the school is famous, or to schmooze the powerful parents, to whom they'll invariably capitulate. They delegate discipline to the assistant principal (so the parents will get mad at her instead of him).

Whenever I do time with one of these principals, I inevitably find myself staring at the walls of his office, which are decorated with those inspirational posters you see advertised in airline magazines. He'll be leaning back in his chair, playing with his tie as he pontificates. Or she'll be micromanaging her staff while strenuously denying doing so, or blaming someone who questions her leadership capabilities.

If you're fortunate, you'll go through your child's entire education without either you or your offspring ending up in the principal's office. However, the chances are good that sooner or later you'll end up paying the principal a visit. Let's suppose that both you and your child have tried to solve a problem with the teacher but gotten no satisfaction. Or perhaps you've received the dreaded call that your child is being charged with a serious infraction—one that might result in heavy disciplinary measures. It's time for that visit. How do you handle it?

Preparing for Your Meeting

When you're getting ready to meet with the principal, you want to be calm and collected, a mature adult interested in hearing all parties out equally, holding your child accountable for bad actions or articulating why she is suffering at school, and working out a thoughtful, fair result. In reality, you're more likely to be burning with righteous indignation, convinced that the school personnel are a bunch of butt-covering boneheads, and either wildly overprotective because your child has been hurt, or embarrassed by whatever your kid did to get you there in the first place. In short, you're anything but calm and collected. So how do you get there? Review this checklist:

- In this meeting you're entitled to have your perspective respected in equal measure with that of everyone else involved. No one has the right to tell you or your child, "You just took it the wrong way" or "Your child is too sensitive."
- Other people's rights in this meeting are exactly the same as yours.
- If your partner/spouse or ex attends the meeting with you, what role in Perfect Parent World is most applicable to your partner/spouse or ex? How will this impact the meeting?
- What role in Perfect Parent World is most applicable to you? How will this impact the meeting?
- How are both of you going to get the support you need from each other so you can be proud of how you behave during the meeting?

Rules of Engagement

No matter the reason you're in the office—whether you've been called in or you initiated the meeting—you have four goals, as beautifully articulated by Julie Baron, counselor extraordinaire at the McLean School in Potomac, Maryland, one of my all-time favorite schools:

1. Maintain your dignity.
2. Feel competent as a parent.

3. Hold your child accountable and communicate that accountability in a manner that demonstrates that your actions support your child.

4. Establish (or reaffirm) a collaborative relationship with the school.

Your position on the social ladder will affect how you approach this meeting. A Queen Bee, Sidekick, or Banker might find it hard to treat the administrator respectfully because it can feel like her competence as a mother is being questioned. A Wannabe parent will often want to please the principal but not intend to follow through with whatever agreement is made. A Steamrolled Mom or Caveman Dad will let the principal have control over the entire situation. Parents who used to work and now stay at home have to be careful that their fear of coming across as a "typical stay-at-home parent" doesn't sabotage their effectiveness. Parents who have always stayed at home might feel they have no authority with these "professionals"; conversely, they might feel so invested in their child that they can't hear what the administrators are saying.

Problem: The Punishment Doesn't Fit the Crime

Let's revisit the hypothetical example I raised in the Introduction. Your daughter Tara takes a Tylenol before gym class because she has her period and feels crampy. The gym teacher catches her and reports her to the principal. The school has a strict no-drugs policy that was stated in a student contract Tara signed in the beginning of the year—and that means all drugs, including acetaminophen. The penalty is automatic suspension. Okay, you really do respect the school's antidrug policy; you don't want anyone trying to sell Tara marijuana in the girls' bathroom. But isn't this taking things too far? Why should your daughter receive the same punishment as a kid caught trying to sell crystal meth? Tara is a terrific student with a spotless record—is the school actually going to ruin her chances for college, her life?

I realize that schools can have rules that don't seem to be based on common sense. I'd agree with the parents in this situation that punishing Tara for bringing Tylenol to school is ridiculous. But that's not the issue. Tara knew the rule; she even signed a contract stating that she agreed to abide by the rule. Therefore she has to accept the consequences.

But in my experience, school administrators do apply common sense to these situations.

Most schools have some flexibility on violations, even ones as serious as possession or use of drugs. It's been my experience that if your child breaks a rule—even a big one—most educators make allowances if it's truly a mistake. Children generally get kicked out of school not when they break school rules but when they lie about it and encourage other people to lie about it.

> *What some parents don't seem to get is that we'll understand when their kid makes a mistake. But to encourage a child to lie, or refuse to admit that your child lied to get out of taking responsibility for what he did . . . that's not what I allow as one of the leaders of this school. That's where I take my stand.*   Steve, principal

When Administrators Change Their Minds

Serious infractions demand an immediate response from all members of the school community who were involved. The problem is that an administrator often makes a decision without being fully informed. This isn't necessarily the administrator's fault; students frequently "forget" important information, or it takes them time to find the courage to step forward with it. As more information comes to light, the administrator might find it necessary to change the original consequence. Unfortunately, people outside the situation often assume that the consequences were changed because the administrator was somehow paid off. However, I've found very few instances of that in my work.

> *We had a student who was incredibly wealthy and had lots of problems. We had her on a contract and medical leave. Kids were convinced that I was letting her go (not kicking her out of school) because she was rich, but I never caught her drinking or drugging. I told them they could call me the next time she was drinking or drugging but I can't kick someone out of school on hearsay.*   Chris, high school principal

What is much more common is that a couple of days after the initial decision is handed down, the administrator learns with greater certainty who was responsible for what. When disciplining students, a good administrator will say at the conclusion of the first meeting, "And if there's anything you've forgotten to tell me after this meeting, you know you can always come back and tell me," which gives the students the opportunity to "remember" what really happened without being caught in a lie.

> *I've changed my mind [about punishments]. Two girls wrote very provocative and inappropriate things on the door of their friend's room. I met with one of the girl's dads and found out that the other girl was responsible for the more offensive things. So I changed his daughter's suspension to a warning.*   Kim, high school principal

Problem: The Entire Class Is Punished for an Infraction Committed by a Few

Let's say a group of kids trashed the gymnasium after the last basketball game. And let's also say that the principal responded by canceling the spring prom. Only a handful of kids vandalized the gymnasium, and a handful more knew about it but said nothing. Why should the whole class be punished?

Okay, I completely understand why you're feeling burned on behalf of your daughter, who had nothing to do with the vandalism, didn't know anyone who did, finally got asked to the prom by the guy she likes, *and* found the perfect dress. On sale. And now there's no prom. Before you prepare to do battle with the principal, stop and focus on the larger issue. You *want* this kind of principal, someone who insists on students' accountability. More often, principals in these situations say and do nothing because they fear the parents. Thank your lucky stars you have a principal who insists that your daughter and her fellow students take responsibility for their actions. Moreover, students and their parents love to take ownership of an event at school when it's good—like when the football team wins the championship. Adults need to remind themselves and teach their kids that if they want to take ownership when things go well, they must do the same when things go badly. I promise you that the lessons about integrity she learned from the principal will outlast her disappointment over a canceled dance.

Problem: You've Gotten No Results from the Teacher

Ideally, you've made an honest effort to communicate with your child's teacher. If you've reached a genuine impasse, or if you feel that the teacher's conduct has been disrespectful of you or your child and the teacher refuses to acknowledge it, then it's appropriate to speak with the principal.

What do you have the right to expect if the teacher has been disrespectful? At the very least, an apology from the principal with a promise that he or she will follow up with the teacher.

> *I have mandated an apology [from the teacher to the parent]. I give the professional courtesy that they'll do it and then tell them that they need to call the parent and tell them what happened. Typically when I see teachers reaching that point, it's about other things going on in their lives and they get to a breaking point.*
>
> Carlton, high school principal

What if the Principal Doesn't Fix the Problem?

Perfect Parent World is far from perfect, and as this story demonstrates, principals don't always know their lines or respond on cue.

> FATHER: *Eric got into an argument with a kid: the kid called Eric a "dirty Jew," and Eric hit him. The lunchroom monitor saw Eric hit the kid and Eric got mandatory in-school suspension because there's a zero-tolerance policy for hitting. I wrote a letter saying I can support the zero-tolerance policy for hitting, but there should also be a zero-tolerance policy for bigotry. I said that this kid's bruise will heal, but the humiliation of being called a dirty Jew in front of his friends is going to linger a lot longer. The school just doesn't get it. . . . The assistant principal was a coward and lied to me and said that the other kid was getting the same punishment as Eric, but Eric sat in all-day suspension and the other kid served a lunch-hour suspension. I wrote to the principal and assistant principal and no one ever wrote me back. . . . I thought it was okay for him to hit the kid, because when you're a boy, answering back verbally isn't sufficient. What's he gonna say, "No, I'm not"?*

MOTHER: *But you can't go around hitting people in the streets, so you have to learn how to handle it. . . . The woman who took him from the lunchroom said to him, "I know you shouldn't have hit him, but what he said to you was wrong. And you had every right to be very angry."*

This story illustrates how the rules of Boy World influenced the behavior of everyone involved. The first boy used a religious slur to put the other boy outside the "Act Like a Boy" box. His target retaliated by hitting him because that fits into the "Act Like a Boy" rules to express anger. The adults also bought in to the tenets of Boy World. The school minimized the incident (boys will be boys) and the dad (an exceptionally wonderful man, by the way) believed that his son had no choice but to physically retaliate.

If something like this happened to your child, what would you do next? I think the most important thing is to give your child a place to voice his experience. If he feels dismissed by the principal, he needs to meet with that person or write him a letter requesting a response. In an ideal world, he'd receive an apology from the principal, and the school would change its policy. However, you have to prepare him for the possibility that he may not get the acknowledgment he wants.

Should you take your case to the superintendent of schools? That depends. How much do you want to fight this battle? Have you perceived a pattern of abuse? Sometimes parents feel they've failed if they don't take something to the superintendent or initiate legal action. I disagree. If you feel your child has voiced his opinion, and you've voiced yours, you're not a failure if you haven't taken the most extreme possible action. If you decide there's a pattern of bad behavior and you do want to press your case, make sure that your child has a prominent voice in the process. Ask him, "What would a tolerant and inclusive community look like to you? If it happens again, what's the best way for the school to handle it?" You can't control the school's response to your situation, but you can help your child be heard.

Sometimes principals' incompetence is dazzling:

Three girls started bullying my daughter in fourth grade. They'd pull her hair, throw her down, and then she got a rainbow note of hate.

They wrote all the reasons why they hated my daughter in the shape of a rainbow and each girl had her color. At first my husband and I told her to be as nice as you can; show them what it's like to be a good friend. We were delusional.

The next year the other girls' behavior continued. I had to beg my daughter to go to school, she missed assignments, and she wouldn't go out for recess. Then one day the teacher left the classroom for a few minutes and the girls attacked her again. When she [the teacher] realized what had happened she told the principal.

The next day I took my daughter to school late because she couldn't sleep the night before. As we were walking to her classroom, the PA system went on asking for my daughter and the other girls to report to the principal's office. He talked to the three girls first as we waited. Then he had them wait outside while he talked to us. He asked my daughter, "What would a perfect day at school be?" She didn't know what to say. "If you had a day filled with rainbows, sunshine, and butterflies, what would that look like?" I thought to myself, "Are you freakin' crazy?" My daughter said, "I just want to feel safe at this school." Then he told my daughter to go tell the girls they could go back to their class now—and my daughter could go with them. You might as well feed her to the sharks!

His idea of consequences after three violations for bullying was to make someone eat in his office. He suggested that my daughter could do office work during lunch or a "special project—she could pick up trash at lunch." I asked him, "What if this were your daughter?" He said he would cry a lot. If he felt powerless to help his own child, how could he help mine?

We transferred schools and my daughter is doing so much better. After our first teacher conferences this year, I broke down and cried, I was so grateful.   Jenna, middle school mom

While this was a miserable experience for this girl and her family, there were three positive outcomes:

1. The girl went through an experience where she needed her parents and they came through. I'm sure that she doubted her parents' sanity when their first suggestion was to just be nice to these girls and show them what a good friend is. However, the parents realized their mistake and be-

came her advocates—so this girl learned that her parents are fallible but that they can recognize their mistakes and move beyond them. They tried to work within the system, and when that didn't help they moved her to a better place.

2. The girl received a written apology from one of the girls, whereupon her mother called the mother of the girl who'd written the letter. That family also removed their daughter from the school at the end of the year. Because the girl's parents took effective action, another family took responsibility for their daughter's bad behavior.

3. The Parent School Board Association became involved and is trying to improve the school. They wrote a letter to all the parents suggesting ways to address the problem and asked the mother to review it.

It's tempting to write off the principal in this case as beyond help, but the truth is that too many principals have never been trained in adolescent social development. Without such training, it's understandable that the principal would excuse the bullies' bad behavior as "just what girls do." And if he considers it normal behavior, he wouldn't see it as deserving of punishment. He did grasp that the victim needed to be separated from the perpetrators, but his choices further ostracized the victim. By trying to "sell" the girl on office work—or trash collecting—as an acceptable substitute for fun, safe recreation at recess, he sent a clear message that if you complain, you'll be removed from your peer group. This in turn sent a message to the entire school about what happens when you break the unwritten rule that you don't complain about socially powerful bullies: *You* will be the one who is punished.

One of the trademarks of a bad principal is that when a student has been bullied, the principal "punishes" the perpetrators by making the victim change classes, change schedules, or stay in the office at free periods or recess. A good principal will check to see if the victim needs or wants to change his or her schedule, but will also see to it that the *perpetrators* are the ones who are separated from the group.

When you think you're getting the runaround from a principal, your best approach is to speak as plainly as possible: "I'm feeling like I'm not getting straight answers. I know that you can't tell me everything because you have to respect confidentiality, but I have to feel like you're giving me straight answers. " If your honest approach isn't met with equally straight-forward responses, then you might consider taking your issue to the principal's supervisor, the superintendent of schools.

LANDMINE!

Be careful about zero tolerance policies as a cure-all to stop bullying in your school. For example, if a child comes to school with a knife in her backpack because she's being bullied relentlessly and the school isn't addressing the problem adequately, a zero-tolerance policy means that child will be suspended or expelled. Although children who bring weapons to school should certainly be held accountable, zero tolerance in this case punishes the target and won't stop the real problem—the students who are bullying this child so badly that she becomes desperate enough to bring a weapon to school. The bullies will then turn their sights on another target, with everyone understanding that the perpetrators won't be punished.

Write-in Campaigns

Parents who are very angry at the administration for disciplining their child will often encourage other parents to write in to the school administrator either to plead the child's case or to attack the head of the school: "We'll take our children out of the school unless you . . ." "We have no choice but to share with our community that we believe your leadership is taking the school in the wrong direction."

I've seen some write-in campaigns for just causes, such as correcting discriminatory practices, but here's what I observe more often: Entitled or Wannabe parents ask their friends to write in to help rescue their child from the consequences of his or her bad actions. Very few of these friends want to write the letters. Usually they're just too afraid to tell the parents what they really think: that the school was right to expel their child. Some parents say they'll write and don't, for the same reason. And many, many parents will approach the head of the school privately and thank them for disciplining the unruly child. These reactions can be straight out of the Queen Bee's playbook, with the powerful parents in charge and the Wannabes trying to appease them.

I do believe there are times when you should write a letter on behalf of another family. However, don't base your decision on how close you are to the family; do your best to decide based on the merits of the situation. Can the family document a pattern of behavior where the school administrators have been unresponsive or disrespectful? Has the family exhausted all the school's stated procedures without getting a fair hearing? Will your letter help foster a system of universal fairness and respect, or are you pleading for special treatment? As I've mentioned before, I tell kids they should never sign a petition unless they're prepared to see it on the front page of their local paper. Would your letter pass the same test?

WHAT PRINCIPALS WANT PARENTS TO KNOW

When I say, "Let me look into it," it's not a blow-off.

Brandon, principal

I'm incredibly anxious when I have to expel a student. I'm worried about being sued. I've been sued. We're still dealing with a lawsuit from two years ago over a disciplinary case. All the time and money that goes into that is just such a waste. Jane, head of school

I believe that no parent or student is more important than anyone else. But I know that some parents think that certain people can walk into my office at any time and get anything they want. I also know that the parents who are perceived here as having influence in my office are Jewish parents or parents who volunteer the most for grade activities. As an African American woman who is an administrator at a primarily wealthy white school, it can be really hard, but I just have to do my best work and be fair. Suzanne, head of school

If You Send Your Child to Religious School

Parents often send their children to religious schools to protect them from what they see as the negative influence of popular culture. They believe that the school has a particular responsibility to champion certain values, such as dignity, forgiveness, and honesty.

Unfortunately, I've talked to many parents who have sent their kids to religious schools of all kinds—Jewish, evangelical Christian, Catholic, Muslim—where the school hasn't lived up to its stated values. These parents feel an especially keen sense of betrayal.

> *I send our kids to a Jewish school and the teachers just won't deal with the bullying that goes on here. There's this attitude that our kids are different—they wouldn't do such things. Meanwhile the kids are doing it every day under their noses.*   Nan, middle school mom

> *I sent our children to a Catholic school because I believed they would share my values and I could trust them to look after my daughters— which they didn't. The principal announced over the PA system that he wanted to see my sixth-grade daughter. When she walked into his office, three girls from her grade were sitting there. He told my daughter that these girls wanted to talk to her and then he let them loose. They berated her for an hour and he never intervened.*
>   Christine, middle school mom

Conversely, I've met wonderful teachers and administrators at religious schools whose spirituality informs and strengthens their commitment to their professions.

> *We are a Christian school and sometimes I'll have parents in a meeting where I have to discipline their child and they'll say to me, "We're a Christian school, so we believe in turning the other cheek and forgiveness, so why does my daughter have to be punished?" I just say the most Christian thing we can do is to hold their child accountable.*
>   Karl, middle school principal

Before that next parent-teacher conference, phone call from the guidance counselor, or summons to the principal's office, take yourself on an imaginary tour down the school hallways. Remember the smells from the cafeteria, the sight of the students careening from classroom to classroom, the sounds of chatter and ringing bells. Think about the times that you handled things well—encouraging your child's voice, expressing your concerns respectfully, appreciating the daunting job educators have— and give yourself some serious credit. Now think about those times when you didn't. Resolve to make amends and help your child learn the lessons that will never appear on an achievement test but that are just as vital.

Field of Nightmares

Kids and Sports

I've gone through recreational sports with all three of my kids. Most parents who coach don't want to have a good time—they want to win. Not to have a good time, not to learn the game, not to grow as people—only to win. It's totally destructive in every single possible way. I don't know why parents stand for it, and I'm one of the parents who does [go along with it]. But you can't take your kid out, because if you do, your kid isn't participating in the peer group, isn't getting exercise, and isn't getting recreational activity.

Harold, father of three

Athletics and team sports present a wonderful opportunity for our kids to develop character, confidence, fitness, and ability. But we also know that they can be powerful weapons in Perfect Parent World for people to bully and dominate other kids and adults. We read about or see the screaming parents who threaten the coaches, players, or other parents. We cringe when we hear a coach bullying a kid half his size. We see mediocre players get more playing time than others (especially if our kid is the one not playing) and suspect their parents of rigging the system. We hear about extreme cases of parents and coaches being injured or even losing their lives over a kids' game. Perhaps even more shocking, such cases don't strike us as out of the ordinary because we see them as yet another symptom of how out of control everyone is, yet we still don't think the problem will ever land on our doorstep.

As a competitive athlete in junior high, high school, and college, I know firsthand how satisfying it can be to be a part of a team, to have a great coach to look up to, to feel confident because of your athletic abilities. I also know what it's like to play on a team where players undermine and intimidate each other, and to suffer under a coach who makes you feel worthless.

When things go wrong, everyone's intentions are usually good. Coaches who demean kids don't believe they're being tyrannical; they think their approach builds kids up. Parents who scream on the sidelines don't hear themselves publicly humiliating their own or other people's children. Parents who become coaches don't believe they favor their own kids. Parents who help out with the booster club and raise money for new uniforms are often unaware that they come across as wanting their kids to get preferential treatment.

When parents talk to me about kids and sports, I've found that they often assume the worst about everyone else—"All the other parents care about is winning," "There's no respect for the coaches anymore"—but it's the very rare parent who can admit when he or she has behaved badly. I've had the opportunity to talk with a lot of wonderful coaches, and many of them are frustrated that parents assume the worst of them or treat them with disrespect. When I asked them what parents think of coaches, they said things like "cold-hearted," "in the pockets of the richest parents," "easily manipulated by the parents who kiss up to them the most," "bullying," or "doesn't care what the parents think."

There's so much to be gained from seeing that our kids enjoy and grow from sports that it's clearly worthwhile to address these problems and repair these relationships. In this chapter I'll discuss the tremendous role coaches play in shaping your child on and off the field, and walk you through the conflicts that commonly arise among parents, coaches, referees, and other adults on the sidelines. I'll also explore how Perfect Parent World convinces you to never challenge people when they're out of line.

CHECKING YOUR BAGGAGE

- Think back to when you played sports in school. Now remember the moment that was most humiliating to you. Did it involve a coach or parent?
- Now recall your most uplifting moment on the playing field—how were your coach, parents, and the other parents involved? Recall again that moment of humiliation—what would it have meant to you if someone had defended and protected you?

OUR ATHLETES, OURSELVES

Why do we get so wrapped up in our kids' games? I believe that part of the answer lies in a role reversal. In *Reviving Ophelia*, sociologist Mary Pipher discusses adolescents' typical embarrassment about their parents in the context of what she calls "Imaginary Audience Syndrome." Visualize yourself sitting in the audience watching your child perform in a play. At the end of the play, you proudly clap, along with every other beaming parent in the auditorium. Your child, however, hears only you and is completely embarrassed by how you clapped. Of course, no other kids care—because they're too busy being embarrassed by their own parents. And no other parents care—they're too busy clapping for their own mortified kids. In other words, your child is intensely embarrassed that everyone else is an audience for your weird behavior—but no one else has even noticed because they're all too focused on themselves.

In sports, I think the same thing happens except that the roles are reversed—now it's the parents' turn to act like narcissistic teens. When we watch our kids on the field, we may cheer for the whole team, but we also worry about what people think about our kids, whereas in fact the other parents are just as preoccupied with their own kids. When he strikes out, misses the shot, or falls behind, we cringe or make excuses. When someone else's kid messes up, we wonder why he's getting more playing time than our kid. If our kid mixes it up with another kid on the field, how will we cope with the other kid's parent? In Perfect Parent World, our kids' athletic performance is yet another barometer by which we feel our parenting skills are judged.

My Competitive Spirit Is Better Than Yours

We've come a long way from the pickup games of stickball our grandparents (most likely our grandfathers) enjoyed. Title IX has brought more girls into sports than ever before and there's increased funding and greater variety in all kids' sports. But along with these positives have come more avenues for ramping up competition in Perfect Parent World.

Nowhere is this more evident than in the growth of "travel" or "select" team sports, where kids typically have to try out to make the team, where the games are more competitive than in the typical recreation league, and where parents' participation and attendance are usually greater—sometimes even required. The kids on these teams enjoy the sense of being among the elite—after all, they made the cut—and they often get better uniforms, better-credentialed referees, paid trainers, and other perks. They also make sacrifices: additional practices every week and longer trips to play other teams. Often the parents make the sacrifices right along with them, but these sacrifices are encouraged in Perfect Parent World because they show that your child is a star and you're willing to do anything to give your child every opportunity (remember Chapter 5). Some parents even brag about this—"Oh, I had to get up before dawn again to drive Ryan to the rink" or "I take Gina to elite gymnastics five nights a week; it's just crazy, but her coach thinks she could be an Olympic qualifier."

These elite teams can be terrific opportunities for kids to grow within their sport as they receive more instruction on skills, push themselves competitively, and experience the thrill of all that hard work during practice coming together in good team play on the field. However, select teams also tend to attract kids and parents who are more driven. This competitive spirit can morph into truly destructive behavior that includes pushing kids too far, allowing unsportsmanlike behavior, and worse.

Our challenge isn't to eliminate competition; it's to erase the equation of athletic ability with entitlement or superiority. We can't stop children from being competitive, and I don't think that's a useful goal. Healthy competition can motivate us to do our best, to try our hardest. What we shouldn't do is allow a competitive urge to become an excuse for unethical behavior. Children are capable of competing hard, feeling good if they win, feeling bad if they lose, and behaving ethically no matter what so long as their parents support them and never let them think that because they are athletes they are above the rules.

Learning to be a gracious loser is a precious life skill that serves a person far beyond the athletic field. I don't believe our kids learn self-esteem in a world that tries to pretend there's no difference between a winning effort and a mediocre one. (I'm reminded of a *Doonesbury* cartoon in which a kid comes home from Self-Esteem Camp, arms laden with trophies applauding accomplishments as trivial as making his bed.) They learn true self-worth by pushing themselves to achieve their personal best, and by knowing and accepting that their best effort might not always result in a win.

When we try to erase the idea of competition or disguise it by giving every player a trophy, we're telling our kids that losing (or, more to the point, appearing to lose) is intolerable both to them and to us and that they can't handle it. We're also buying in to the cultural message that winning is everything. In essence, we're telling them that they should sacrifice everything to achieve victory and that if they lose, they should cover it up. Our kids need to learn to handle frustration and disappointment. This isn't an issue of ability. If we tie our children's sense of self-worth to their achievements—"I'm nothing if I'm not good at football, soccer, etc."—then we risk raising kids who are so terrified of failing in front of us that they'll do anything to win (or, at the opposite extreme, who'll do nothing to win, opting out of competition completely).

My dad did a great job of always being supportive of us playing sports. It was a huge priority in our lives. On the con side, I don't think my dad was a tremendous athlete in high school, and there was an immense amount of pressure to get a scholarship and that was very hard to deal with. He told me that he made a decision when I was a sophomore starting on the varsity team, and I had a 4.0, that I was gonna get a scholarship. I didn't get the scholarship. What was devastating about that is that it felt to me like I had failed.

John, high school coach

Of course, we're not the most powerful mediators of our kids' experiences in sports. Just as teachers are the authority figures in the classroom, coaches are the authority figures on the playing field. These men and women are leaders with tremendous power to shape our kids' attitudes toward competition, fair play, and hard work. Our relationship with them may be intimate or hands-off, but it's crucial that we understand how they approach coaching, and how and when to step in when we disagree with the decisions they make.

THE SCOUTING REPORT ON COACHES

My Little League coach brought a flat of flowers to practice on Mother's Day so that each player could give his mom some flowers. He even brought bags for the flowers for the kids who biked to practice so we could carry them home.   Wesley, college athlete

When I first tried out for football, they put a strip of tape on my helmet which meant that I wasn't allowed to even try out for a skilled position. It was a total disgrace. So later I had a coach who said, "You want to be quarterback? Great! We'll have a day when everyone can throw." I gave it everything I had. It felt really good that everyone would have a chance to prove themselves on merit.

Byron, athlete in his twenties

In an ideal world, our children's coaches would be trained in everything from sports psychology to adolescent development. But that's rarely the case; coaches are often pressed into service from other school departments or from the ranks of volunteers, including other parents (a case I'll discuss below). While I believe most coaches share a love of their sport and a desire to help kids excel in it, chances are that your kid is going to experience a few duds.

What makes a good coach? Someone who can get your kid through the storm of adolescence, help him or her channel energy and aggression in positive ways, and see where he or she fits beyond the social rankings within the school—a particular challenge because athletics is so often tied to social status for kids and adults alike. A good coach does the following:

- Sets clear expectations when it comes to trying out, performing, and all-around behavior
- Chooses players based on merit and gives everyone a chance
- Never verbally or physically abuses players
- Disciplines players by making them work harder and do more physical conditioning
- Holds players accountable for their actions on and off the field (including good sportsmanship), during the season and in the off season, and doesn't allow their parents to make excuses for them or get them out of team or school responsibilities
- Doesn't encourage players by demeaning their opponents or anyone else
- Keeps his or her cool with irate parents
- Tells players: "This is a game. If you truly try your best, then I'm proud to be your coach."

A bad coach reinforces the worst stereotypes of athletic success: winning at all costs, the acceptability of demeaning others in service of "team building," etc. A bad coach reinforces the "Act Like a Woman" and "Act Like a Man" boxes. He or she:

- Plays favorites rather than giving kids a chance to prove themselves
- Knows his power and protects it at all costs—even at the expense of your child's welfare
- Withholds praise and gives players the cold shoulder so as to control them (as one coach described his methods, "The more I'm a jerk to this kid, the more he'll try. And if he quits, he's dead to me.")
- Values winning more than good sportsmanship
- Demeans players with cruel nicknames and punishes underperformance or disloyalty to him with verbal or physical abuse

There do seem to be two schools of coaches. New-school coaches have been educated more progressively and are more knowledgeable about sports psychology. They treat kids fairly and don't demean them. They've probably had a bullying experience (as a perpetrator, bystander, or target) when they were young athletes themselves and feel passionately that this abuse will not be allowed on their teams.

Old-school coaches seem to fall into two subcategories: the ones who let kids know that they strongly value both good sportsmanship and good citizenship and those who believe that athletic ability and achievement justify unethical behavior.

The biggest challenges parents have discussed with me have to do with old-school coaches who bully. Let's take a closer look.

COACHES WHO BULLY

A coach is an ambassador for the school. Schools typically seek out coaches who reflect their culture. If a school's culture is entrenched in Boy World and Girl World, it will attract and support the kind of coaches who don't feel respected unless they're super-winners. The principal might talk a good game about the importance of fostering good values, but in the end, he or she will likely condone a bullying coach's behavior so long as the coach is leading the team to victory. Many parents ask, "Why is the principal doing nothing?" Sometimes it's because the principal agrees with the coach's tactics, but in my experience it's more often because he feels intimidated. He might fear that if he takes a stand, parents who agree with him won't back him up, and parents on the coach's side will attack him. As I said in Chapter 1, he becomes the cultural rule breaker—that's why Entitled parents can attack him so viciously.

This same school pride and drive toward success are what allow athletes to get into trouble and get away with it; the coaches will look the other way or even condone it when the kids get caught drinking, hazing, or engaging in other unacceptable behavior. The principal, parents, and larger community will do nothing. (To turn the African proverb sideways, it takes a village to raise an Entitled athlete.) So coaches who bully and degrade kids in the belief that this will get the best out of them tend to survive. Under these coaches, kids learn that they're worthless if they don't win, regardless of effort. When kids' sense of self is tied so closely to their performance, they become willing to do whatever it takes to win, which might include taking illegal drugs to enhance performance, sloughing off their academic work, or cheating, whether on the field or in the classroom. This kind of cheating is driven by their desire to feel worthy. After all, most kids aren't raised to be cheaters—what does it take for them to override their ethics? Only the belief that they are worthless in the eyes of their community if they don't win.

I don't think most bullying coaches set out to belittle and dominate; I believe they really think that their approach, which they might even describe as "tough love," is the best way to motivate players. I'm all in favor of waking kids up and pulling the best out of them. However, there's a difference between strongly communicating to your players what they're doing that hurts the team and degrading them. I'm not advocating that coaches be warm and fuzzy to get their point across. But there's a middle ground between being warm and fuzzy and making players feel like dirt.

> *One of my best friends on the team was constantly being made fun of by the coach. On the bus ride home, my friend just started bawling. I told him, "The coach is an idiot, that's just the coach," but my friend couldn't stop. Then he tells me that his dad just moved out, his parents were getting divorced. That coach could have been a role model when my friend was losing his role model. I hated that guy.*
>
> Nick, high school athlete

Although both male and female coaches can be bullies, it's particularly appalling when coaches belittle male players by comparing them to girls and/or gay men or by insulting their girlfriends. Here are some coaches' comments that athletes have reported to me:

- "You throw like a woman."
- "You're all acting like a bunch of fags out there."
- "What are you, a pussy?"
- "You're going to wear skirts to school next week."
- "Imagine the other guy having sex with your girlfriend—take him down."

I know many men may see the first quote and say, "But the fact is that most men throw better than most women. There's nothing wrong with saying that." Whether it's said innocently or not, here's the problem: When you tell boys that they aren't good enough by comparing them to girls, that starts them down the slippery slope of disrespecting women in general and becoming ashamed of anything they do that allows them to be compared to women. Those comments are some of the first "Act Like a Man" messages toddler boys receive.

Fast-forward a few years and boys don't need violent video games to grasp that society defines masculinity in a violent or degrading way when they get these messages from coaches or see it with professional and collegiate athletics. This kind of talk perpetuates the worst aspects of Boy World (where you demonstrate your masculinity by emasculating another guy or dominating a woman), and if we're serious about raising boys with good character, then we need to speak out about it.

TALKING BACK TO TALKING DOWN

If you learn that the coach is disrespecting your kid, you've got to get involved. There are four ways you can find out about it: you overhear it, someone else tells you, your kid tells you, or you see it yourself. How do you handle it in each situation?

Let's suppose you overhear the kids talking about an incident as you're driving everyone home from practice. If you know the kids well, the least you should say is, "Coach Clark was wrong to do that," and explain very specifically why whatever the coach did was demeaning. Then encourage the kids to talk to their parents about it: "I'm not going to force you to do this, but I expect you to do it, because you have the right to be on a team where no player is treated disrespectfully." Afterward, when you and your child are alone, say, "Let's talk about this; what are we going to do about it?" If your kid begs, "Don't say anything! It's not a big deal!" stand firm. Say, "You and I can talk to the coach, or I'll talk to the coach by myself. What do you want me to say?" Bring your kid in on strategy: "When's the best time to call? When would he be most receptive?" If your child continues to protest—"Promise me you won't do anything! The coach'll get back at me!"—say, "I'll make no such promises, but I'll work with you on it."

Suppose another parent calls you and says, "Did you hear about what happened to Casey?" Don't assume Casey's parents know; it's very common for kids not to tell their parents if coaches have been abusive to them. I'd call the parent of that kid: "Someone just told me that this happened to Casey. I'm so sorry; how can I support you? Your kid deserves to be on a team where he's treated well. I'd like to help make that possible. Just know that I'm here."

If the other parent is calling you about your child, your first reaction will be to get really angry at the coach. Your second reaction will be to question yourself: Why didn't your kid tell you himself? Doesn't your child trust you? You'll take it personally that you had to hear it from some-one else. It's a natural feeling, but understand how hard it is for a kid to tell you, especially if you have a son, because boys are supposed to "take it." Yes, it's true that your child doesn't want you to freak out, but he or she also doesn't want to see you upset. Your kid is probably telling himself or herself, "It's okay, I'm still standing. I can deal with this." Stop yourself from calling the coach right away. I mean it: *Put the phone down.*

When you're calm, sit down with your kid and go through the whole thing as I've described in Chapter 7. Just as I advocated that you take the lead when a teacher disrespects your child, this is another situation where it's appropriate for you to initiate the conversation with the coach. Again, your child may well beg you "not to make a big deal of it." Tough. You have a re-sponsibility to take a stand. Prepare for your conversation using the SEAL (stop, explain, affirm, lock in/lock out) approach I described in Chapter 6.

If you see the coach verbally abusing your kid, you have two choices: speak to him right away or talk to him later. Again, you don't have the right to remain silent. If you speak to him in public directly after the game, you may embarrass him into changing his behavior—or he may become so angry and defensive that he'll take it out on your kid later. It might be better to collect yourself and call at another time, when you'll have the coach's undivided attention. Then proceed using SEAL. (If you're making the call because you've heard the coach said or did something offensive, remember that your first task is to be sure you've gotten an accurate report.)

YOU: *Hi, this is Gavin's dad. Is this a good time to talk? Good. I'm calling because my son reported that* _____. (Give a detailed description.) *Is this true?*

COACH: *Yeah, I said those things. I get a little hotheaded during the games. The kids know me, and they know I don't mean anything by it.*

YOU: *Listen, my kid loves playing on your team, and I really respect how much you've taught him about the game. But name-calling crosses the line, and I don't think disrespect has any place on your team. May I have your word that this won't happen again?*

COACH: *Look, I think you're making too much of this and if you or your son can't handle it, maybe this isn't the team for you.*

YOU: *Coach, I respect your leadership on this team and it was really hard to make this phone call. Gavin didn't want me to because he was worried that it would hurt his chances on the team if I said anything. But I know you're not that kind of coach, so I was willing to take that chance. I'm asking you to assure me that it won't happen again.*

If the coach won't listen to you, or if it happens again, you're within your rights to go to his superior.

> *If you do go to the coach's superior, you can always approach this person as a consultant: "I need advice working with this coach." That way the superior is informed but also knows that you're going to try and deal with it.* Raul, high school principal

If you can't make any headway with the coach, talk about the situation with your child. Make sure he or she understands what you find wrong and offensive about the coach's approach. If your child wants to stay on the team, remember that he or she can learn a lot about how to work with someone who's flawed or difficult. However, it's worth employing a variation of the Friendship Bill of Rights: "What are the top three things I need in order to do my best on the team? What are my experiences?" Then compare and contrast.

Depending on your position in Perfect Parent World, you'll have certain challenges when it comes to confronting the coach. Entitled parents are more likely to excuse bad coaching: "Oh, Coach is hard-core, but anything that makes my kid tougher is better, and that's how we win." These kids don't learn good sportsmanship unless they come to regard the coach as an anti-mentor ("I'll be a good sport because I hate how my coach is a jerk about winning no matter what").

Wannabe parents will be tempted to kiss up to the coach because he or she is in a position of power. The coach will know that he or she can manipulate them. Wannabes are also more likely to kiss up to the parents of the best players, and those parents might try to manipulate the Wannabes later, pressuring them for support if their kid misbehaves and they want to lobby the coach for a lighter sentence.

As for the Invisibles, bullying coaches will dismiss them because they look weak—if they notice them at all. Invisibles will have that sinking feeling that they're back in high school confronting the bully, and the temptation to remain silent will be tremendous. But good coaches love Invisibles because they're usually such great people to work with.

When your kid has a great coach, I hope you'll make the effort to tell that person what a fantastic job he or she is doing. I've given a lot of attention in these pages to bullying coaches. Let's make sure we praise the coaches who do it right—and give a special vote of thanks to the ones who do it as volunteers. Keep that in mind when a parent comes around collecting for the coach's present. And if you're a dad, I challenge you to start the collection process yourself.

COMMON PROBLEMS WITH KIDS' SPORTS TEAMS

Problem: Your Kid Is Getting Lots of Pine Time. Do You Say Anything?

When kids are younger, most coaches try to give every teammate equal playing time. Starting in seventh grade or so, the coaches often decide to give more playing time to the team members with more ability; this is especially likely if your child is on a "select" team as opposed to a come-one, come-all recreation league team. Good coaches should spell out their playing philosophies and expectations of players and parents at the beginning of the season; some even ask parents to sign pledges to signify they understand the ground rules.

It might well be that your child knows exactly how her abilities compare to those of the rest of the team, and while she's probably not thrilled with being benched, she might at least appreciate the reasons why. However, if your child feels she's being unfairly penalized with less playing time, it's your job to encourage her to speak with the coach. Just as you'd prepare her to meet with a teacher, sit down with her and ask her what she wants to do. What outcome does she want? She has two goals here: first, to communicate effectively, clearly, and respectfully, and second, to see if she can change the situation.

In order to have this conversation with your child, you first have to have it with yourself. Maybe your kid is okay with not starting but you're not. Are you convinced that the coach has overlooked her talent? Do you feel embarrassed if you go to a game only to see your child standing on the sidelines? Are you less likely to attend if she isn't playing? What do you say to her immediately after the game? One coach complained, "The players get home and their parents are in the kids' face about it [the game] or in their ear, and it's almost like they get brainwashed to go, 'Hey, the coach doesn't know what he's talking about.'"

Please understand that your natural desire to see your child get the most playing time makes you a biased observer of the game. As another coach told me, "After the game, I'll get one phone call from a parent who's complaining that all we want to do is win, so only the best kids are getting the playing time. Then I'll get a phone call about the same game with the parents complaining that we played all the bad kids, so we didn't play well."

If you're satisfied that the driving force behind the conversation with the coach comes from your child, not yourself, rehearse the kinds of questions she might raise:

- "I'd like more playing time; what do I need to work on most?"
- "Could I please try another position?"
- "Are there any outside programs or exercises that could make me a better player? What other recommendations do you have?"

Help your child decide the best time and place for this conversation. Should it be face-to-face or on the phone? Of course, your child needs to check in with the coach to be sure the time is convenient and ensure she'll have the privacy she needs if she wants to speak with the coach before or after practice.

> ## LANDMINE!
>
> **Only if you have no other option should you or your child run up to the coach right before, during, or after the game. And never blindside him or her in the parking lot!**

What if your child has had this conversation and nothing changes? Should you step in? In general, I'm in favor of letting coaches be coaches; most have good intentions and are doing everything in their power to be fair. The most common refrain I hear from them is, "There's no way to satisfy parents." One father described how a group of coaches even got their sweet revenge:

> *Our dads thought that they could coach better than our coaches. Finally one of our coaches said, "Any father who wants to coach, come down to a scrimmage and we'll let you coach." First they put their kids in, but when they started losing, they pulled them out because ultimately they wanted to win. Afterward they told the coaches, "Don't ever do that to us again."*

Problem: Your Child Gets Cut from the Team

Is it ever appropriate to speak to the coach? Again, I think your child, not you, should have this conversation.

I've interviewed a dozen coaches on this subject. They tell me that when the parents make the call, the conversation typically begins innocently: "I know my kid got cut; can you tell me why?" But that question is quickly followed by another: "How come this other kid got on the team?" Inevitably, the parents compare their child to another child whom they see as a worse player; the implication is that the coach is favoring the other kid. Coaches naturally hear this as a challenge to their ethics or competency.

Just as you don't see the same child her teachers do, you don't know your child as a player the way the coach does. You also have less appreciation of the slots the coach needs to fill, the difficult choices he or she needs to make, and how your child performed during tryouts. It's painful to be cut, but I think you have to respect the coach's decision. Again, I'd rehearse with your child how she can ask the coach what she needs to do to make the team next time.

Problem: You're Not Happy with How the Coach Disciplines Your Kid and/or the Team

Inevitably there will come a time when your child or members of his or her team do something wrong—either they won't live up to their commitments to the team or their conduct off the field will violate the team's standards—and ideally the coach will hold them accountable. How the coach handles this is crucial to what your child learns about values in action. A good coach will hold the guilty players responsible in a fair manner that might embarrass but not humiliate them. There's a very important difference. As one coach put it: "When your kid does something wrong, is held accountable, and consequently feels embarrassed, that's okay. Embarrassment shows remorse—a very good thing. But punishment and/or discipline whose sole purpose is to humiliate isn't something anyone should ever do to anyone else."

I love the following story, because it describes a coach who really got it right:

> *A few years ago, a coach was getting ready to coach his first state championship. His son [who was one of the players] had his eighteenth birthday and the players threw him a big party. There were alcohol and strippers at the party. The cops came and broke it up and because it was a small town, they called the coach: "Your starting team is here partying. Do you want to come get them?" He told them no, [they should] do what they usually do. Then the coach suspended every person who was at that party for the whole game. His starting lineup, his best team, was suspended. They all had to be at the game in a tie, serving water and cheering on the guys who were gonna end up playing. He played a championship game with a third-string team and lost, but it was a huge deal because people were calling in everywhere going, "That is what it's about."*   Angelo, high school dad

When I was just starting out as an assistant coach, one of our boys skipped class. The head coach suspended him from playing in the most important game of the season. He was one of best players on the team. The team lost the game. That really made an impression on me.

Marcus, high school coach

Recently there was a coach in the Northeast who disciplined the kids on the football team when they were caught drinking in the off season. The coach suspended the players because he believed they had committed themselves to a code of conduct, period—not just when they were on the field, not just during the season, but as athletes who were part of the school and the community at large. He ended up going toe to toe with the principal and parents, who at first didn't back him. "This is out of your jurisdiction," they told him, reasoning that if the infractions didn't occur during football season, they shouldn't affect the team. The coach stuck to his position, almost at the expense of his job.

If you think the coach has overstepped his or her boundaries in disciplining the team or some of its players, including your child, take a hard look and decide whether you truly believe the coach acted unfairly, or whether you're just upset because it's your own kid. If you genuinely feel the punishment doesn't fit the crime, by all means speak to the coach respectfully about it. Coaches tell me that they often hear from parents when they've decided to suspend the whole team because a few players have violated the code of conduct—or from parents who feel the punishment is too severe relative to the infraction. In these cases, the coaches are taking principled stances because they want to achieve the long-term goal of student athletes respecting the code of conduct and living up to the coaches' high expectations of them. I could ask for no better coach for my sons.

One head of a school described to me how he'd attempted to discipline a lacrosse player who'd trashed the other team's locker room during an away game. The player's parents insisted that the coach didn't appreciate that it was "just a joke." The head of the school reluctantly let it go. Then two weeks later, this same girl played a particularly cruel trick involving a laxative on another student—also presumably "just a joke."

At that point, I decided to expel her from school. Her parents were total jerks about it. The locker room incident had led me to believe she hadn't accepted responsibility for her action and that they hadn't helped her accept responsibility with their attitude about it. They just kept saying to me, "Don't you get it? It was a joke. What's wrong with you?"

I felt I had to tell them that she could not come back on campus for the rest of the school year, and the parents could not come back on campus unless I specifically gave them permission. They would still come to the rest of the lacrosse games. They pulled their car up onto the field itself on the property of an adjoining church, right up to our property line, and then climbed out of their Suburban, honking their horn when we would score a goal. [The mother] would try to get girls to come over and talk to her daughter until I put an end to it.

Charlie, head of private school

So the question to ask yourself right now is: "If that woman was my friend, would I say something to her? How could Perfect Parent World stop me from saying anything to her?"

PUTTING THE STARTING GUN TO YOUR OWN TEMPLE: PARENTS AS COACHES

The head of our league convened an emergency meeting of all parents. The old coach had just quit, and they told us if we didn't pick a new coach in the next half-hour, we'd miss the registration [deadline] and our team would dissolve. Did any parent want to volunteer? My daughter kept trying to yank my arm up, but I kept it frozen at my side. You would not believe the crap these coaches take from all the parents; no way would I do it. So one mom volunteered and I was so impressed with how she took command of the girls. And then the next month I was asking myself, "How come she doesn't play my daughter more? My daughter's just as good as her daughter."

April, parent of a middle-school athlete

Coaches and parents are often the same people—and this is one of the main reasons why youth athletics is so fraught with conflict. Some parents are drafted because of their expertise, while others are pressed into service simply because the team is desperate for help. Some parents have even ended up coaching teams in sports they've never played. More commonly, parents take up coaching because their kid is on the team. No matter what the circumstance, if you decide to hang the whistle around your neck, you'll realize four things:

1. Even if it were a paid job, there's not enough money in the world to compensate you for the nonsense you're putting up with.

2. Your job is much, much harder if your child is on the team.

3. The kids are watching you very closely and learning more from your actions than from your instructions.

4. Parents are watching to see if you favor your kid.

Before you volunteer, sit down with your child and ask, "What could be the negatives and positives if I coach your team?" But then say, "I know you know this, but just so I'm clear, I'm going to treat you fairly, just like everybody else. You won't get any special privileges." Coaching a team when your child is on that team is exceptionally hard because you'll be more emotionally invested and that will challenge your ability to coach effectively. You might not always be aware when you're favoring your child—but rest assured that the other kids on the team will be watching you like hawks for signs of favoritism, as will their parents, who won't be able to keep from talking behind your back about it. One parent coach recommended benching one's own child for a while at the start of the season: "Especially in those beginning games, make a visible statement that your kid isn't going to be favored. It might not be fair to your kid, but it's more important for the team that everyone sees he isn't going to be favored."

> *[When I was a kid] my baseball coach got into an accident, so my dad came in and coached my team for six weeks. First thing he did was bench me. I was a freshman and he replaced me with a senior. I was so mad. But he told me, "If we want to have a baseball team, you need to do your job and that means you sit." After a few games he would put me in at the end of the game when we were winning.*

Then people started bothering him for not playing me, so then he put
me in.   Hank, elementary school principal and volunteer coach

Fielding parents' complaints about inequitable playing time is inevitable. One coach's recommendation: "Coaches must keep a scorecard so that when parents say, 'My kid only played a quarter of the game,' they can have empirical evidence that he played half the game. There has to be a basis in fact, not 'I don't like your kid.'" This can be a real burden when you're making up the lineup and trying to help the kids in the middle of the game; you may want to enlist an assistant coach or other neutral party to do this recordkeeping. You can minimize trouble by having a preseason meeting with just the parents and provide printed handouts to explain your expectations, how they can speak up if they're unhappy, etc. One coach told me, "It's appropriate for coaches to give out cell numbers to parents to use in an absolute emergency. An emergency does *not* include questions about playing time, strategy, or position."

Be clear about what you most want the kids to learn and remember about being on the team. Ten years from now, the kids you coach won't remember the scores, but if parents' recollections are any indication, they'll never forget the life lessons—positive and negative—they get from the playing field. As one coach put it, "Some coaches will say, 'I'm not paid to lose games or make kids be friends with one another,' but in a sense, you *are* there to teach kids how to be friends and work together." If you're aware of these pitfalls and work hard to be sure every player has a chance to show his or her potential, you'll be one of those coaches kids look back on years later with respect and admiration.

SCREAMING ON THE SIDELINES

Most of us are spectators, not coaches. While we don't have the pressure of creating the starting lineup for the game and fending off unhappy players and parents, we're not out of the hot seat—it's just become the fold-up canvas kind with the cup holder set back from the sideline. Sometimes the action on the sidelines trumps anything on the field. Let's discuss some of the more common issues parents watching games confront.

Problem: Another Parent Loses It on the Sidelines

You're standing on the field watching the boys play soccer when a parent behind you screams, "What the hell are you *doing* out there, ladies? Get it together!" If you're a mother, you're probably thinking, "He did *not* just say that." If your husband is there, you'll glare at him, signaling your complete disgust with the cretin behind you. If you're a father and your wife gives you that look, you'll probably find yourself praying, "Please let this ass behind me go away because if he does it again, my wife will get into it with him and then I'm going to have to get involved." So you'll ignore your wife's look, train your eyes on the field, and shout encouragement to the kids. Which won't fool your wife for a moment. Then the other team makes a goal, so the cretin screams again, this time at your team's goalie: "Are you blind? A five-year-old girl could have saved that shot!" Now your wife has had it and looks at you with laser death eyes, which can mean only one thing: "You'd better go back there and take care of this or I will—and you don't want it to get *that* ugly."

> *Guys who are perfect gentlemen in every other aspect of their lives get to their kids' games and think nothing of humiliating their kids in every way.*   Gabe, middle school dad

> *As a coach, you get approached by parents who challenge you to a fight because they disagree with what you're doing. I've coached for two years now and each year I've had the opportunity to be in a physical altercation.*   Ralph, middle school dad

Or maybe it's even worse: That parent is in the face of the ref, the coach, or another parent, possibly even his own kid. The threat of physical violence looms, or maybe actual punches are thrown. When a fight breaks out, your immediate reaction might be denial: "This cannot be happening." You can find yourself being a silent bystander when you don't mean to be because you're in such a state of shock. The whole thing could be over in thirty seconds—but it might take that long to get over your shock. Don't blame yourself; I've spoken to plenty of mothers and fathers who have experienced this involuntary paralysis.

Whether you've reached a slow simmer because of another parent's obnoxious behavior or been confronted with a sudden explosion, I hope you'll find the courage to confront the offender or at least talk to the kids once you've regained your equilibrium. Floater and Reformed Dads are usually pretty comfortable intervening because they've been calming other people down since they were teens, but even they can be reluctant to take action. Proud-to-be-a-Pain Moms are also pretty fearless about stepping in; their moral outrage will propel them right into the offending parent's face. Many of us, however, are too shocked or fearful to say or do anything. We're tempted to brush it off as a momentary loss of control; we desperately want to assume that it won't happen again. The truth is that it's much more likely to happen again if we don't say anything about it.

Entitled parents are the most likely to mock and insult the referee personally. Some of us make ready excuses for this bad behavior: "Oh, don't mind Oscar, that's just the way he is; he's a teddy bear off the field." One father echoed the experiences of many when he told me, "I have a friend I have to babysit." Dads, hear me loud and clear: Babysitting your out-of-control friend is a good first step, but it's not enough. You have to stop him. It's no excuse if he says, "I just got out of control." We're not allowed to "just lose it" at work or in church, and it's not okay to do it on the field, either. Our boys especially are depending on dads and coaches to show them what courage and dignity look like. While both boys and girls need these lessons, boys may have a harder time absorbing them because Boy World culture says that it's a demonstration of masculinity to get in someone else's face, especially when it comes to sports.

I've asked many parents why they don't intervene when they see other adults publicly humiliating kids. Just as women can recall with pinpoint precision who teased or excluded them in middle school, I've found that men remember with great intensity those moments on the athletic field when they were humiliated—or when people stood up for them. When I asked them why, with these burning memories, they didn't try to stop similar behavior as adults, I often heard these kinds of excuses: "Because someone is going to sue me" or "You never know what's going to happen these days; the guy could kill you."

I think these are all lame reasons not to intervene. People who say things like that are buying in to the belief that since they can't control the situation, they shouldn't do anything about it. They assume that they'll just make a bad situation worse, and they think their fathers and grandfathers didn't have to deal with stuff like this. Frankly, I've talked to men from many generations, and their memories of these conflicts are remarkably similar to what fathers report today. For the most part, when someone acted out, no one did anything then, either. Many of us have been so conditioned to be bystanders that we justify it. And are we seriously going to live our lives doing not what's right but what's least likely to bring a lawsuit?

I also reject the excuse that "I can't change this guy, so why do anything?" The primary reason to do something is that our sons and daughters are looking at us to see what kind of men and women we are, who has the power, who's going to stand up. If we say nothing, we raise children who grow up to say nothing—it's a self-perpetuating cycle.

There is one explanation for not wanting to intervene that I can understand, however. It was said eloquently by a friend: "The most humiliating thing I could think of is a parent making me look bad in front of my kid. So how could I do that to another parent?" But again, this understandable feeling shouldn't convince us to do nothing. Here's a couple of strategies parents have used:

> *I was at my daughter's game when a group of parents were booing the other kids and I just turned around and stared at them with my jaw dropped open, and after that there was no more booing.*
> Malcolm, high school principal and middle school dad

> *You don't need to say much. Since guys are so reluctant to say anything, a few words go a long way. "Let's cool it a little bit." "That's a little harsh." A little goes a long way with dads.*
> Walter, high school dad and coach

> *When a parent is humiliating their child on the athletic field, I often see another dad come up to that kid and tell them something they did that was really good. Or they put their arm around the kid and support them. I think they're role-modeling for the other dad and also telling the other dad to stop without saying it in words.*
> Karl, high school dad

So please review your SEAL skills and say something to parents who go overboard. If you can't bring yourself to do that, say something afterward to the coach. Some coaches tell the referees in advance that certain parents are likely to lose it, and the referees can warn or eject the unruly parents if need be. Other coaches unobtrusively pass out "Your conduct is disrupting the game and disrespectful to the players" cards to out-of-control parents so they can rein in their actions without public embarrassment.

Problem: You're a Little Overenthusiastic Yourself

My mother is a lovely, lovely woman, but watching my brother play soccer she was horrible. She wasn't my mother. So my dad and I refused to stand next to her. We would stand at the end of the field far away from her.　　　　　　　　　　　　Clara, high school student

I think most coaches would say that they're fine with parents cheerleading—except that what they hear from the sidelines is decidedly light on "cheer," and the "leading" also leaves a lot to be desired. Some clever coaches have banished overenthusiastic parents to the opposite side of the field, away from coaches and players. One soccer referee revealed that he didn't have to worry about loud parents anymore; he simply strictly enforced the rule that everyone must stand at least nine feet back from the field boundaries. The parents discovered that it was too hard to shout from that distance. Teams around the country have instituted Silent Sundays, where the rule is that parents may say nothing at all, or at most shout only encouraging things and clap briefly and politely if a goal is scored. Most parents say that Silent Sundays help them realize how often they "helpfully" shout out instructions to their kids, "correct" them if they make a bad play, or otherwise drive the kids nuts. One mother whose enthusiastic exhortations apparently went unappreciated said, "My son ordered me, 'Mom, every day is Silent Sunday for you!'"

If you know you're likely to get carried away, make every game a private Silent Sunday. If you're not certain whether you've been overdoing it, why not ask your child how much he or she appreciates your helpful running commentary in the middle of the game? "My dad was terrible," one teen told me, "and my mom finally banned him from coming to basketball games. He was a federal judge, so I guess he thought he had the right to judge everything." If you simply can't suppress your desire to spread sunshine, you might want to take a page from one mother's playbook: "We worked it out to cheer for each other's kids because our own kids felt mortified if we cheered for them."

Problem: Your Kid Mistreats Another Kid on the Field

As a parent, you should keep your eyes peeled for misbehavior on the field. Don't assume the coach sees everything. If you think you see your kid acting up on the field but the coach doesn't seem to have noticed, don't call a sideline conference on the spot. After the game, in private, talk with your child about what you saw. Call the coach that evening: "Hi, Coach. I'm not sure if you're aware of what happened today, but my kid deliberately tripped another kid. I want to let you know how we're disciplining him, and we completely support you if you decide to bench him. We really want to get your take on it so he learns good sportsmanship."

Let's suppose your child does something more flagrant. I'm not talking about the kind of scuffles that naturally occur when kids play hard. I'm talking about when your child deliberately crosses the line, either cursing the other kid out or getting physical. To make matters worse, the other parent is watching. What do you do? If you say nothing, that parent is going to hate you. Walk over to the other parent immediately and say:

YOU: *On behalf of my child, I'm sorry he pushed your kid.*
OTHER PARENT: *Don't worry about it. It's no big deal.*
YOU: *Well, if you're comfortable with it, I'd like John to apologize to your kid after the game.*

Whether your kid is ten and you can still sling him over your shoulder or sixteen and a hundred pounds heavier than you, you still have to walk him over to the other kid and make sure he apologizes. (Remember what I said about wanting your children to fear you? Imagine a 6'4", 200-pound junior apologizing under the watchful eye of his mother.) Regardless of what the coaches or referees do, you're the ultimate arbiter of your child's participation. Even if your child has already been disciplined with a benching or a red card, he still must apologize. It can be as simple as him walking up to the other kid while the crowd's dissipating and saying, "Hey, dude, sorry about that."

If the coach hasn't taken any disciplinary action against your child following a flagrant display of poor sportsmanship, this is one of the few times when I think it's appropriate to go up to him or her immediately after the game and ask, "Coach, did you see what Johnny did? Do you have a problem with it?" If the coach saw it and did nothing, make it clear that you'll back him or her up in imposing any disciplinary measures, including benching.

Let's suppose the cleat is on the other foot. A kid has roughed up your kid. Assume the coach will hold the other kid accountable until you're proven wrong. If you believe that the coach isn't taking action, find his contact information and call, following all the rules of engagement we've talked about in the earlier chapters—that is, no calling this coach during dinner and accusing him of being a bad coach as soon as he picks up the phone.

WHAT DO COACHES WANT PARENTS TO KNOW?

I'm keenly aware that you are there to watch your child play, but it's most important that kids look forward to coming out and playing. Everyone gets that opportunity, even at the expense of losing the game.

Kids on the bench want more desperately to play than the kids who are playing. A good coach has sensitivity to that difference and will give every kid a chance to play.

I know when parents are sucking up to me. Most parents pick up their kids and go. The suck-ups begin with a smile on their face and chitchat for five minutes, then they try to suck you into their social circle—"Come over to my house for a barbecue." Everything should be on a "Mr.-and-Mrs." basis.

Just remember that you're not entitled to get your kid more playing time if you're sitting in the booster club.

What's helpful is giving out directions to away games, manning the phone tree, and bringing refreshments—not assistant coaching.

WHAT DO PARENTS WANT COACHES TO KNOW?

I know my kid isn't going to be the star of the team; just let him feel that he's part of the team.

I can disagree with some of your coaching techniques but still think you're a great person and be grateful you're my kid's coach.

Parental competition in athletics was probably obvious to you before you read this book. I hope now you have some specific strategies to understand your own behavior and how to respond to other parents and coaches. So the next time you're on the sidelines and you see something you don't like, you can step up to the plate.

"If She's on My Committee, I Quit"

Parent Volunteering

Executive Committee • Grandparents and Special Friends Day • Halloween Carnival Committee • Cultural Arts Committee • Harvest Festival Committee • Booster Club • Global Awareness Dinner Committee • Winter Concert Committee • Holiday Gift Sale Committee • School Play Committee • Gift Wrap Fund-Raiser Committee • Parent Curriculum Review Committee • Student Newspaper Committee • Authors and Artists Day Committee • Spring Fling Committee • Mother's Day Boutique Committee • Father's Day Plant Sale Committee • Teacher Appreciation Day Committee • Moving-Up Day Committee • Yearbook Committee • Book Fair Committee

Your pen is poised over the sign-up sheet the mother on your left just passed you. Yearbook Committee? Does a ten-year-old really *need* a yearbook? Who knew the school had so many committees? Well, you *should* have known. For the last three years, you've made a New Year's resolution that you'd get more involved in your child's school, but it just didn't happen. This year will be different, though. You paid attention to when the next PTA meeting was scheduled, and you dutifully arrived fifteen minutes early. You walked in, got your Styrofoam cup of coffee, smiled at some people you vaguely recognized, and sat down in the back of the auditorium, wondering why you didn't drag a friend along so you wouldn't feel like such a loser sitting by yourself.

The president called the meeting to order only ten minutes ago, but you're already drumming your fingertips on the armrest. Can't these people just move it along? You could have made fifteen thousand decisions by now at the office. You look back down at the sign-up sheet. Why do so many of the same names appear over and over? Who are these women with so much time on their hands? You're lucky if you can even dig the flyer for one of these events out of the bottom of Carly's backpack, let alone serve on the committee. (Come to think of it, there's probably even a Flyer Committee they forgot to mention.) Wait . . . Book Fair Committee. Now *that's* something you can help with. You love to read, you've been in two different book clubs for years, you know the local bookstores well, and you're really organized. You write your name down and pass the sign-up sheet to your right.

Forty-five minutes later, the president breaks everyone into their committees, so you eagerly walk over to the Book Fair group: five women chatting, heads tilted forward. Although everyone greets you warmly, you feel like the new kid at school trying to eat lunch at the cool kids' table. You introduce yourself and say, "I could call some authors—I really don't mind getting on the phone with people." Five beaming smiles shoot back at you and one of the mothers says, "Thanks! That's so nice of you! We have it all taken care of. But we always need someone to rip tickets at the door." And then they go back to talking, completely shutting you out.

We all know that most school functions and community organizations such as religious youth groups and Scouts wouldn't exist without parent volunteers. These are the people who get things done, who serve as important conduits of information between the school and parents. I've worked with a lot of great people on these committees. However, I've also spoken to a lot of parents who had terrible experiences in these groups— experiences so bruising that if they ran into their archnemesis fifty years later at the grocery store, they'd still be so angry they'd burst a blood vessel.

Perhaps you never planned to become involved with any parent association, Scout troop, or other communal effort. Or perhaps you've been looking forward to donning your booster club barbecue apron or den mother uniform since your child was born. But if you get involved in these organizations, your ability to enjoy the experience and do good work will depend completely on how you handle the inevitable conflicts with the other parents. It's worth the effort. Take another look at the list of committees that opened this chapter; they're all drawn from events at real schools. Did you know that parents at many schools organize a mass casserole-in to show the teachers their appreciation? You might balk at the expensive, often ugly gift wrap you're forced to buy every year, but did you realize how many thousands of dollars that single fund-raiser can bring in so that the school can buy books or computers?

Yet it's hard to work together in groups. We volunteer because we want our schools to be better and our kids to get the best. Given our good intentions, we feel especially irritated or hurt when our group turns into a model of confused inefficiency or a hotbed of gossip. We promise ourselves we'll never sign up for anything again. At other times, we may have overinvested ourselves in such groups. We can behave badly, then be tempted to rationalize the behavior because "we're doing it all for the kids."

In addition, working in these groups can bring us right into the thicket of restrictive rules that govern Perfect Parent World, forcing us to stand up to Queen Bees or hold our own against Desperate Wannabes. It can call up the filters that promote misunderstandings between parents who work and those who stay at home. It can highlight the absence of volunteer fathers, a problem that sends two messages. When dads stay away (or are shooed away), it suggests that the school groups are women's work, so if men participate, they're only doing it because they don't have something more important to do. The lack of dads means that parent volunteer committees lose not just needed labor, but the vitality that comes with men's participation. Worse, when power becomes consolidated among a very few, it's those voices that often set the school or community agenda. Second, it suggests that all mothers, no matter what's going on in their lives, should participate or else they just don't measure up in Perfect Parent World.

How can we make working in these organizations more fulfilling so that more parents get involved? How can we break free of the rules of Perfect Parent World so that our contributions to groups like these make us feel good about our community? And how do we confront parents who abuse power, play favorites, or pressure us to help beyond our means?

This chapter will explore these issues and discuss how to handle problems that commonly arise when we work together.

CHECKING YOUR BAGGAGE

- What are the top three reasons you have for wanting to join the PTA or other parent volunteer group?
- If your friends are members, how has that influenced your decision to be involved? What role do your friends play in Perfect Parent World?

BEING A GOOD LEADER

We had an incredible leader. She made us all stop and remember our work was for all the children, not just for your individual school or child. We all worked together to pass the budget. She had this no-nonsense way that combined with her passion and commitment so that we in turn were more inclusive and cooperative.

Roselle, PTA member

Obviously, if you're going to be an officer or hold a similar position of power in a group, you have a special responsibility to make sure your actions benefit everyone in the community. Here are some guidelines to keep in mind.

Remember That People Are Watching You

Other parents will watch you carefully, especially at the beginning of your tenure. They're looking to see if you favor people you're close to or if you orchestrate events to put your own child in a more advantageous position. But as the two comments below illustrate, we may not always recognize this angling for favoritism as a bad thing because we see it as for our kids' benefit:

As an active member of the school, I'm on the PTA. I don't want to abuse that position, but for all intents and purposes, I do. I spy. I have covert little lunches. I pop in for lunch.

Harriet, PTA board member

I don't want to [use my position on the PTA] but I do because I have a higher calling . . . being an advocate for my child.

Joelle, PTA board member

It is your responsibility as the group leader to recognize moments when you might be taking advantage of your position.

Make concrete gestures that show what kind of leader you are. For example, if there's a parking space in the school designated for the PTA president, score yourself some political points by not parking there or asking that the sign be taken down. You'll park just like everybody else. Rest assured that word of this will spread.

Please be aware that kids are watching you, too. They look at you as an example of how people handle positions of power, for good or bad. You have a tremendous opportunity to be a positive role model for fairness, a good work ethic, grace under pressure, and inclusivity.

Be a Sensitive Fund-raiser

As discussed in Chapter 4, it's all too easy for people of different socioeconomic classes to make assumptions about each other that in turn make it more difficult to work together. Some people think nothing of putting on an event where everyone is expected to give a certain amount of money that is way beyond what most people can afford. Some people with more money are always seen as the go-to people, and when they don't give, people think they're being selfish.

You have to make everything affordable. You don't have to have gala fund-raisers. One of the schools in our area has an art auction where a gallery comes in; I don't think we would ever do that. People would feel imposed upon, it would be beyond them, and then they'd feel excluded. We do an event with our local restaurants. All you can eat and *drink for $20 per person. We get 1,300–1,500 people. A neighboring school has a gala black-tie thing, but only 300 people come. We raise just as much money and it's much more egalitarian.*

Corinne, PTA member

Of course it's important to raise money for your organization's needs, but it's equally important to ensure that as many parents as possible feel like valued members of that organization. If you want to approach parents of greater means for greater contributions, do it privately so that you don't pressure families who aren't in the same privileged position.

Don't Be a Micromanaging Dictator

No one likes to work in a dictatorship. From what I hear in cities and towns across the country, there are many PTA presidents who are particularly challenged in this area. If you're in a leadership position, it's probably because you have strong opinions about how to do things, you can mobilize people easily, and you don't rest until the job is done well (remember I said Queen Bees have a lot of positive characteristics). This can make you a wonderful leader—or the kind of person who insists that everything must be done exactly as you want it or it won't be good enough. The best leaders always surround themselves with competent people to whom they delegate responsibility, trusting that they'll do their tasks well—even if they do them differently than the leader envisioned. Your goal is to be inclusive. Why not let someone new be in charge of the dance decorations, even if they want to use those Mylar streamers you find so hideous?

I joined a committee for a Harvest Brunch—the first parenting group I joined since quitting my job to stay home with my daughter. Three of us moms were new to the committee, and when we walked in, the other ten moms made us feel like nothing we said had any value. The Queen Bee Mom was incredibly micromanaging: "My pet peeve is when parents bring in napkins that don't match." She said there wouldn't be any coffee for the brunch because it was too much trouble to set up. "We have to have coffee," I said. "It's a brunch and people are going to expect it." She told me, "The coffee serving issue is too complicated. You'll see that when you've been around for a few years." I could tell a lot of moms agreed with me, but they were afraid to back me up. I said I'd be happy to pick up some boxes of coffee from Dunkin' Donuts, but the Queen Bee Mom wouldn't pay any attention. I had to step out of the meeting and when I came back, she was on to the next point in her agenda. "What about the coffee?" I asked, and she was furious at me. I used to go to meetings where we'd be deciding to spend hundreds of thousands of dollars on advertising that would affect millions of people, and here we couldn't even discuss whether to serve coffee at a brunch.

Merrilee, elementary school mom

Why do so many leaders in PTA, Girl Scouts, and other youth groups micromanage? Because most of these leaders are women and the rules of Perfect Parent World can operate with extra force when that's the case. Specifically, I see two issues that are particularly challenging to women in these situations. First, Girl World teaches women to communicate ineffectively when they're in conflict with someone, and second, for some women these groups are the one place outside of their home where they feel a sense of authority, accomplishment, and ownership.

For example, suppose you're a married woman who used to work and made the choice to stay at home with your kids. As much as you hate to admit it, you resent that some people think of you as "just a mom." Now that your children are a little older, you have more time on your hands. You choose to get involved in your son's church youth group and find that you enjoy the work and get positive feedback about it from people in your community. You're giving back to the community but you're also getting public recognition as a competent leader—one of the things that has most likely been denied to you as a stay-at-home mom. It's natural to feel good about this. Everyone has the right to want recognition for hard work. The problem is that your emotional investment in this group can become tied to your identity to the point where it can become difficult for you to share power and listen to constructive criticism.

If, on the other hand, you're an Invisible, you might find yourself suffering in silence when you work with a leader who doesn't appreciate you, takes credit for your work, or talks behind your back.

I think the reality is that stay-at-home moms can be particularly vulnerable to these problems. Women who work are less likely to see their participation in these groups as a vital part of their identity. I'm not saying this to disparage women who stay at home or choose to focus their energy on one community project. What I'm saying is that the more you invest your energy in one group, the more power it has over you. And if you're a stay-at-home mom reading this and thinking, "Wait a minute, what about the working moms?" don't worry—I'll get to them later in the chapter.

Put Effort and Thought into Your Recruitment Drive

Our school has a lot of migrant workers and they won't come to the PTA. They move around and they never had a voice in school before, so they don't join.   Eleanor, PTA member

Frankly, I saw myself on the fringe. As a single mom, I was trying to make a living and put food on the table. A lot of these women had the time and I'm grateful for it because they got things done and I couldn't help out.   Irene, elementary school mom

If you aren't getting the participation you'd like, have you asked people when they can meet? Every community is different, but one PTA I know got a lot more participation when they changed their meetings from after school to lunchtime. Have you asked as many men as women to be involved? Have you assumed that fathers don't want to be part of the PTA and therefore you have not tailored recruitment strategies specifically for them? Have you asked people why they don't want to join and really listened to their answers? Have you talked to other PTA members about how to make new people more welcome? Have you done special outreach to specific groups within the larger community of your school?

Remember That You're the Head Cheerleader, Not the Enforcer

In the words of a woman who served on the PTA for most of her children's lives: "You're doing a positive thing, but it's not life-and-death. The leader's responsibility is to give some perspective. If something isn't 100 percent perfect, big deal! We got it done."

Do What You Can to Break Down the Divide Between Working Parents and Stay-at-Home Parents

It's only natural that anytime mothers join forces, there will be some who work full time, some who work part time, and some who stay at home. Remember that our filters strongly affect our interactions with people — especially those who have chosen a different path than we have. No matter how broad-minded we are, all of us make such judgments.

You might have read what I wrote about stay-at home moms and thought, "Wait a minute, it's the working moms I have a problem with." I know, and I've heard from a lot of you.

If you're a working mother, ask yourself, "What are the first words that come to mind about the stay-at-home mothers in my community?" If some are negative, do you think your interactions with stay-at-home moms ever betray your negative preconceptions? Have you volunteered with stay-at-home moms? Was it a positive or negative experience? Why?

In my work with PTAs and other groups, I've observed that two different types of working mothers tend to participate. The first type of mother is patronizing; she believes that stay-at-home mothers aren't as interesting, capable, or smart as she is. Not surprisingly, stay-at home mothers aren't the only people she patronizes. She can be bossy and condescending with almost anyone. She assumes people will listen to her, agree with her, and do her bidding. One father reported that a working mom came to a meeting to describe her "incredible idea," which she would have known was something the PTA had been doing for years if she'd bothered to ask first. Then she sat back imperiously, expecting everyone else to scurry into action. This kind of working parent is prone to professional name-dropping ("I've got a breakfast meeting with the president of corporate blah-blah-blah"). It's important to her that everyone else recognizes her standing in the "real world."

The other breed of working mom sees the PTA and other parent organizations as simply another kind of job, part of her responsibility to be involved in her child's life. She's much more of a team player.

As a divorced, working mom of three boys, being on the PTA or a Boy Scouts troop leader was something I had to do. I saw it as part of raising my children. And it was a very positive experience for me. [It was] very supportive and all of us worked together.

Dana, mother of three

Now let's turn to stay-at-home moms. If you're a stay-at-home mom, take a moment and challenge yourself: What's your attitude toward the working mothers who volunteer with you? If you have negative preconceptions about them, do you think the working mothers know? Do you feel that they look down on you? Have you wanted to say something to them about it? If you haven't, what stopped you? If you have, how did it go?

In general, I'm more likely to hear drama from stay-at-home moms. There are more fights over fiefdoms and more tightly held grudges. The stay-at-home moms gossip more, then deny that they gossiped in the first place. Stay-at-home moms who are Queen Bees succeed in dominating anyone in these groups, especially if they have more money than their peers. But the stay-at-home moms who aren't Queen Bees and thus don't have a lot of social power can have a harder time challenging working moms because our culture accords working parents higher status. These stay-at-home moms worry that they won't be taken seriously, and they can come across as intimidated or defensive. And regardless of whether they worked or stayed at home, many of the women told me that the one way they didn't want to come across in their conflicts was as a "hysterical stay-at-home mom who lives her life through her kids." Look back at the "Act Like a Mom" box and you can see why women fear this image—the out-of-control, out-of-the-box mother.

So it makes sense that the best parent group leaders are the ones who actively try to break down the divide between these two groups, assigning mothers from both sides to work on the same committees and making sure that everyone's contribution is valued.

Express Your Appreciation Often

Remember to thank parents for their contributions, no matter how small. Be generous in giving credit and offer your appreciation in public so that as many parents as possible get a moment in the spotlight. You don't need to hand out expensive bouquets to every contributor; a creative note in the PTA newsletter or heartfelt announcement at the meeting will encourage members to stay and bring in new recruits.

How to Be a Good Soldier

If you want to join the PTA or any group like it, here are some guidelines to remember:

You're There to Help, Not Shine

You'll be most helpful if you ask to be put wherever your help is most needed, not where you'll be the most visible, where you can wave to your child, or where the work is the most pleasant. If you're new to the group, offer to help with the dirty work that no one else wants to do. As one PTA volunteer told me, "You're only entitled to do the more fun things after you do the boring, dirty jobs. And even then, you shouldn't take advantage."

Expand Your Efforts Beyond Your Child

Your responsibility as a member of a parents' organization is to the overall welfare of the school community, not to your child. Consider volunteering for a project that has nothing to do with your child.

Don't Abuse Your Hall Pass

When you're at the school doing PTA work, don't attach yourself to your child's class. You're not there to monitor your child, you're there to work. Put yourself on a once-a-semester drop-in diet. If your child is younger, he or she may be thrilled to see you waving frantically through the window, but older kids are more likely to be mortified, and the teachers will think you're either sucking up or checking up on them.

COMMON PROBLEMS PARENTS FACE ON COMMITTEES

Problem: You Can't "Just Say No"

"LeAnn? Hello, this is Jeanine Conrad, PTA president. I'm calling because we're *desperate* for someone to oversee the Bangor Elementary *Bugle*. If I can't find any parent to run the newspaper, we're going to have to close it down—and it's the longest-running elementary school newspaper in the state and the kids will be absolutely crushed. Everyone else has said no. Can I please count on you to save our paper? The kids and all of us on the PTA would be so grateful."

Oh, the guilt. How could you say no to *that*? Sometimes the problem isn't that your contributions to communal efforts aren't valued, it's that you're so good that you get taken advantage of. Committee leaders pounce on the easy marks, the parents they know can be counted on to do even the most annoying work—this is one reason why the same names turn up over and over on committee rosters. You want to give back to your community, but the satisfaction of contributing can easily turn into resentment when others continually cajole or even bully you to participate.

What do you say to draw the line when you're already overcommitted? Easy. Like this: "No." (As the saying goes, " 'No' is a complete sentence.") Okay, I lied. I know it isn't easy to say no when people ask for your help. But please remember that whether or not you're a great parent isn't determined by how many committees you're on. If you volunteer for something just because you think you should, but you really don't want to or have too many other things going on, you'll be more likely to become resentful or frazzled and less able to do a good job.

Also remember that you don't have to become the president of the PTA or dedicate forty hours a week to help your school. If you want to help out but your time is tight, lay out your parameters from the outset: "I'd love to help, but I can only give an hour a week." "If you need someone to design flyers or anything else I can do on my own time from home, please feel free to call." "I can't help out until ___, but after that, my schedule really frees up." If you get persistent calls from the poor soul designated to drum up help, remember that giving her a firm no is better than a wishy-washy "I'm not sure—can I get back to you?" You need offer no explanation. "Sorry, I can't help out, but thanks for asking" is sufficient. And if you find yourself saying yes to something, then having to breathe into a paper bag the second you hang up the phone, you've made a mistake. Take another deep breath, pick up the phone, and dial the person right back: "I know I just said yes when you called. I wasn't really thinking things through. The truth is, I simply can't do this right now. Sorry, but you'll have to find someone else." Then hang up the phone and take a few more breaths into that bag. Remember that the quality of your parenting isn't determined by your ability to say yes to this request.

LANDMINE!

If you don't want to volunteer for something, don't say, "I can't. I work." Every parent on that committee works, whether it's inside or outside the home.

Problem: You're Getting Trashed by Other Members of Your Committee

You can encounter bullying or mean gossip in any group. However, the worst conflicts tend to occur in the very organizations you think should be exempt (church groups, this means you) and they're the hardest to resolve. You'll never see bullying with nicer smiles and sweeter words than you'll see in one of these groups. When it happens, you often won't see it coming; you might not be sure it even happened until you walk away. Here are the most common complaints I hear among mothers on committees:

- "She's trying to use her position to get the best teachers for her kids."
- "She picked her good friend to head up the committee even though there was someone else with more experience."
- "She's spending the funds in an inappropriate way."
- "She was supposed to get approval to spend that much money."
- "She's impossible to work with. It's her way or no way."

When you hear whisperings of gossip about you, you'll be tempted to fall back on Girl World tactics. Queen Bee Moms and Bankers might want to go into full-scale attack mode. They'll strategically consider who their friends and enemies are and develop a reconnaissance plan to uncover who said what. They might even spread gossip about their presumed accusers to make them realize that they miscalculated by going after the top dogs.

A Sidekick Mom might go crying to the Queen Bee Mom to ask for her protection because no one defends her friends better than a Queen Bee.

Wannabes will get incredibly upset but will try to keep doing nice things for the most powerful people in the hope that they can take advantage of the situation. Invisibles don't generally end up in this situation because they'll avoid leadership positions like the plague. But if they do, their strategy will probably be to resign rather than deal with this unholy mess.

None of these strategies is ideal. If you get even a whiff of this kind of gossip swirling around the group, you have to address it directly. First, examine the accusations and see if there's any merit to them. If there is, you need to fix the problem immediately. However, you have the right to make mistakes without being trashed.

Problem: You're Dealing with an Evil Tyrant Masquerading as a Helpful Parent Leader

> *When my kids were in theater, I volunteered to sew costumes. The Queen Bee Mom was very adept at getting people to confide in her. She then used this information to discredit or ridicule you to her small group of friends. I've seen her talk such trash about another woman that had volunteered to do the job and did it in a different way than Mrs. Queen Bee wanted it done. The only reason I was tolerated at all was that she needed the work done and I stupidly came back every day. Initially I went because I felt I should do my part since my kids were involved and then it became more a sense of protection for my kids. When she started in with me about this one woman, I told her, "What does it matter? Just because someone does something differently than you doesn't mean they have to be criticized." That shut her*

up, but when other people came into the room, she started in on it again. I just stood up and said, "I've already told you that there is no need to destroy this woman. She did what you asked her to do. It was one less thing you had to do. Just because someone does it differently than you would does not make her awful." Then I walked out of the room. After a few minutes, I walked back in and all talking ceased, which was pretty uncomfortable. And from then on I was ostracized.

Celeste, middle school mom

You shouldn't have to pay such a high price for getting someone to stop talking trash. But you also need to be smart about how you handle it. Celeste confronted the Queen Bee Mom in front of her court. The Queen Bee Mom felt defensive and reacted like any leader whose authority is challenged, be it a PTA president or sixth-grade Queen Bee: She did what she needed to do to consolidate loyalty and allegiance from everyone else. So if you find yourself in a similar situation, confront the offender one-on-one using SEAL (stop, explain, affirm, lock in/lock out).

YOU: *Angela, can I talk to you for a minute?*

ANGELA: *Of course! What can I do for you? You know, that costume you made for Danny yesterday was so amazing. Where did you get that fabric? Anyway, what did you want to talk about?*

YOU: *Thanks. Look, one of the reasons the play is so great every year is because of you. You always make sure that everything gets done. But yesterday when we were working on the costumes, it really upset me when you were talking about Ana. I know she doesn't do it the way you might want her to, but I think she's doing a good job.*

ANGELA: *Well, I'm sorry you feel that way about it. I didn't mean to sound harsh, but honestly, I'm not very happy with her work. She's not like you. I know I can depend on you to get it done right.*

YOU: *Well, thanks, but still . . .*

ANGELA: *Don't worry about it.*

You think you've had your grievance addressed, but in reality Angela just worked you—and most teen girls could tell you how in a heartbeat. Angela started and finished with a compliment, and in Girl World you aren't allowed to be angry with someone who flatters you. In Perfect Parent World, compliments have the same derailing effect. So you backed off and didn't finish the conversation. Let's finish it now.

YOU: *Well, I am worried about it. I'm thrilled that you like my work, but we're a group here. We need to respect each other's work. If you don't like what Ana's doing, you need to find a way to tell her respectfully, in private, and not talk about her to other people. Please know that I consider this conversation private and hope that it will stay between us. I want to keep working with you.*

ANGELA: *Okay, I see your point, but I still think you're making a little much of this.*

Suppose you walk back into the room where Angela and two other mothers are now working and realize from their fake smiles and the sudden pause in the conversation that Angela has been mocking you. The one-on-one confrontation hasn't been successful; now you need to speak to the group.

YOU: *Look, I'm guessing I just made a lot of people uncomfortable, but when we talk behind each other's backs, I don't want to be here. I like being here, working here with you all. I want to be comfortable here. I don't want to worry about what people will say about me as soon as I walk out the door.*

It's important to establish boundaries with other parents even in situations that don't affect you directly. You've probably gone to a parent meeting where someone hijacked the floor regarding a particular issue, dumping all over people who held a contrary view. You likely decided not to say or do anything; you didn't have strong feelings on that issue, so you said to yourself that you should let the people who care duke it out. Yours was part of a collective response: "Oh, her again. Just hear her out; she always does this." With a sigh of relief, you stepped away, satisfied that it wasn't your problem.

Although you might have the luxury of leaving PTA meetings and heaving a sigh of relief that you didn't have to deal with obnoxious parents, there's someone else who will: your child. He or she will have to deal with these parents in a host of ways—from accepting their curriculum changes to putting up with their children. And since kids often behave in ways similar to their parents, should you really sigh with relief that you don't have to deal with these people when your child goes to a school where their children feel they have the run of the place?

Problem: How Do You Tell a Parent That You Don't Like Her Leadership Style?

> We have an annual rummage sale. Last fall, there were three parents in charge. By the third day, one of the women came to me in tears. This woman felt that she was being totally snubbed. She didn't like the behavior of the two and how they were interacting with the other parents. So she came into my office and basically said that she wanted to resign from the parents' association, that she did not feel welcome, that she realized that she wasn't of the same social status, that they were putting it in her face by the way they were acting.
>
> Miranda, middle school principal

If you're on a committee and see someone being excluded, don't assume that the leader is being a cliquey Queen Bee Mom. She may be naturally more talkative with other members of the group she knows better. The outsider may not be as fluent in communicating how she feels, or she may have assumed that the Queen Bee Mom is unapproachable. Address the Queen Bee Mom in private and say something like this:

YOU: *I'm having a great time in your group. However, I've noticed that Susan is feeling like she's not being given the opportunity to help in the way she'd like. I happen to know that she's a terrific artist, writer, and designer, and we could really use her skills. Could we find a way to rope her in more?*

QBM: *Oh, absolutely!*

YOU: (One week later, when there's been no change): *Hey, remember when we talked about Susan? I can't help but notice that things haven't really changed for her. What's your take on this? I really think she feels hurt and underutilized.*

Even if the Queen Bee Mom thinks you're making too big a deal about the problem, she's banking on your silence. Your speaking out has put her on notice. Ideally, the Queen Bee Mom will take action; it's possible that she honestly forgot about it. But if she doesn't change her behavior, you should seriously consider leaving the group. Be honest in your exit interview: "As much as I appreciate being here, I'm resigning because I don't want to be part of a group that excludes someone."

HOW TO BE A GOOD CLASS PARENT

Many parents prefer being a class parent or class representative because their efforts have a direct impact on their kids. It's for this very reason that things can get ugly.

> *In first grade there was great competition to be class mother. Whoever was picked would be in charge of class parties, Valentine's Day, and Field Day. These were the only parents allowed in the classroom the day of the party. Our PTA had one person who was in charge of choosing all the class mothers. We had two moms competing with each other and one dropped out because she couldn't take it. It was seen as a really cliquey group. It was very hard to break in.*
> Carmen, elementary school mom

> *It was constant one-upmanship. Our principal banned goody bags because the class mothers were competing so much. One class would walk out of the classroom with fabulous goody bags while other kids got nothing.* Therese, elementary school mom

If you're elected a class parent, this isn't a license to have numerous impromptu parent-teacher conferences instead of your one-per-semester allotment ("Oh, I'm so glad I ran into you. I wasn't happy with Devon's grade on his sedimentary rock report—do you have a sec?"). I'll say it again: It isn't a hall pass to pop into the classroom whenever you please.

It is, however, a great opportunity to make all the other parents in your class feel included. Your duties can start with something as seemingly minor as finalizing the class list, the one circulated to all the families with the kids' names, addresses, and phone numbers. Think it doesn't matter if you don't get all the contact information for a name or two? Think again. These are the kids who won't get as many calls from classmates with questions about homework or opportunities for play dates. They won't get party invitations in the mail if the other kids don't know their address. A seemingly harmless omission on the class list can snowball into major exclusion. Likewise, you won't reach out to these parents if you don't know how to contact them. If a language barrier is keeping you from completing the list, call the principal's office and enlist help. After you've completed the list, call every parent—try to speak to both parents in two-parent households—to introduce yourself. If the parents are divorced, make a particular effort to include both addresses on the class list and share all information—especially logistics—with the parent who does not have primary custody.

Don't rely on the same familiar names when you're rounding up help for class parties, chaperones for field trips, and the like. Make it your business to phone the parents with whom you've never spoken to find out how and when they can help.

When it comes time to collect money for a class present for the teacher, be sensitive about different families' abilities to contribute. Some class parents like to leave things very open-ended: "We're collecting for a gift for the teacher. We'd love it if you want to send in a contribution but there's no pressure." Other parents prefer to offer some guidelines: "We're suggesting a donation of five dollars. Some parents give less, some give more, and some prefer not to give at all. Please do what feels comfortable for you."

LANDMINE!

If you're middle-class, please be sensitive when preparing goody bags, treat bags, etc. If you fill them with expensive items, poorer families might feel that you've assumed that they can't afford such niceties, and they might see it as a handout.

Getting More Dads Involved

It's really pretty depressing to see that women are still doing all the work on the PTA. Our school board is where the important decisions are made—and the board is mostly men. It's clear that the people who are important don't perceive the PTA as important. You can just tell from the vibe and the way things are structured; each month, the PTA reports to the board and it's the last thing at the meeting. What's important [to them] was the principal's report, not how Grandparents' Day went.   Joe, middle school dad

I got involved when my daughter was in kindergarten. I wasn't uncomfortable in a room full of women. As I got more involved, I wanted more women on the board because that was the men's domain and the PTA was the women's domain. The board now has 40 percent women, but the PTA is remarkably dominated by women. When I look at the class reps, there are maybe two men.

        Dylan, middle school dad

So far I've talked about mothers volunteering because—let's face it— parent volunteerism is one of the most clear-cut examples of the unequal division of labor between moms and dads. I know some fathers do participate. We just need to look at how and when.

Parent groups have the same benefits and problems as do middle-school friendships—and I refer to middle school because parents often segregate themselves by gender for volunteer jobs just as boys and girls segregate themselves during early adolescence. Moms tend to organize events and work out social logistics; dads usually sell the Christmas trees and build the playgrounds.

This generally reinforces two dynamics. First, more women end up working on long-range projects such as organizing a book fair, which can take months of preparation. Longer-term projects create more risk of drama, since they bring groups of people close together—sometimes too close. However, because it's the women who usually take on the long-term projects, conflicts that arise are too often dismissed as "mothers being difficult." The dads hear about the drama from their wives, thank their lucky stars that they're not involved, and have a clear example of why they wouldn't ever want to participate themselves.

Second, more men are attracted to short-term projects; for example, "Come to the school at 7 a.m. this Saturday and clean up the playground." Cleaning up might sound like drudgery, but for the most part activities like these are fun: They offer instant gratification and everybody feels as though they pulled together for a good cause. And these events are often too time-limited to offer much opportunity for exclusion, badmouthing, or other negative fallout. As the two quotes introducing this section indicate, the lack of gender equity (more men on the school board, more women on the PTA) often means that the invaluable contributions of the PTA are denigrated as "women's work"—which makes it that much harder to enlist men.

I asked fathers in several focus groups why they didn't participate in more school activities. Here are some of their responses:

> *Why would you want to hang out with women who are working on something they're incredibly uptight about? What are they uptight about? Their children. Any venue where women can be in a leadership position—especially women who don't usually get that opportunity—those women are going to exercise power.*
>
> Harold, elementary school father

> *That is an overtly sexist comment to assume that all women are uptight about their children. And men aren't? It's not to say that there aren't kernels of truth there, but I joined the PTA to be involved in an organization with insights into my children's lives because so much of their time is spent at school.* Max, middle school father

> *Why would they want to be aggravated by a group of women? And I always thought of the PTA as something people joined to get special treatment for their children.* Norm, middle school father

If you're a parent leader, make it your mission to reach out to more fathers for long-term projects. Make sure that at least half the members of the overseeing committee are men. Offer creative solutions for how dads can stay involved in long-term projects even if they can't come to every meet-ing. Likewise, reach out to more women for the shorter-term projects; there's no testosterone required to bag a Christmas tree or flip a burger at a rally.

It can be difficult to break down these gender barriers. Back in the eighties, author and mother Mary Kay Blakely wrote a hilarious essay about her dogged attempts to get dads to contribute brownies to an up-coming bake sale. When they begged off, she pressed on, explaining how they could buy brownie mix and make brownies in a single pan. Still the fathers fought her tooth and nail. Many mothers report that things aren't much different today. One mom told me that when she called one house to ask the parents to send in ten dollars for the teacher's gift, the father, a full-time professional, immediately volunteered to put his wife, another full-time professional, on the phone. "There's no need," the mother told him, "This is the entire message — just send in ten bucks with Joey on Monday for the teacher's gift." "Wait," he kept telling her, "Just let me put my wife on." They went several rounds like this, with the mother insisting that she didn't need to talk to the wife, before the husband gave in and said he'd take care of it.

It's worth persevering to erase these gender disparities. It's not just that our children need to see their dads fully invested in their schools and that dads need to discover the satisfaction of being a greater part of the school community. The larger issue is that when dads don't, they reinforce the belief that men's work is more important than women's work and that "mother's work" is the least appreciated of all.

THE PUNAHOU PFA

The Punahou School in Hawaii is an independent school of 3,400 stu-dents with an international reputation for excellence. Their grounds are extraordinary. There are state-of-the-art theaters, well-equipped science labs, and athletics facilities that rival those of the best universities in the country. But the most impressive thing on campus is an enormous banyan tree that stretches into the sky. Halfway up the trunk, a white line is painted. Any child above the second grade may climb the tree, but only as high as that white line. In the many decades that the kids have been scaling the trunk (without harnesses, nets, or cell phones), the most severe injury has been a broken arm. Why don't more kids hurt themselves? Don't they fall? Absolutely—they fall all the time—but the spreading arms of the banyan catch them.

The banyan tree is a perfect metaphor for the Punahou PFA. Like any parent organization, this PFA has had stumbles, but the infrastructure is sound enough that it remains strong, and very few parents are bruised by the experience of working in this community.

How did this come about? I spoke with Linda Goto-Hirai, the president of Punahou's Parent-Faculty Association, and observed the respectful way teachers, administrators, and parents worked with one another. Years ago, these adults made the decision that Punahou needed to commit itself to becoming a more diverse community. The PFA began to actively solicit working parents from all different professions, with different life experiences, and gave them leadership roles. They canvassed parents to find out the best times for meetings, whether it was before work or during lunch. They spread the word that joining the PFA didn't mean making a lifetime commitment—parents who could spare only an hour a month were as welcome as those who could volunteer every day. Goto-Hirai decided that "as head of the PFA, it's my responsibility to make sure that this is a school for every child." Gradually, the PFA came to reflect that diversity, and today it is a truly democratic enterprise. (Would you be surprised if I told you that Goto-Hirai surrendered her PFA parking spot?)

I know these people have had disagreements—when I was there, the question of instituting uniforms was being hotly debated—but underneath the disagreements was a foundation of mutual respect and trust. (I've worked in plenty of schools where as soon as the PTA people leave the room, the teachers and administrators collectively sigh in relief.) The Punahou School is a superb example of what parents can achieve if they commit themselves to the long-term goals of inclusion and diversity.

There's so much to be gained when the experience of parent volunteering goes well. It's one thing to believe that our communities are held together through the relationships of all the members—students, parents, teachers, and administrators. It's another to experience this coming together firsthand, with the pride of knowing that you've contributed and in a way that you can be proud of.

You Are Cordially (Not) Invited

Coping with Kids' Parties

One of the sixth-grade girls is having what promises to be the blowout birthday party of the year. The whole middle school is talking about the theme: come as your favorite celebrity. Reputable sources (that is, parents who arrived early in the after-school pickup line) have confirmed that the party will entail (1) encouraging guests to dress up exactly like their favorite celebrities in their favorite music videos, TV shows, and movies, down to the skimpiest outfits and latest piercings; (2) a real red carpet, with paparazzi-style photographers snapping the kids' pictures as they head into the party, and (3) more photo ops inside the venue, to be turned into a video montage to be played at the end of the party with photo souvenirs as party favors. The invitations came in video form, with highlights from the birthday girl's life set to a bouncy beat. The video concluded with the birthday girl telling viewers, "So as you can see, the party's gonna be great—but hurry up and RSVP, 'cause space is limited!"

Some of the parents are elated—what a cute idea! Some are jealous—they'd planned on that theme and now Jenny's mom has taken it. Some are horrified but don't say anything because they don't want their kids banished to social Siberia. Some are furious that their kids have been left off the list—and they're either plotting payback, sending emissaries while praying for divine invitational intervention, or dropping obvious hints. A few are so appalled about the excess that they can't talk about anything else. When teachers hear about the party, they just roll their eyes.

The drama escalates when the girls and boys who received the coveted videos start telling friends whether their parents will or won't let them go—all of which is duly reported back to the other parents. Girls and their mothers argue about how much to spend on outfits and whether they're too sexy. As the party date approaches, parents arrive at the after-school pickup line earlier and earlier to find out the latest developments. It's clear that the party has become a referendum that reveals which parents are taking the high road and refusing to let their children go and which parents think everyone should just relax and let the kids have a good time.

The front- and back-room machinations by kids and parents alike rise to such a fever pitch that the principal asks to meet with Jenny's parents. As he attempts to explain why some of the parents are so opposed to the party, Jenny's mother interrupts: "If there are parents who don't want their kids to come, so be it, but they have no right to stop us from doing what we want for our child. And is it so bad that we want to do something special for our daughter on her twelfth birthday? I had five miscarriages before she was born—she was a precious gift to us, and other parents don't have the right to stop us from celebrating this very special day."

Game, set, and match.

I'll come clean: This party vignette is a composite of three real situations. However, I have no doubt you've heard of parties that are even more over the top, for even younger kids. Chances are you've been on both sides of this great divide as host or guest.

Before you became a parent, you probably didn't think much about children's parties—except perhaps that you wanted to avoid them. But once you had a child, the well-meaning inquiries began: "How are you going to celebrate Mark's special day?" If you thought, as I do, that if your child isn't old enough to know it's his birthday, then the parents should give each other gifts and call it a day, you were treated to scoldings from friends and family. Maybe you gave in to the pressure and threw a little family party with hats and a homemade cake. But by the time your child was old enough to know it was his birthday, the cozy gathering with cake and party hats had morphed into a more elaborate affair with a guest list and fancy goody bags.

In Perfect Parent World, parties—giving them, having our kids invited to them—can become a barometer for parental fitness. Slowly but surely, the parties we throw for our children can be transformed from personal expressions of love into public demonstrations that we are good parents. And when our kids are excluded from parties, we convince ourselves that our anger reflects not an overinvestment in our children's popularity but proof that we care about our kids being treated right.

In this chapter, I'll offer some guidance on how to keep these occasions in the proper perspective and on an appropriate scale, how to help your kids learn the life lessons they offer, and how to deal with other parents when the party mood sours.

Field Work for Your Party Ph.D.

It's time for some reconnaissance. Do you know how to pick out the Queen Bee or Dominator in a crowd of kids? Can you spot who's at the top of the social totem pole? Your goal is to become more conversant with kids' group dynamics so that when your child has a party you'll be more likely to head off problems at the pass or address them more effectively if they arise. You'll also be able to respond to parents' concerns more knowledgeably. Imagine that you're the Jane Goodall of children–an impartial scientific observer of kids' group dynamics.

Begin your field work at the nearest elementary school playground. Don't start off watching your child with her peers; you're not an unbiased observer. Take a look at another group of elementary school children playing. Whoever is farthest away from the supervising teachers has the most social power. The closer a kid is to the teacher, the less social power that child has.

Now move on to the middle and high school kids. Observe them during pickup, waiting for the school bus, hanging out at the mall, or in their most natural habitat: in front of a movie theater on a Friday or Saturday night. The kids who have the most power will be literally the center of attention, ringed by other kids of lesser social status. Watch each child's body language; you don't need to hear what they're saying to each other to understand whose voice has the most power.

Now try observing your child with his or her peers. What can you tell about the social pecking order? When your child has a party, you're going to apply these same observation skills.

Golden Rules to Minimize Party Drama

The same rules apply whether you're having a party for a child who's five or fifteen — it's just a little harder to make sure the rules stick as kids get older.

- *Examine your criteria for the guest list.* Have you encouraged your child to add any names because they're the "right people" to invite or because you're hoping for reciprocal invitations from that friend or family? Ask yourself: "What do I most want my child to learn from how I make up a guest list?"
- *Consider inviting everyone in the class.* As your child gets older, this usually becomes less feasible. In that case, come up with logical parameters. Perhaps your child can invite everyone in drama club, or from his class at religious school, or from his bunk at camp. Agree on a maximum number of guests and don't allow your child to sneak extra people onto the list later.
- *Even if you do invite "everyone," don't assume that the party will be drama-free.* If your child is a Queen Bee or Dominator, Wannabe, or Sidekick, he or she will use the party to reinforce the group's social pecking order. You should be just as concerned when you see girls huddling together in groups at a party as you would be to see boys and girls coupling off.
- *Power corrupts.* A well-meaning sweetheart of a child can turn into a Machiavellian tyrant at the drop of an invitation. While it's perfectly appropriate for your child to limit the number of people at your house for a party and invite whomever he or she wants, keep in mind that your child can be tempted to use the situation to settle old grudges, begin new ones, and flex a little social power.
- *If your child is going to have a small party, know that someone will*

probably be hurt that he or she wasn't invited. That doesn't mean you have to invite that child, but you have to teach your child how to handle the situation ethically.

- *With younger children, go over the rules of being a good host.* Explain that your child has to be welcoming to every guest and share his or her toys. Once your child is in middle school, the two of you should come up with clear, written guidelines about your and your child's hosting responsibilities. The number one guideline is that everyone should feel welcome. Ask your child what "everyone should feel welcome" does and doesn't look like.

Some questions to ask your child:

- "Are there any people who will be surprised or hurt if they don't get an invitation? How are you going to handle that?"
- "Are there people you feel you should invite but don't really want to? Why?"
- "Are there people you aren't inviting but want to? Why?"
- "Are you inviting people who will exclude other people or do things that would make you nervous or would be against our family values?"
- "What will you do in that situation?"
- "When do you want me or another adult to get involved?"

Controlling Pre-Party Chatter

Annie's twelfth birthday was coming up and I really wanted to do something special for her, so I got her tickets to a concert she really wanted to go to. Then she asked if she could bring a few friends and I thought we could make it a really special occasion. So I pulled strings and we got six tickets so she could invite her closest friends. But then the school called me and was really upset because I shouldn't have done it. Was I so wrong to want to do something special for my kid?
                Colleen, middle school mom

On the face of it, this parent's confusion is understandable. Why was the school trying to stop her from doing something special for her daughter?

The girls weren't going to miss any school. Here's the problem: Those tickets were the most sought-after tickets of the year if you were a twelve-year-old girl. They were incredibly expensive and they gave the birthday girl immense power to decide who among her friends was worthy of an invitation.

Please understand that no matter how mature your daughter is, if she's one of the anointed in such a situation, there's *no way* she isn't going to talk about it the moment she gets to school. If she sees someone walking down the hall wearing a blue sweatshirt, she'll say something to the Unchosen like, "See that sweatshirt? I'm going to get one exactly that color at the concert next week."

The truth is that even a simple home birthday party has that same potential, and it's your job to make sure your child doesn't take advantage of her power as the host. Consider having the following conversation with your child to lay out your expectations:

1. "I expect you to keep the talking about your party to a minimum. I know I can't control every word that comes out of your mouth, but I need you to be aware that other people might feel hurt or excluded because they weren't invited. You're allowed to invite your friends, but you aren't allowed to make other people feel bad in the process. This is my law."

2. "I expect you to honor both the spirit and the letter of the law. This means you can't do anything obnoxious like obviously try to cover up that you're talking about the party with your invited friends by falling silent, starting to whisper, or running away when someone who wasn't invited comes up to you. I consider that unacceptable behavior."

3. "If I find out that you have used this party, which is my gift to you, to make someone feel bad, I will cancel it." (If you issue this threat, you *must* make good on it, no matter how much your child wails, tantrums, or apologizes.)

Avoiding Totem Trouble

Every year a girl in our town has a birthday party with the most ridiculous party favors. Her family is much wealthier than everyone else. This year all the kids got fleeces. All the kids suck up to her all year to make the guest list.   Denise, middle school mom

JUMPING OFF THE BANDWAGON

Take a minute to acknowledge the social pressure you might feel to outdo other parties you've attended or which your child has described, and ask yourself these questions:

- Think of the most excruciating child's party you ever attended. Remember all the irritating details—what do you think they reflected about the hosts?
- Think of the best party you've been to (especially one that was celebrating a rite of passage such as a graduation, a religious milestone, or a birthday). Why was it so good? What do you think it reflected about the hosts?
- If a Floater or Reformed hosted a party in your community what would it look like? How can you make sure that a party you host would resemble that?
- Are you worried that your child will be disappointed in you if you don't give a fancy party? Have you had a discussion with him or her about it?

Please understand that even the sweetest child won't be able to resist showing off a party favor; these favors fall into the same category as the valentines, candygrams, and carnations kids exchange at school as barometers of popularity (which is why I think it's a terrible idea for schools to have them—even if it's for a good cause). So under no circumstances should you give out favors that the kids can wear or bring to school the next day to show that they were part of the lucky chosen. This especially includes anything with the guest of honor's name on it (sweatshirts, bracelets, etc.) or portable stereos, iPods, and gift certificates to the trendiest stores.

TYPICAL ROADBLOCKS ON THE ROUTE TO PARTY CENTRAL

Problem: Your Child Wants to Invite a Kid You Hate

Okay, maybe *hate* is too strong a word, but you don't trust a hair on this kid's head. First, you have to ask yourself why. Does he or she dress a certain way that drives you nuts? Get over it. Does he or she behave in a way that sends your antennae due north? Then you've got a legitimate reason for concern. Perhaps you've seen this kid in action and you know that his or her presence at the party will cause problems.

Sit down with your child and ask if he or she has any general concerns about how any of the guests might act during the party. If your child fingers the same kid you're worried about, ask: "So, how should we deal with it?" You might decide you need to supervise more (there's always the snack tray to refill or more soda to fetch). Do you need to come up with a code word that your child could use to indicate he or she wants you around more?

If your child doesn't express worries about any kid's behavior, give him or her a heads-up that you do have a concern. Present your evidence: What exactly have you seen that gives you concern about this child? If you haven't seen him or her in action but have heard horrible stories from other parents, say to your child, "Listen, maybe these stories are completely wrong, but tell me if we have cause for concern here. Either way, I'm going to be extra vigilant. Let's come up with a few ways that I can check in on things regularly without getting in your way."

When your child is older, if the kid you're concerned about has a reputation for violence, bringing drugs to parties, or bringing other people to the party without permission, I think you're within your rights to forbid your child from inviting him or her—which, by the way, doesn't mean that the child won't come. But you have to be sure you aren't buying into unsubstantiated gossip. If you're going to do something so potentially hurtful, you'd better be very sure of your information.

Problem: You and Another Family Have Scheduled Parties on the Same Day

In a perfect world, kids who receive invitations to two events being held at the same time would be true to their word and attend the party to which they RSVP'd first. But the reality is, too many kids violate this rule—often because their parents allow it. They'll ditch one party in favor of the other or pressure one host to change the date. If your child is lower on the social totem pole, it's likely that friends will bail out in favor of the party hosted by the more popular kid. So call the other parents immediately.

It's not a show of weakness to say how awful you feel that kids are bound to ditch your child's party for the other kid's party.

YOU: *Hey, is this Rebecca's mom? Hi, this is Ray, Jill's dad. Do you have a minute? Are you having a party for Rebecca on the eighteenth? Well, Jill also has a birthday this month—I know, they get old so fast—and we scheduled her party on the same day as yours.*

REBECCA'S MOM: *Oh, I'm sure it won't be too much of a problem. They hang out with such different groups, don't they?*

YOU: *Actually, I think this is one of those times we need to give the girls some guidance. Since the invitations went out, kids who were invited to Jill's party found out about Rebecca's party and they started backing out or saying they'd come by later.* (If Rebecca's mom protests that Rebecca isn't more popular than Jill, wait until she finishes.) *So now Jill feels terrible and I don't really know what to do and I want to ask you if we can work together to figure this out.*

What exactly should you ask for? There are three options. You can host the party together, you can host separately, or someone can change the date. If the other parent refuses to share or to move the date, take the initiative and be gracious yourself. If you can't move the date yourself because money has already been spent and people have already RSVP'd, then explain what's going on to your daughter so she can revise her expectations. Now, if someone ever comes to you with this dilemma, please do everyone a favor and do the right thing. The best thing to do would be to call or e-mail a letter to all the parents signed by both families that describes the situation and your expectation that children will honor their first commitment.

Problem: Your Kid Doesn't Make the Cut for the Guest List

It's genuinely painful when your child is left off the invitation list. This mother's story is a typical one:

> *There are nineteen kids in my son's class and ten were invited to a birthday party. He didn't make the cut. He was devastated. I didn't*

know what to do. I want my child to realize and accept that he won't be invited to everything—and that's okay—but at the same time he's ten and he was so sad. I called a friend of mine who's a good friend with the birthday girl's mother and got an invitation. Did I do the right thing? Flor, elementary school mom

No, this mother didn't do the right thing, but I certainly understand her motivation. She felt terrible for her son—any parent would. But let's break it down. She's sad for her son because his feelings were hurt. He's at an age when she can't kiss the hurt away, but she still wants to. She knows she should help him to make peace with the fact that he won't be invited to everything, but her anxiety about his being a social outcast is intolerable, leading her to pull strings to get him invited. She convinces herself that what she's doing is okay because "if the kids just got to know him better, they could be friends." Meanwhile, in the eyes of the other parents, she's behaving like a Desperate Wannabe.

If you're ever in a similar situation and you're tempted to wrangle an invitation, ask yourself what your goal is. After all, your child already knows he wasn't invited; you can't undo the hurt of the original rejection. And if he desperately wants to go to a party where he isn't wanted, that's a flag: He's acting like a Pleaser or Wannabe who's willing to sacrifice his dignity to ingratiate himself with the "right" group.

If you wrangle the invitation, here are the messages you send to your child:

1. This social occasion is so important that he simply must go; if he wasn't invited, it's because he isn't good enough. From this he learns that being invited to a party is a reasonable measure of his worth.

2. Being excluded calls for the parent's immediate action rather than discussion or reflection. But wait: Maybe your son wasn't the host's close friend. Was he among his ten closest friends? By picking up the phone immediately, you've missed one of those "teachable moments" all the parenting books rave about—the chance to discuss why it's okay to be excluded, and why your child thinks it happened.

3. If he doesn't get his way, Mom or Dad will come to the rescue—which makes the situation worse. Can't you just hear the birthday boy complaining to his friends, "Can you believe his mom called and got my mom to invite him?" Then your child is going to be made to feel like an even bigger loser.

Yes, it stings when we see our kids excluded. Sometimes we have no idea why our perfect child is being left in the dust, and sometimes we know all too well. But no matter what the real or imagined reason for the exclusion, we know our kids hurt when they're left out. The silence of a phone that doesn't ring is deafening. Maybe we're not thrilled by the idea of our teens trolling the malls or movies in huge packs, but we ache when each Saturday night finds them listlessly watching TV alone. We long to fix things. However, we're often blind to how our desire to smooth our children's social lives can set them up for bad relationships in the future.

I'm going to share a conversation that I had by e-mail and later by phone with a mother who found herself, against her better judgment, micromanaging her daughter's social life. This mother spoke to me about her reaction when two popular girls in her daughter's class of twenty excluded her:

> *I'm telling you things I would never admit out loud and I know there are other parents out there like me. I do manipulate my daughter's social life. I plot and I scheme. I'm almost like a PR agent pushing my kids, like this is my daughter and, you know, hello, she's here. But it's all subtle, kind of like you're building up your clients. It was all through a little planning, little sleepovers and get-togethers. The kids who I especially would have liked for her to have been friends with always got an invitation to our house. My daughter was oblivious that the other girls weren't accepting her. I saw it and it upset me that she was in that situation. . . . I was obsessed with one child in particular and her little sidekicks. What is it about this girl and her friends that they're excluding my child?*

I asked this mother, "Why do you want your daughter to be friends with people who aren't nice to her?" Her reply was one I've heard from hundreds of parents: "I don't necessarily want her to be friends with them, but I want her to be accepted." What many parents don't appreciate is that in Girl World and Boy World, "being accepted" can mean accepting other people's right to treat you badly.

My next question was "What do you mean by 'accepted'?" She gave me the expected response: "I want her to be accepted for who she is." This certainly sounds like something we'd all want for our kids, but let's probe a little further: What does acceptance look like to you? What does it look like to your child? By my definition, acceptance means that people allow you to be you—however silly, goofy, or awkward that may be. Unfortunately, that doesn't happen very often in middle and high school; in fact, the higher you move in the pecking order, the less likely it is. The more regimented and controlled the behavior, dress, and other markers of your social status, the less you're free to be who you are and still stay in the good graces of your tribe. This means that for many children, "being accepted" means *not* being who they really are—exactly the opposite of what this mother says she wants.

By pushing her daughter to be friends with popular girls who don't accept her, this mother is teaching her child that these girls have the power to determine her worth, and that the girls who *do* accept her daughter "for who she is" don't matter because they aren't high enough in the social pecking order. She is also inadvertently priming her daughter to see her as superficial (even though she isn't) and to buy into her philosophy that you can determine your own value only through the lens of others' regard. I asked the mother to do a cost-benefit analysis of her daughter being friends with the girls who are rejecting her. In other words, what does she gain by having those popular girls accept her? What does she lose? Here is the mother's reply:

> [If she was accepted] I would feel vindicated in a way. We want our kids to have what we didn't. I wasn't an unpopular kid, but I wasn't the most popular. I was just one of these kids that flew under the radar. I take it personally. Instead of fixating on the twenty other kids that think my daughter is lovely and sweet, I fixated on the two kids that didn't like her. I wanted to know, was my child different from somebody else? Why is it that my daughter isn't good enough?

Now we're at the heart of it. Remember what I said about how we never quite leave seventh grade behind? Inside this mother lurks the teen who believed that if she could just be accepted, all her problems would be solved. And now she is transferring that belief onto her daughter. Her good intentions are creating a situation where her daughter will suffer in much the same way she did.

Problem: Your Child Doesn't Want to Invite an Old Friend to a Party

A mother related the following problem:

> *My twelve-year-old daughter, Katie, is having a birthday party and doesn't want to invite Amanda, one of the girls from the neighborhood. Katie's grown up with Amanda, but lately Amanda has been really mean to her. My husband and I talked to her about it and we felt really strongly that she shouldn't have to invite someone who's been mean to her. Katie didn't invite Amanda but one of the other mothers whose child was invited called me and was very angry that we had done this. Now a lot of the people in the neighborhood think we were horrible. The party is coming up in two weeks and I can't figure out what to do. If we invite Amanda, we're telling Katie that it's okay to give in to peer pressure and invite her—even though Amanda is so mean to her. If we stick to not inviting her, then everyone hates us. I guess I did something wrong, but how do I fix it?*

I hear versions of this story all the time and there's a pattern. The birthday girl's mother is almost always perceived as a Queen Bee Mom. Starbucks & Sympathy Moms typically talk behind the Queen Bee Mom's back but rarely confront her directly. Invisibles don't usually say anything to the gossiping women, and even if they do, they are dismissed. If anyone does speak to the accused Queen Bee Mom, it'll be the Wannabe because she needs to feel like she's "doing the right thing" and wants to be in the center of the drama. It's rare that the mother of the child who's not invited will speak directly to the Queen Bee Mom; if she does, she's likely to be so nervous and angry that she doesn't present her case well.

The birthday girl's mother most likely doesn't see herself as a Queen Bee Mom. She feels justified in not inviting a girl who was mean to her daughter, but she's still uncomfortable about how to handle it, so she has a fern moment and doesn't deal with the other parents directly. The dads are likely to hear about the situation from their wives. They may empathize, but they're likely to chalk this up as one more example of women blowing things out of proportion. This is a classic illustration of why mothers end up hating each other over what seems like a small thing (of course, it only seems like a small thing when it isn't your child being excluded) and why fathers disengage from their children's social lives.

Both Amanda's and Katie's parents have legitimate reasons to be angry. The birthday girl has every right to exclude someone who's been mean to her. If you were Katie's parent, you wouldn't want her to invite someone who treated her badly because then she would be valuing the relationship and appearances over her right to be treated with dignity within that friendship.

You should affirm your child's right to make the decision and guide her in handling it in a responsible way. Encourage and prepare her to have a conversation with Amanda using SEAL. Your goal is to walk Katie through the process of articulating to someone who hurt her what she wants (or doesn't want) from the relationship. Ask your daughter if there are any circumstances under which she would feel comfortable inviting Amanda. Would she change her mind if Amanda apologized sincerely? If Amanda apologizes but it's obviously not sincere, will Kate still feel comfortable not inviting her? Let her make the decision either way. Keep in mind that while Katie may be the best kid in the world, she still may be tempted to use the party as a way to settle grudges or bully her once-and-possibly-future friend back. Your responsibility is to make sure that she doesn't do this or to hold her accountable if she does.

Have Katie arrange a one-on-one meeting with Amanda (no partisans or seconds standing by), either face-to-face or on the telephone, but not by instant messaging, text messaging, or e-mail.

KATIE: *Amanda, I need to talk to you.*

AMANDA: *What's up?*

KATIE: *Are we speaking in private?* (Girls often harass other girls with threeway calling or listening in, so make sure it's just them on the phone.)

AMANDA: *It's just us.*

KATIE: *Good. I wanted to tell you that I don't like it when you talk behind my back and laugh at me.*

AMANDA: *What are you talking about? Are you serious? When? Name one time. And anyway, I was just joking.*

KATIE: *Yesterday when I walked away from you and Carly in the hallway was the last time, but it's been going on for a while. I feel like I try to tell you to stop and you don't listen. My birthday is coming up and I'm having a party. I'm telling you how I feel because I don't want to invite you, but I wanted you to hear it from me and know the reason why.*

Katie is not the only one who needs to use SEAL in this situation. Since the kids have known each other for a long time and you're neighbors with the parents, you need to call the parents. This is where the rubber meets the road. Here are some guidelines for communicating with other parents so the situation doesn't blow up in your face. As always, the phone rules apply; don't launch into the conversation as soon as the other parent picks up the phone, don't assume the other parent knows what is going on with his or her child, and assume the other parent is a good person and loves his or her child as much as you love yours.

Under no circumstances should any permutation of the following issue from your mouth at any time during the conversation:

"I don't know how you're raising *your* child, but in our family . . ."

"There's a lot I could tell you about your daughter, but I'm not going to stoop to that level."

"Maybe your child's jealous of mine, but that doesn't give her the right to be so nasty."

"There are other parents in the neighborhood [or school or church] who agree with me."

Here's how such a conversation might go:

YOU: *Bob, is this a good time to talk? Amanda and Katie are having a problem that I need to talk to you about.*

BOB (sounding scared): *Why don't you call Marie at work? She's so much better at these things than I am.*

YOU: *Oh, I'm sure you and I can work this out. Anyway, Katie's birthday is in two weeks and she doesn't want to invite Amanda. We've talked to Katie about this because Amanda has been a good friend for such a long time, but she feels that Amanda has been so mean to her that she really doesn't want to. Katie's planning on telling Amanda tomorrow, so I'm calling to give you a heads up.*

If you're the mom and the other mom answers, you're operating with the narrowest margin of error. Just stick with the guidelines and the script and you'll make it through with your head held high. If you're a dad making the call, you'll have the advantage because most parents will be shocked you're calling in the first place. If the other dad answers, he'll probably be too embarrassed to get his wife because it'll look like he isn't man enough or capable enough to handle this conversation. If the mom answers, she'll be completely thrown off to find herself speaking to a father—and if you handle yourself well during the conversation, she'll be distracted by her growing frustration toward her husband because he isn't as cool as you are.

Now for the other parent's response:

OTHER PARENT: *It can't be that bad, can it? I think the girls can work it out. Amanda will be so hurt if she's excluded. That can't be the right thing to do.*

YOU: *I feel terrible about this situation, I know Amanda's a great kid but Katie has been having a really hard time with her recently and it's her decision. She's going to tell Amanda tomorrow, and although we think Katie has the right to invite whomever she wants to her party, she must do so in an ethical way. So if she doesn't or you think we should sit down with the girls, just let me know.*

Now let's suppose the conversation takes a southerly turn:

OTHER PARENT: *Well, that's not what Amanda is telling me. She just said last night that Katie is talking behind her back.*

The pounding in your temples reminds you to breathe. Remember that this parent loves her child as much as you love yours. You've just said that Amanda is mean and horrible. Allow that person a moment to react. Then take a deep breath and continue:

YOU: *I know this is hard to hear and it was really hard for me to call you. I feel bad about this, too. Amanda has been welcome in our house since you first moved into the neighborhood, but I have to respect that Katie doesn't have to invite someone who's making her feel bad. I also want you to know that I know these things can go both ways. I'm going to talk to Katie about being mean to Amanda; I want to be sure she treats her respectfully and is accountable for her actions.*

A situation that seems reciprocal presents a great opportunity for both sets of parents to sit down with the girls and explain what you expect as they negotiate this bump in their friendship.

OTHER PARENT: *I'm so sorry. I totally understand, and I'll talk to Amanda. I hope she can earn Katie's trust again. Thanks for calling.* (Don't laugh! This really does happen!)
YOU: *Thanks so much for understanding. This was really hard for me and I can't tell you how much I appreciate what you just said.*

After you hang up the phone, make a mental note that this is a parent you want to be friends with—even if your kids aren't.

What if you didn't do the prep work described above, or what if you did and it's still really messy and suddenly you're getting nasty glares from your neighbors? Call Amanda's parents and say:

YOU: *We had a problem that we didn't handle well. Katie told us that she didn't want to invite Amanda to her party because Amanda was being mean to her. We felt like she had the right to do that, but we should have called you and talked to you about it first so you could talk to Amanda and she wouldn't feel so surprised. As a family, we need to apologize for hurting Amanda's feelings because Katie didn't invite her to her party. Can we talk about this and then talk to the girls?*

Note that you aren't apologizing for not inviting Amanda. You're apologizing for how you handled it. You're preserving your child's right to make decisions, but you're taking responsibility for handling it in a thoughtless way.

Now let's suppose you're one of Amanda's parents. It's Saturday morning and you're doing a little yard work when Marcia, your neighbor who's always just a little too curious about what everyone's doing in the neighborhood, comes up to you.

MARCIA: *Good morning! How are you all doing?*

YOU: *Fine. It was such a crazy week but there's not too much going on this weekend. Just got back from Home Depot—they had a great special on azaleas. I went a little overboard but they're so beautiful I couldn't help myself.*

MARCIA: *They really are beautiful. . . . But I'm so sorry about Katie's birthday party. I really can't believe Amanda wasn't invited.*

YOU (panicking, but not wanting Marcia to know you're in the dark, and wanting to get as much information as possible out of her): *Yeah, I know. Amanda's really upset about it but I always tell her she can't be invited to everything. When is it supposed to be, anyway?*

MARCIA: *The fourteenth. I just think it's terrible. The girls have been friends forever. Amanda shouldn't be treated like that. My Beth was really upset about it when she came home yesterday and told me about it. I think all the girls are really upset about it.*

YOU: *Don't worry about it. Amanda is strong enough to handle it. It's just a shame that some people can't be a little more gracious.*

Marcia leaves—is there just a little extra spring in her step?—and you return to your plants, steaming mad. How dare Katie and her parents cut out your daughter! Why? And all the girls know? That means that every-one in the neighborhood knows.

So you wait, expecting some explanation from Katie's parents. None comes. You run into them walking their dog and they say hi and that's it. You can't believe they're so rude. What do you do?

First, talk to Amanda. Get her in the car with you, tell her she looks a little down, and ask if everything is okay. If she spills, skip ahead. If she doesn't bite . . .

YOU: *Beth's mom told me that Katie's having a birthday party but I haven't heard you talk about it.* (Wait for ten seconds to give your daughter a chance to respond.) *Are you invited?*

AMANDA: *No, but whatever, I don't care anyway.*

YOU: *Well, maybe you don't care, but if it happened to me, I'd be hurt.* (Wait a few seconds. If your daughter admits she's hurt, continue:) *I'm so sorry. Do you want to talk about it now or later? I know you're hurt, but why do you think Katie wouldn't want to invite you?* (If she says "I have no idea":) *Well, what do you think she'd say?* (If she doesn't want to talk about it:) *Okay, well, if you want to talk about it, I'm here. And it doesn't have to be me. I just want you to feel there's someone you can talk to.*

Even if Amanda was horrible to Katie, you might still be furious at Katie and her parents for excluding her. Calm down, remember they love their daughter as much as you love your daughter, and call. Keep in mind that they're going to be nervous, perhaps even defensive, when they hear from you.

YOU: *Is now a good time to talk?*

THEM: *Sure, what's up?*

YOU: *Tell me if I'm wrong, but I think Katie's having a birthday party in a couple of weeks and Amanda wasn't invited. Can you tell me why not?* (Hear that your child is a miserable troll.) *Okay, that's really hard to hear, but I'm glad you told me. Would Katie feel comfortable telling Amanda why she's angry? I don't think Amanda knows, and I want her to have the opportunity to hear it and do better.*

THEM: *I don't think Katie feels comfortable talking to Amanda alone. Katie feels like she's tried to talk to Amanda and it doesn't get anywhere.*

YOU: *If Katie doesn't feel comfortable speaking to Amanda alone, then I would be happy to bring Amanda over to your house and we could do it together. Look, I know this is hard, but if Amanda is being mean to Katie, I want her to admit it and stop.*

Problem: Your Child Issues an Invitation, Then Withdraws It

Your daughter invites someone to a party and in the time between the invitations arriving and the party date, the two girls have a huge fight in which the other girl was truly horrible to her. Ideally she should be able to say to the girl, "Obviously, we aren't getting along. Do you still want to come to my party? No? Then that's settled." If the girl says yes, your daughter should say, "Then we need to work this out before the party."

Your child could take matters into her own hands and disinvite the person and then tell you that the other person suddenly can't make it. Changes like this to the guest list, especially in middle school, are red flags. Call the other parent to make sure you're getting accurate information. I can hear parents crying foul over this—isn't it micromanaging, the very thing I've been telling you not to do? In this case, I'm guilty as charged—because I think the principle of accountability is so important that I do want you to make sure your child takes responsibility for following through on commitments.

What if you discover from the other parent that his child is the brunt of your child's mean behavior? In that case, your child should apologize immediately, as outlined in Chapter 6. In fact, I strongly recommend that you go over to the other child's house and have your child apologize in front of the parents—and reextend the invitation.

What if you discover from your child that he doesn't want the other kid to come anymore because this kid's attendance is going to spell trouble for the party? Perhaps the problem child is planning to bring uninvited guests, or start up a game that makes your child uncomfortable, or worse. (Think of Spin the Bottle and then magnify it by one hundred—it's called "Nervous." A boy runs his hand up or down a girl's body until she halts the action by calling out "Nervous!") In this case, have a conversation with your child about how the two of you can work together to handle each of his concerns. If you have a good relationship with the other child's parents, discuss the issue with them, too. Chances are they'll find out anyway.

As I discussed in *Queen Bees & Wannabes*, it's your role as a parent to be the "Eternal Out," the ever-present excuse your child can always use: "I wish I could let your friends come over, but Mom says I can only have five guests." "Sorry, my dad would kill me if he found out." You can have prearranged signals that mean "Hey, help me break this up" or "Time to send everyone home." By all means, give your kid permission to roll his eyes every time you walk into the room with yet another lame excuse to spy on him and his friends—another load of laundry, you're just looking for that book, etc.

Problem: Your Child Accepts an Invitation, Then Decides Not to Go

Parties can be a wonderful opportunity to teach your child about the importance of honoring commitments. Please teach your child the following party rules:

- If he accepts an invitation to a party, that's an ironclad commitment. If a better offer comes along, too bad. He may not accept it, leave the first party early to go to the second, negotiate with the host of the first party to change the date, or any permutation thereof.
- No brokering invitations for other people. For example, "I know he was thinking of inviting you, but then he had to invite Carlos and Brian and that's all his mom said he could have, but let me see what I can do."

Unless you have a silent sufferer for a kid, if you hear about a change in party plans from your child, it's probably because he's being ditched.

However, if you discover that your child is the ditcher—the one backing off plans after he's already accepted an invitation—you need to take action. It could be that your kid just doesn't feel like going, but chances are there's something more going on. Perhaps he's on the outs with the host and is afraid that if he goes, he'll be excluded or ridiculed. Or he could be worried about what's going to happen at the party, from sexual games to vandalism to drinking and drugs. (I'll discuss these issues in depth in Chapter 11.) Being a ditcher doesn't necessarily mean that your kid is ruthlessly blowing someone off. He or she could have a perfectly good reason, but you won't find out unless you know to ask.

Perhaps your child wants to back out of attending a party because the friend giving it never leaves his side and he's looking to put some space between them. I've seen plenty of kids who need to separate because their interests have diverged, one person has become too clingy, or the friendship just seems to have run its course. Kids might make these decisions for legitimate reasons, but they need to learn to bow out gracefully. Typically, they send nonverbal signals that they think or try to persuade themselves are crystal clear, but the target of the signals is baffled or oblivious ("I totally ignored her at lunch, but she just doesn't get it and thinks we're still best friends"). I've talked to thousands of boys and girls about why they have such a hard time communicating in these situations. Paradoxically, kids' desire not to give bad news straight up to friends ("I don't want to hurt your feelings, but I want to spend more time with other people") leads them to ramp up the nonverbal behavior to an often dizzyingly cruel degree.

Even if your child's friendship with another child has run its course, if he accepts an invitation to that friend's party, he's obliged to honor his commitment. You then need to have a serious conversation with your child so he knows how to behave when he gets there: no eye rolling with his new friends over what a loser the old friend is or similarly obnoxious behavior.

As your child gets older there could be other more complicated reasons for wanting to bow out of the party. Suppose your child tells you it's because the friend is lying to his parents about where everyone's going, or planning to indulge in some illicit activity such as sex, drinking, or drugs. These are clearly good reasons not to go. It's also a good idea to talk to the other parent: "Jake just told me something that I thought was important to tell you. He thinks someone is planning to bring pot and their brother's Ritalin and Prozac. If you talk to Chris about this, could you please not say my son told me? Thanks so much. And please know if the situation is ever reversed, you can always call me." You might want to rely on the English teacher's pet peeve, the passive voice: "It was reported to me that . . ." so your child won't be implicated.

Problem: Other Kids Accept Your Child's Invitation but Don't Show Up

> I had a student who was constantly being teased by the other kids. I was so worried about him because he was such a pleaser. In sixth grade, he had a party and a lot of the kids who said they would come didn't. One of the few kids that did was made fun of, too, and the student felt terrible, because he knew the kid who had done the right thing was being punished through guilt by association. I never met the dad and the mom was so fragile. She wanted her son to be accepted but at the same time she didn't because if he was accepted by the other kids, then he would leave her.
>
> Gina, middle school counselor

There are a lot of reasons why plans change at the last minute. Emergencies do come up but imagine how horrible it would feel to be this child and his parents. If you have a Floater kid, realize how much power your child has to make the other children honor their commitments. So sit down with your child (no matter what her social position) and tell her that if she is ever in this situation, you expect her to make you proud and do the right thing.

Problem: You're Going Broke Buying Presents

Gift giving can become a competitive sport among both kids and parents. Some kids "order" presents when they issue invitations. Others deliberately inflate the guest list to receive more loot. Kids want to elevate or solidify their own status by giving the status item of the moment to the guest of honor. What's clear is that you can drain your wallet dry if you don't set up boundaries, and it also creates ridiculous expectations about what a normal gift should be.

If you're new to the party circuit, ask some trusted friends to give you guidelines on appropriate spending limits. Give your child a fixed budget and ask his or her help selecting a present that meets it. Middle school kids can be encouraged to go in on a bigger present together so that each family invests less in the pot. (Once they're in high school, kids usually buy the presents themselves.)

Problem: Your Child Has Been Invited to an "Alternative Prom"

I'm not referring to parties that parents have organized in protest of the outrageously overpriced school-sanctioned events. I'm talking about parties that parents sponsor because their child has been disciplined by the school and isn't permitted to go to the real prom or graduation party.

It's easy to feel sympathetic toward these parents. They almost certainly feel that the school has unfairly punished their child over a minor infraction. They don't want their kid to miss out on an important rite of passage, so they're sanctioning a home-grown version of the prom to which they're allowing their kid to invite lots of other kids. Should you let your child attend? I'd say no. If you let your child go, you're in effect saying that you support the parents in their belief that their child doesn't have to be responsible for his or her actions. After all, the child violated a school rule, and the school has found him or her accountable. I suggest that you call the parents and have a conversation like this:

YOU: *Hi, is this a good time to talk? I know your whole family has been really upset about what happened with Adam—I'd be upset, too. But as your friend and someone who likes and cares about your kid, I have to tell you that I think having an alternative prom is contrary to what I know about you as a parent. I know you want Adam to be a responsible person, and having this party for him doesn't allow him to take responsibility for his actions. He's a strong, capable kid because you've raised him to be that way.*

OTHER PARENT: *If this were your kid, you'd be doing the same thing. Adam says he didn't do it (whatever it is) and I believe him. So we're handling this as a family and, frankly, it's our decision.*

YOU: *It's your decision, but I think our friendship depends upon us telling each other when we disagree and this is one of those times. It's hard for me to say this to you but it's that important to me. I hope you understand why we don't feel we can let Melissa go. Thanks for hearing me out.*

I've spoken to many parents who disagree with the parents who have these alternative parties, but don't do anything about it because they don't think it's any of their business. I want to be clear: It *is* your business. When parents openly disrespect and defy a school-mandated punishment, it sends a very clear signal that they don't believe they have to obey the rules. Very likely, their kids share the same sense of entitlement, which is probably why they got in trouble in the first place. That makes your child's school and, by extension, your child unsafe. And the next time your kid—and the other kids you care about—could very well be the target of these kids' misbehavior. So speak out and use parental peer pressure to stop the Entitled parents' bad behavior.

SPECIAL EVENTS: CELEBRATING YOUR CHILD'S "BIG DAY"

Parents are going all out to celebrate their children's "big days": sweet sixteens, bar and bat mitzvahs, quinceañeras, graduations from elementary school or middle school or high school. I'm not going to fuss at you for wanting to do something special for your child—oh, wait, yes I am. Nowhere has Perfect Parent World made its mark more clearly than in rite-of-passage parties where parents can rationalize unchecked egoism, blatant social competition, and spending outrageous amounts of money.

The Theme

If the party is meant to mark a rite of passage in your child's life, please consider that that is a fitting and sufficient theme. There is no reason to ornament your child's achievement with Yankees paraphernalia, Mardi Gras beads, or anything else. I've spoken with many clergy members who feel that overlaying a theme on top of a bar or bat mitzvah, confirmation, or other religious occasion detracts from the significance of it.

The Budget

It can be particularly hard to keep your child's expectations to a modest scale or to rein in your own vision when you've attended lavish celebrations for other children. I've known families who've gone way beyond their means to put on parties for their children because they felt the children "deserved" it, because they wanted to "hold their heads high in their community," because "that's how everyone does it," or because they "didn't want to look cheap."

Ask yourself and your child: "What message do we want this celebration to convey? What family values do we most want to reflect?" If your child has come home from other parties laden with expensive booty, he may think he has to do the same with his guests. He or she gets a voice here, but you're the benevolent dictator who ultimately makes the call.

If you've decided to keep the celebration on a smaller scale, make sure that the way you talk about it doesn't make any other families feel uncomfortable for making different choices. "We're doing the party this way because it's the best fit for our family's style" is a sufficient explanation.

Hour 523: Guests Held Hostage

Special-event parties are rife with opportunities for abuse of power, from group photo ops to candle-lighting ceremonies. The decisions you make with your child about these mini-events will determine whether guests feel welcome and included or reminded of their exact distance from the center of the party. They will also determine, not incidentally, whether your guests are genuinely entertained or bored to tears. Here are just a few situations to consider:

- *Videos.* The high points of the young host's brief life (one hopes not from the moment of birth) are up there on the screen. Perhaps the montages are set to music. Perhaps images of family, friends, and other loved ones are included. Will the video be a short but sweet five minutes or sixty excruciating minutes? Will it play in the background while the guests enjoy their meals or dance, or must all action come to a halt as the tape rolls? Will it feature many of the guests, who will enjoy seeing themselves, or will it star a largely unknown cast of characters?

- *Open mike night.* Will a very few preselected people be called upon to pay tribute to the guest of honor, or will every guest with even a glancing relationship to the host feel free to step forward and speak with no time limit? Please consider whether the audience will glory as much as the speaker in the tale of how the kid at the mike enjoyed sharing a bunk with the guest of honor three summers ago.

- *Candle lighting.* This ceremony, wherein the young host calls up special family members and friends to light a candle in honor of the day, can be a delight, especially if the host has written endearing tributes to those people. Or it can be horrible as all of the child's cohorts (camp friends, church friends, temple friends, school friends) storm up in symphony and tussle over who gets to stand closest to the host and candle. There's a tightrope to walk here between brevity and inclusivity. I'd encourage your child to limit the list to family members and let friends enjoy the ceremony by proxy.

Bar and Bat Mitzvahs

We've been saving for her bat mitzvah since she was born. We saved $15,000. The DJs and balloon people, it's unbelievable. People are asking, "What's her theme?" Then I'm sitting with my mom on the couch last night and she's getting teary-eyed, and she says, "You haven't even asked me about inviting my friends." . . . I don't want to invest my body and soul in this, I don't agree with it. It's been very hard.   Dina, mother of a seventh-grade girl

When I had my bat mitzvah, it was an incredibly positive experience— which was strange because I hated pretty much every minute of Hebrew school. It was a rite of passage in the best possible way and I don't think it occurred to my parents to have a fancy theme party. Fast-forward five years later to my brother's bar mitzvah. By this time, Perfect Parent World had gotten to my parents. I'll never forget the ice sculptures at the food stations and the enormous band.

As an educator, I have watched parents compete with each other through these parties to absurd levels. I have also watched non-Jewish parents observe this competition with mixed horror and disbelief. And as a Jewish person, it deeply pains me to know that this competition, narcissism, and display of wealth often provide the first and most enduring image non-Jews have of Judaism.

Many parents—both Jewish and not—have told me that they abhor the excessive amount of money spent on lavish bar and bat mitzvahs but feel uncomfortable speaking up about their feelings. Non-Jews especially are terrified to say anything, lest they be considered insensitive or anti-Semitic.

I hope this chapter has convinced you that teaching your child how to give and attend parties with social savvy isn't a trivial issue. Parties are invaluable training grounds for putting values into action and for teaching kids that you can have a lot of fun even when limits have been set. Your child will need these skills—as will you—when the punch bowl gets replaced by a keg, when an illicit cigarette becomes a joint, when a friendly game of cards turns into strip poker. As kids grow up, parties become one

ON THE BIMA: HANDLING BAR AND BAT MITZVAHS

Tom Weiner has been a rabbi for twenty-one years, most recently at Congregation Kol Ami in White Plains, New York. He shared his thoughts on how to prepare yourself and your child for bar and bat mitzvahs.

PLANNING THE PARTY

You want that day to be a reflection of who you are as a family—the best possible reflection of your values and of Jewish values. The best time to begin thinking about it as a family is third or fourth grade, before it's an immediate issue. People are often very conflicted. Out of love, they don't want their child to feel less than, different, left out, or less loved, so for all of those complicated but wrong reasons, they tend to give in and throw these big blowouts.

Twenty years down the road, when somebody mentions this day, what do you think your primary memories will be? If your child supposes that he'll think with pride of the moment when he stood on the *bima* and read from the Torah, the beauty of having his grandparents bless him, the pride on your faces, or the sense of accomplishment he felt that he did something he first thought was impossible, then you're doing the right thing. If your child says that what he thinks he'll remember best is the Shirelles singing in your backyard in a big white tent or that the captain of the *Queen Elizabeth II* let him take the wheel of the ship during the bar mitzvah party, then something's wrong.

You don't have to pick a theme. The theme is Shabbat or bat mitzvah. It doesn't need to have an additional theme of the New York Knicks with four members of the team showing up. I don't know how *Star Wars,* NASCAR, or princess-for-a-day enhances in any positive way what's already taking place.

If you opt for a more elaborate celebration, remember: You are in control of this day. Not the child's friends, not the party planner, not the band leader, not the photographer. Sometimes professionals will use some pretty serious high-pressure tactics and you have to keep reminding yourself that you hired them and you can tell them to do what you want and not do what you don't want.

A bar or bat mitzvah is really a very simple, modest thing. Before you're thirteen, there are a lot of Jewish responsibilities you don't have because you're a child. The bar or bat mitzvah is a basic way of saying, "We're going to let you take this first step into adulthood of reading the Torah before the community, a privilege not open to children. We're going to trust you with this significant responsibility. May it be the first of many as you grow into adulthood." You're creating the beginning of something, a vessel that the young person has the rest of his or her life to fill meaningfully or not. We tend to treat these occasions like retirement parties, but the bar or bat mitzvah is really more like your child's first day on the job.

WHAT KIND OF GIFTS ARE APPROPRIATE?

You can give a kid a GameBoy that will be immediately exciting, then tossed away and meaningless in a few months. Or you can give that child an incredible book or piece of art or Judaica that at the moment they might not be totally thrilled with, but which in twenty or thirty years will call up a meaningful memory of your relationship and that day.

WHOM SHOULD FAMILIES INVITE?

The bar or bat mitzvah should not be used as an extension of Mom or Dad's professional life. Sometimes there's a large group of clients or associates whom the kid doesn't even know. That also puts extra pressure on the parents to have their work faces on as opposed to thoroughly celebrating with their child and loved ones.

Sometimes kids' invitations are a reflection of the worst aspects of social pressure in school. Err on the side of inclusion. If you have a class of twenty-four kids, don't invite twenty-two of them—that's just hurtful and wrong and antithetical to what the day is about.

ANY FINAL WORDS FOR PARENTS?

This launching should be modest, with a certain amount of humility and trepidation for entering into the responsibilities of Jewish adulthood. The bar or bat mitzvah is a wonderful opportunity to tell your child publicly how much you love him or her, to help your child build self-esteem and master something new and big and scary. A celebration afterward is more than appropriate, because the kid's worked hard and deserves it, but the message should be: "We love you, you're terrific. *Now* what are you going to do?"

of the prime ways they test-drive newfound interests in alcohol, illicit drugs, and se—

You know, let's wait to discuss those in the next chapter.

Sex, Drugs, and Rock 'n' Roll

Just Say, Oh No!

It's early Sunday afternoon when the phone rings. The voice on the other end of the line is so angry and upset you can barely make out what the person is saying.

KAREN: *Marlene? This is Karen, Michelle's mother.*

YOU: *Hi there. What's up?*

KAREN: *Are you aware of what happened at your house last night?*

YOU (hesitantly): *Sure, the kids came over and watched movies. Dan and I were here the whole time.*

KAREN: *Really? That's hard to believe from what Michelle just told me.*

YOU (starting to get a little annoyed): *I'm sorry?*

KAREN: *Michelle was so upset about what happened, we could barely get it out of her.*

YOU: *Karen, can you just tell me? Because I have no idea what you're talking about.*

KAREN: *While you were somewhere in the house, the kids were drinking and smoking pot. Apparently your children cut out the seat of a recliner so they could hold beer in it. Michelle doesn't drink, so she walked into another room, and I can't even bring myself to say what Michelle saw when she walked in on some boys and girls there.*

YOU: *What? I—I—*

KAREN: *How could you let this happen under your own roof? What do you plan on doing about it? I think the other parents need to be told immediately. We thought we could trust you—what kind of parents let their kids do this?*

When I hear parents have these conversations (which I do—usually in very uncomfortable emergency parent meetings after a party gets completely out of hand), I feel terrible for every parent in that room. They're all there because they're scared for their children's safety, and this should be a time when parents come together—but they don't. Why do these situations so often end up with the parents alienated from one another or feeling unfairly judged?

Karen has good reason to be angry and upset. But as understandable as her reaction is, it does more harm than good. There are no foolproof ways to guarantee that your child will handle partying responsibly. Frankly, most of us learned to party responsibly by making a lot of mistakes. Chances are there's one type of alcohol you can't stand to even smell now because your body still remembers an unfortunate interaction with it.

Adolescence is about trying new things, exploring, making mistakes, learning, and moving on. In the process, our kids learn what their limits are and which friends will truly stick by them. Too many of us ask our kids to do the impossible: We want them to go through that normal process of trial and error for everything *except* alcohol, other intoxicants, and sexual activity, which many adolescents believe fall into the category of normal experimental behavior. As parents, we're so worried about the short- and long-term consequences of such experimentation that somehow our dialogue—with our kids, with other parents—never gets beyond a superficial politically correct discussion.

In this chapter, I'll discuss these topics and help you find some ways to talk about them more openly. Since we tend to have unique concerns about drinking, doing drugs, and sex, I'll consider each subject in turn. However, it can sometimes be a little artificial to separate these concerns because you'll often want to use a similar approach when you talk to your child and other adults about them. Here are some general considerations to keep in mind:

- There are a lot of teens who don't drink, do drugs, or have any kind of sex before they're eighteen.

- Now that I've said that, don't assume I'm talking about your child.
- It's possible for a child to go to a party and not drink or do drugs. Actually, these kids are very valuable commodities at parties because they can be designated drivers.
- If your kid doesn't like big groups, he'll be less likely to have or go to the parties that worry you so much. In contrast, if your kid loves to be in groups . . .
- It's possible for a kid—your kid—to drink or do drugs and not run off the rails. You may have even had this experience yourself as a teen. Not only is this not reassuring, but paradoxically, it might make you even more confused about policing your child.

Having "the Conversation"

Do your kids know where you stand about drinking, drugs, and sex? Have you had the Conversation with them? No, not the one about where babies come from, although I hope that you started having that conversation with your child when he or she was in elementary school and that you have returned to it regularly. I'm talking about the conversation in which you communicate your values about drinking, drugs, and sex. It's a conversation you'll have in various depths at various stages of your child's life, ideally beginning before your child has to deal with these issues—not when you find the homemade bong in his or her closet. It's where you talk about your beliefs and expectations, set ground rules for behavior, and lay out the consequences for violations of those rules.

Let's talk about the alcohol-and-drugs part of this conversation first and then talk about sex. Parents are freaked about how to have this first conversation for a couple of reasons. Here are the questions I field most often.

Should I Tell My Children if I Drank or Did Drugs?

I don't think you should lie to your kids, although there are people whose opinion I respect a great deal (both as professionals and parents) who disagree with me. However, I think it's better to decline to answer the question or limit how much you tell. You're allowed to say you consider it your private business, just as you might choose not to talk about other personal issues, such as your sex life. You don't have to share everything with your child and make it a Hallmark moment.

Most parents fear that if they admit their previous experiences yet say that they think alcohol and drugs are bad, they'll lose all credibility; after all, they're still alive to tell the tale. Give your child some credit. Just because you're standing in front of him in one piece doesn't mean he won't understand if you share experiences where you made mistakes and learned from them. Have you watched people you know struggle with alcohol or drugs? How did that change your relationship with them? Did you ever find yourself in dangerous situations or with people you didn't know well or trust because of drugs or alcohol? Many parents with whom I've spoken relate their experiences (sometimes heavily edited) to their kids while emphasizing that drugs are much more potent than in their day, that they had some horrific experiences because of drinking and drugs or had good friends who did, and that they've rethought their views on drinking and drugs from an older, wiser perspective.

How Can I Forbid My Child to Drink or Do Drugs if I Did Them? Isn't That Being Hypocritical?

No, it's being a parent.

From the conversations I've had with many parents, I'd think that most of you were partying constantly when you were young. Many parents admit to me with a giggle and a wink that they once did drugs—implying that they were huge partyers when they were younger. I suspect that there's a small part of these parents that wants to seem hip to their kids. You might go to bed at 9 p.m. with a newspaper on your chest now, but there was a time when you were cool. If you're one of these parents, the danger is that your desire to seem cool will blur the boundaries between you and your child. You might find yourself telling your child more than he or she needs to know, which could make it harder to enforce discipline if your kid breaks the rules you've established.

I think many of us are profoundly ambivalent about discussing the subject with our kids because we're not entirely sure where we stand. No, we don't want our kids running out and getting drunk or wasted, but we can't quite find it in ourselves to see this kind of experimentation as an out-and-out evil. Perhaps we ourselves dabbled and came through it unharmed. Perhaps we privately (or even publicly) believe that pot should be legalized, or that it might not be such a terrible thing to let our kids get rip-roaring drunk and sick to their stomachs so they'll "get it out of their system." Or perhaps we've sat down with our teenagers and watched a movie with drugs and drinking in it and found ourselves belly-laughing because it's genuinely funny. In the next instant, we're consumed with guilt: The movie makes drinking and drugging look like tons of fun, and isn't laughing along a kind of tacit admission that we did the same kind of thing ourselves, because how else would we know to scream with laughter as the characters on the screen have an attack of the munchies? Isn't enjoying that movie an endorsement—even an encouragement—of this kind of behavior?

You might choose to admit your ambivalence when you talk about this stuff with your child. Here's how one mother explained the issue to her son:

> *"There's the real world and the ideal world. In my ideal world, the drinking age would be eighteen, the way it was when I was your age. But it's not. I personally think it's ridiculous to put people in prison for smoking pot, but I don't make the laws. I might not agree with the school's zero-tolerance policy for drinking and drugs, but tough. We've explained the law and the school's rules to you thoroughly. If you're so lazy, stupid, or irresponsible as to break them and you get caught, you're gonna swing. This is something I really need you to get. If you violate these rules, there will be serious consequences, and Dad and I won't be able to get you out of them. And even if we could, we wouldn't. It's all on you now: You have to make smart choices when we're not around."*

Recognizing your ambivalence is an opportunity for you to clarify—first to yourself, then to your child—what your values about alcohol and drugs really are. We've all had experiences where our actions didn't reflect our values. This is a chance to sort out why and help your child understand your position.

What if I Mess Up the Conversation?

Give yourself the right to make mistakes. These conversations are hard. For many reasons, you might not be as articulate as you'd like when you talk to your kids about drinking, drugs, and sex. Don't worry about it. Some parents think that if they say something wrong during the Conversation, their child is doomed. When I ask parents why they're so scared, they usually don't have a concrete answer. Do they think that if they do it wrong, their child will become an alcoholic or a drug addict? You'll be successful if you communicate the following:

- Your child can come to you (or another adult ally) for help.
- Your child can make mistakes and learn from them.
- Your child's actions have consequences—and you'll enforce those consequences or allow others to enforce them.

You don't need to have the full-blown talk at every turn, but do take advantage of opportunities as they naturally arise. If your child sees someone get drunk at an adult party—even if it's a member of the family—don't shy away from the resulting conversation. How did this person behave? How did his or her drunkenness affect others?

If your position is that drinking, drugs, and sex are completely wrong and strictly forbidden, then please know that your policy will make it almost impossible for your child to ask for your help if he or she breaks your rules. Please make sure that your child understands that even though you take an absolute stance against alcohol, drugs, and sex, your love for him or her is unconditional. Make sure your child has another ally to go to if the need arises.

Having the Conversation with Other Parents

If we want other parents to respect our point of view and help us enforce the boundaries we've set for our child, we have to communicate our values. Afraid you'll sound prissy, stuck up, superior, old-fashioned? Get over it.

The rules of Perfect Parent World affect our ability to guide our teenagers safely and wisely through the hazards of sex and drugs because they stop us from reaching out to one another lest others see us as lousy parents with out-of-control kids. Our position in the social pecking order can make it hard for us to stand up to a Queen Bee Mom or Kingpin Dad, or take a Wannabe or Invisible seriously when that parent is trying to alert us to a problem with our child. We can have filters in place that allow us to replace a wise judgment of the situation with a judgment of someone else's parenting abilities. And when we're talking about drinking, drugs, and sex, we have to multiply the degree of difficulty.

Let's start breaking all this down, while first admitting that we may be genuinely confused about the right position to hold and how to communicate that to our kids and other parents.

I don't think there's a more contentious debate among parents than what the rules should be when it comes to teens drinking—and by extension experimenting with drugs and sex. Most parents publicly embrace one of two basic approaches. The first camp reasons something like this: "The kids are going to drink anyway, so they might as well be safe while they do it. I'd rather have them drink under my roof, where I can keep my eye on them. It's naive to think kids won't drink, and if they're doing it out of the house, then they'll be more likely to drink and drive. It's the kids who have to hide it who drink irresponsibly and get into trouble."

The opposing camp says: "Underage drinking is illegal. That's all there is to it. I'm not condoning it, and any parent who does condone it is irresponsible and can't say no to their kid."

If You're an Under-My-Roof Parent

It's a fact that many young people will drink and experiment with drugs. Like the parents I described at the beginning of this chapter, many parents who let their children drink under their roof are well-intentioned. The trouble is that, more often than not, the parents I've known who have this policy aren't able to hold their ground with their kids. It's the kids who end up in control of the house, not the parents.

One of our students had a mother who really wanted to be the popular mom. He told me that he came into his living room during a party

to see his mother upside down, held up by his friends, drinking from
the keg.   Megan, high school principal

Another problem with the under-my-roof philosophy is that it assumes that if a parent is in the house, kids won't abuse alcohol or drugs (or engage in sexual activity). Likewise, it assumes that if parents aren't in the house, kids will run amok. In fact, although it's good to have an adult in the house, it isn't a guarantee that bad stuff won't happen. In spite of your best efforts to supervise the kids, you can be distracted or fall asleep. Seriously, if you go to bed at 10:30, as I do, you're not the man or woman for the job. Remember that the cool kids don't show up at any party or get-together until 10 or 11 p.m. at the *earliest*—which is exactly when most parents go to sleep. Coincidence? I think not. A very wise parent once told me, "Nothing good happens after midnight." She had a point.

Let's be clear: All the kids in the grade, school, and often the neighboring schools know which parents allow drinking in their house. These are the houses where you can get away with stuff. It's not as if the kids go to these places thinking, "Wow, this parent really respects me and wants me to be safe, so they're allowing me to drink. For sure, I'll do so responsibly." They're much more likely to think: "Excellent! We have a place to go where we can do whatever we want and no one will bother us!"

I honestly believe these permissive parents are trying to be responsible. Contrary to what other parents may think and say, they don't want their children to be alcoholics. They're understandably confused, and because it's so difficult to have an honest conversation on this topic with other parents, they don't have the opportunity to think through their feelings and consequences of their actions.

If You're a Zero-Tolerance Parent

The strict zero-tolerance parents don't have it any easier. I've heard from many teens that their parents' absolute stance has driven their drinking activity underground—or into cars, which is exactly where we don't want it to be. These kids learn the benefits of sneakiness—and they learn that they can't talk out their confusion with their parents lest they get punished.

If you're a parent with this philosophy, you might feel that you have no choice but to stand firm behind the law and school rules. You don't want to condone illegal activity, and you don't want to send your kids down a slippery slope at a time in their lives when their judgment is pretty wobbly. At the same time you might worry that your absolutism will come across to your kids—and, let's face it, to other parents—as a lack of faith in your kids' judgment or an inability or unwillingness to grapple with the realities of kids' social lives.

If You Don't Know Where You Stand

I believe most parents fall into a sort of no-man's-land between the zero-tolerance and the only-under-my-roof parents, although they usually won't admit it in public. This silent majority is scared to death to admit their ambivalence because they don't want to be judged as uptight by the first group or as too lenient by the second. But if they did admit it, they might describe their viewpoint as something like this: "Many of us grew up when the legal drinking age was eighteen. I wish it still was; you'd have a shot at teaching your kids to drink responsibly while they're still living with you. Instead, we don't teach them and then they go off to college and get themselves into all kinds of trouble. That makes no sense to me. I'm genuinely confused; part of me wants them to make their mistakes while they're still at home, but part of me wants to say, 'I might not agree with the law, but you still have to respect it.' I have no idea what to do."

The parents who are most vocal about their opinions are generally the ones who are absolutely dead set against drinking. I've found, however, that some parents who claim to have a zero-tolerance policy let their kids have an occasional glass of wine at dinner, a sip of champagne on New Year's Eve, or even a little bit of a margarita on a family vacation. They don't see any contradiction between their public stance and their actions. Frankly, I don't have a problem with this; I don't think these parents are being hypocritical or sending the wrong message. When I press them to articulate their views, they generally stumble around before admitting that what they really take a hard line on is teens drinking irresponsibly.

Both the zero-tolerance and the drink-only-under-my-roof parents have valid points, but that's not really the issue. What matters is that parents on opposing sides of this debate can't seem to talk to one another. They're afraid to say what they really think because they worry other parents will judge them. And they're right.

> *Parents who forbid their children to drink can be very harsh on the parents who don't because they make the assumption that these parents are irresponsible and haven't talked to their children about alcohol.* Nadene, counselor

> *I talk to our parents all the time about drinking and initially we always have a problem that no matter what the parents say, it's always about their belief and anything different from that is suspect—not different, suspect.* Wilma, high school principal

The truth is that parents of both sides of the issue will have kids who'll make very poor choices, and then people on the opposing side will use our children's experience as proof that their side is right and the other side is wrong—no matter what side they're on. That's one of the reasons why we can be embarrassed and won't want to tell our friends—even though they're probably going through the same thing with their kids. All of this parental judgment keeps parents from closing ranks and makes it that much easier for teens to take advantage of the situation.

TYPICAL PROBLEMS PARENTS ENCOUNTER

Problem: You Don't Know How to Handle the "People in Europe" Issue

"People in Europe drink wine during meals and their kids aren't alcoholics." You might have heard other people say this and you might believe it yourself—or your kid might have even advanced the argument. You shouldn't have to be European (although it does give you a pass) to admit you like to have wine at dinner—with your children present. Feel free to stand up and admit that you're one of those folks who have a glass of something at dinner. I'm one of those people. I personally believe that kids benefit from seeing parents drink responsibly—not to get drunk, not "because I had such a horrible day," not out of force of habit, but to enhance a meal or social occasion.

Should you allow your child a little glass as well? I know plenty of families who do so because it's consistent with their values, and I don't think the police are waiting outside their door, but do be aware that there will always be some teens who abuse the privilege. And what if your teen has a guest over for dinner—is it okay for you to serve the guest as well? Out of respect for the other child's parents, I say no, unless you've checked with them to see that they don't mind. Just discuss it with your child beforehand so that you don't have to have an awkward conversation when the friend is at your table. And if your child says your decision to refuse to serve his or her friend is illogical or hypocritical, that's okay—*it's still your decision to make*. What you don't want to happen is for the friend to come home and tell his parents how cool you are because you let him drink wine at dinner.

Problem: Should I Call the Other Parents if I Catch My Child and His Friends Drunk or Stoned?

Well, wouldn't you want another parent in your situation to call you? Of course you would, and of course you should call the other parents. Before you do, however, unless someone's life is in immediate danger, collect yourself and get your strategy together. The more calm and collected you are, the better you'll handle the situation.

Some kids will try to escape out a window or back door, so if you can, take a roll call before you announce yourself to the kids, and note any escapees. Tell the kids that you'll be phoning other parents. Your child and her friends may beg and whine: "You don't understand! My parents will kill me!" Don't be deterred. It was your child's choice to drink or do drugs in your house, you said it was against the rules, and the decision to break your rules has consequences.

If you caught the kids defying your rules under your own roof, it might be especially difficult to make this call, since you might find yourself on the receiving end of some unpleasant responses from the other parents, especially if they're Queen Bee Moms or Kingpin Dads. ("How could you fall asleep knowing the kids were having a party?" "I don't know if we can trust our kid to be under your roof again." "We don't want our kid hanging out with your kid anymore.") Face the music and make the phone call.

How and when you call the other parents is important. In my best-case scenario, you call the other parents before you "catch" the kids red-handed. You describe what happened, lay out the consequences for your child (don't say anything about how you feel the other kids should be punished; that's not your responsibility), and explain the additional actions you'll be taking ("I'm calling all the parents involved").

YOU: *Hi, Anne—it's Ross. Look, I need to talk to you. The boys came over after school and are hanging out in the family room downstairs. I just walked by and they're drinking. They don't know that I know yet—I wanted to call you and the other parents first. So could you come over? Then when the kids are sober I would like the parents to meet together with all the kids—maybe tomorrow night, my house? We can talk about it more later, but I just really want to present a united front to them.*

After you've alerted the other parents, go get the kids and bring them into the kitchen or living room together—somewhere they can look at each other and be miserable but not conspire to divide and conquer the parents. For that reason, don't leave the kids alone in the room without a responsible adult present. Tell the kids that you've caught them, that you'll discuss consequences with your child separately, and that you've alerted the other parents.

In private, discuss with your child the consequences for violating your rules, which also meant a violation of your trust.

Problem: The Other Parents Punish the Infraction Differently

Your kid and their kid get caught—drinking, drugging, whatever. What if you find out that the other parents are dealing with it in a completely different way? Most parents I meet worry about what to do when other parents are more lenient than they are. Suppose you ground your child for a month while the other parents simply warn their child not to do it again? And suppose their child e-mails your child two seconds after that conversation and says, "Dude, I totally got off!" So what? You can't control how other people discipline their children, but you do have control of three crucial issues:

1. What you communicate to the other parents. By explaining the consequences you're imposing for your child, you're communicating the seriousness with which you take the matter.

2. What you communicate to your child. Explain that what you saw is against the rules. Explain what you want instead. Explain the punishment. Affirm that you love your child. If your child's friend has received a different punishment, explain that that won't in any way change how you're handling things. If your child objects, let him or her rant and stand your ground.

3. What you communicate to your child's friend. Say everything to the friend that you've said to your own child, but don't impose a punishment; that's for the other parents to do. Explain what he or she did that you didn't like. Explain what you want instead and what you expect when he or she is under your roof and with your child. If you feel that this kid is a good friend and respects what you're saying, affirm that he or she is still welcome in your house ("Mark, I love having you around the house, but you have to follow my rules, just as Will does"). If you don't feel that this kid will respect you and your demands, feel free to say the following:

YOU: *Mark, I've told you what I need you to do if I'm going to feel comfortable having you in my house, but I'm not feeling like you're getting what I'm saying. And I know that your parents have chosen to punish you less severely than I'm punishing Will.* (Mark protests with some form of "No, it's cool, I get it!" Wait until he's finished.) *I want you to be absolutely clear about where I stand. When you're in my house, I think of you as my kid—which means I demand the same of you as I do my kid. If you act irresponsibly again and I catch you, I'll have no alternative but to ask you to leave until you can earn my trust back. I don't want that to happen, but I have to feel that you're taking my rules seriously and that you care about Will's welfare.*

While we're on the subject—and this goes for both of you—if you act irresponsibly outside of this house and hurt yourselves, each other, or other people, I will be extremely disappointed in both of you. Will, as my child, you also have the added burden that I will hold you fully accountable and punish you accordingly.

If the other parents give their child a lame punishment, you should be worried. Most likely that child's risky behavior will escalate and there's a very good chance he could bring your child down with him. I wouldn't outright forbid your kid to hang out with him—that's likely to encourage sneaking around behind your back—but I would have a conversation with your son about the circumstances under which he would agree to leave Mark's presence immediately and get help. For example, your child should agree not to hang around another kid who's involved in:

- Drugs and alcohol
- Vandalism
- Other self-destructive behavior, such as jumping off roofs or other high places (I'm not kidding), drinking and driving, street racing, etc.
- Bullying (ask your child if he thinks this is possible and if so, what would it look like)

LANDMINE!

Don't use the word *bullying* in talking with your kids. Say, "Could he do something to someone where you think you should intervene?"

Problem: Should You Let Your Kid Have a Party?

There's a very fuzzy line between "having a few people over" a get-together, and a party, and many kids try to game the system by insisting that they're not having a party, they're "just hanging out." What kids call it is immaterial, because things can spiral out of control whatever the size of the gathering.

Suppose your child wants to have a party before the prom. You figure this is a great chance to take pictures of everyone in their finery and keep a close eye on things. You might not be able to control what happens at the prom—you're not naive, you've heard the stories—but you can run a tight ship with all the kids at your house.

Or can you? You should know that most kids view pre-parties as more fun than the actual prom and will work overtime to sneak in some drinking or drugging so that by the time they get to the prom they're drunk or high enough to chase away their social jitters. In fact, they may really go at it, since a high tolerance for alcohol and drugs gets big points in Girl World and Boy World. You'd be hard pressed to find a high school student who isn't well aware of the free availability of alcohol, pot, and drugs such as crystal meth or the prescriptions in so many families' medicine cabinets. How will you prepare yourself and your child?

If you're a parent who thinks it's better to have the kids drinking in the safety of your house, here are some things you should realize. First, if you're hosting a party and there's going to be alcohol, you're in effect hosting a sleepover, because you don't want those kids drinking and driving. It's best to have a lot of sleeping bags, unless you've arranged for parents to pick up their kids at the appointed hour. If there are girls and boys invited, that means you're agreeing to a coed sleepover. Are you okay with that? Will the girls be sleeping in one room and the boys in another? How will you enforce that, and what will you do if they disregard the sleeping arrangements? Do the other parents know about your plan? Are they okay with it, too?

Do you have any medications, relaxants, or stimulants (for example, diet pills, Xanax, Valium, Vicodin, Percocet) in your medicine cabinet that a motivated teen could use to enhance his or her inebriated state? If you do, take them out of your house before the party or put them in a safe (unless you plan to stand in front of the medicine cabinet during the entire party, which isn't a good idea because then you can't supervise the kids).

Whether the sleepover is single sex or coed, I can almost guarantee that there will be some drama in the wee hours of the morning when one of the girls will absolutely insist that she has to leave *immediately*. If you're lucky, a girl who's had too much to drink won't drive herself home.

But unfortunately, one of her less-inebriated-but-still-drunk friends will probably offer to drive her home—and you'll have a drunk teen behind the wheel. Perhaps you've anticipated this and told the kids that you'll drive anyone home at any time. But it's 3 a.m. when the drama hits—do you really think they're going to wake you? I wouldn't count on it.

One more reminder: Serving alcohol to underage teens isn't just unwise, it's illegal. And as if what happens under your roof isn't trouble enough, you could be held liable for any harm or injury they cause or incur.

Problem: You're Afraid Other Parents Are Going to Have a Party and Serve Alcohol to Underage Kids

What should you do? Just straight up ask them. I don't care if your child kicks and screams; it's your job to ask some basic questions of the parents at any house where there's going to be a party. You have a right to know whether adults will be present, whether they're inviting a few kids or it's a big blowout, whether there's a curfew planned, and what the refreshments and entertainment will be ("I just wanted to check in with you about the party. Will you be home for it? Do you plan on having alcohol at the party? No? Great! My kid is really looking forward to going and we'll see you there"). If the parents say, "Well, yes, we'll be supplying beer, but we'll be here," don't interrupt them. If your rule is that your kid can't go to a party with alcohol, then your kid isn't going to the party. Tell the parents that you don't allow your child to go to parties with alcohol, so thanks for the invitation, you really appreciate it, but your child won't be attending. You don't need to make the other parents feel like fools. Your decision is sufficient. I know that you might worry that your child will be ostracized for not going to the "cool" parties. If your child has other opportunities for socializing (sports, drama, school clubs), he or she will be fine. What's more important is that you're putting your values into action.

Problem: You Don't Trust the Parents of Your Child's Friend

It's possible that your child will have a friend who has a genuinely irresponsible parent. It's possible that the other parent has an alcohol or drug problem. And I'm not only talking about a guy in his underwear drinking a twelve-pack in front of the TV. What about a mom who's wasted on Xanax? What do you do?

This was actually a situation I experienced with one of my closest friends in middle school, and it was scary—but her house was also the place where we wanted to hang out the most because her parents gave us the most freedom. Her mom and dad were both alcoholics and the air would crackle with tension when her dad came home. Within moments they were screaming and throwing things at each other. I didn't tell my parents, who didn't know my friend's parents well enough to see it for themselves. If you find yourself harboring similar concerns about her friend's parents, sit her down and discuss it:

YOU: *Honey, I need to talk to you about something and it's not about you. Now that you're getting older and spending more time at friends' houses, I want you to know that I really like your friends but there may come a time when maybe one of your friends has a difficult home situation. Maybe a parent will express their anger or frustration in a way that makes you feel uncomfortable. Maybe a parent will act strangely because they drink alcohol irresponsibly or take other drugs. I want to be clear that I'm not talking about any parent we know specifically; I just want you to be prepared if you're ever in this situation. You can talk to me about it and together we'll figure out the best thing to do.*

Sometimes children in these homes get so fed up with their parents that they'll do anything (including getting into trouble themselves) to get help from other adults.

One of our ninth graders came to a school dance drunk, so we called the parents—and his dad was a board member. Both parents came to the school drunk and the dad hit the kid. We called Child Protective Services and his older brother picked him up. The next week the student told me that he had come to school drunk on purpose so that the school would call his parents and they would see what he was dealing with at home.   Malcolm, high school principal

Problem: You Want to Go Out of Town.
Can You Trust Your Kids?

If you have older teens and you want or need to go out of town overnight or for a weekend, I wouldn't trust your children entirely. Help them out. Ask your neighbors to drop by around 11 p.m. Tell them not to knock, just walk right in and go to the kitchen or out back (because that's where the alcohol will be) or where the best TV in the house is (because that's where the kids will be hanging out). If you believe in full disclosure, tell your kids before you leave that you've told all the neighbors that you'll be out of town and that they have authority to come into the house without knocking whenever they please. Talk to your neighbors about what you want them to do if they walk into your house and see the kids out of control. Call you first? Call the police right away?

Now you have to pick a calm neighbor—someone who likes teens, isn't going to freak out, and can be a leader in a chaotic situation. This person should have no problem yelling at your kids or busting the party up—but his or her general attitude can't be hostile and the person shouldn't be a power freak. Don't assume it has to be a dad. Size helps, but a steely-eyed, determined mom can make any kid whimper.

I'm assuming that you have at least one neighbor you can count on to be a surrogate parent while you're gone. If you don't yet have this kind of relationship with any of your neighbors, I hope you'll work to develop it. The reason why I love my neighborhood is because I have these kinds of neighbors. I know that if any of my neighbors saw my children doing something dangerous or something they know I wouldn't approve of, they'll put a stop to it. My go-to guy in this situation is Joel, father of Dean and Grant. He's six foot four with a shaved head and a beard, and he can be seriously scary if he wants to be.

If my sons ever had a party while my husband and I were gone, Joel would unhesitatingly walk right into my house and shut it down—and even the most obnoxious guys would be terrified. Frankly, his wife, Lisa, would be pretty tough in that situation, too. That's peace of mind that an alarm system can't give you.

I think it's also a good idea to call the parents of your child's closest friends and tell them you're going out of town. Ask if the kids can hang out at their house while you're away, or ask that they keep their antennae up if the kids go out.

If you know that your child doesn't have the maturity to resist a party, don't put temptation in his or her way. Have a relative or trusted friend stay in the house while you're gone, or ship the kids off somewhere.

> *I wouldn't go out of town and leave my kids at home. I really don't trust them. I think they're good kids and usually make good decisions, but I also know that that they lie to me and pull the wool over my eyes. There's no one more skilled and manipulative than my girls. Every night when they come in I meet them at the door. I'm talking to them and looking at their eyes. I'm smelling their breath. I wouldn't even leave the house when the kids were in college. If they knew we were out of town, they would come back home and have a party of biblical proportions.* Cameron, father of teen girls

> *We had friends whose daughter had a huge party while they were away. As a consequence, they took away their daughter's driver's license for six months. Her mom asked her, "Was it worth it? You waited so long to get your license, and now you can't drive for six months because you disobeyed us." She said, "Yeah, it was totally worth it, because if my friends found out you were out of town and I didn't have a party, I would have totally lost face."* Maureen, mother of teens

Of course, many kids would never dream of hosting a party when their parents are away. Others might invite a few friends over to watch a movie, but then word gets out and suddenly a hundred of that kid's close personal friends are knocking on the door. Or maybe he or she isn't planning any kind of get-together, but the herd just descends because kids have a sixth sense that way.

And how's your sixth sense? Is there any way to tell that your child is planning a party for while you're gone? Here are a few warning signs:

- She's too nice to you, a little too helpful.
- She asks about your schedule (i.e., when you won't be around) with studied nonchalance.

- If you're going out of town, her friends may call more than usual the night before you leave. You'll be at a disadvantage if your child has a cell phone, since her friends can call to discuss party plans without you having a clue. They can also do it by e-mail. In fact, this is one of the rare times when I think you should spy on her e-mail and instant messaging. A parent's out-of-town trip can be too tempting for even the most honest, upstanding kid.

Let's say you've come back home. You walk into your house and your parental antennae go up, but you don't see obvious signs of anything funny. How can you tell if your kid had a party? Here's what I would look for:

- The pantry, freezer, and fridge are empty—maybe there's some frozen diet entrées, but that's it.
- As you pick up over the next few days, you find mysterious items of clothing around the house.
- The outside of your house is littered with cigarette butts—and you don't smoke.
- The place reeks of air freshener.
- The house is cleaner than when you left it; the carpets are so recently vacuumed that you can see the vacuum marks and all the trash cans in the house are empty. (You can also check your outdoor garbage cans for signs, but a smart kid will put the incriminating evidence in the neighbor's trash—especially the neighbors they like the least.)
- There's not one roll of toilet paper in the house.
- Your child is very nice to you.

Problem: You Think You Caught Your Kid, but You're Not Sure

Of course you want to believe that you have the kind of relationship with your child in which he or she will always tell you the truth. Some parents were outraged when I suggested in *Queen Bees & Wannabes* that their daughters might not always be little angels (I believe my exact words were "Your daughter is a liar and a sneak"). However, it's a reality that some kids lie to their parents at some point. Sometimes it's just to protect their sense of privacy, not necessarily to deceive. But regardless of motive, most teenagers stick to what they see as the fair ground rules of lying:

- Every lie is based on a grain of truth. Your child will use this truth-let later if he or she is caught and will hang on to it for dear life. That's why kids can be so self-righteous when they're caught. From their point of view, the one little truth they told trumps the ten lies they wrapped around it. And if your kid is angry with you about something, that justifies the fib in his or her mind.
- A smart teen will wrap a fib in so many details that you'll get confused. That's why, if you suspect your child is lying, you have to talk to the parent who's hosting the party or any other adult who will be present.
- Your child will offer an innocent, bare-bones description of an upcoming event at a time when you're too exhausted or distracted to concentrate on the conversation. Later your teen can plausibly claim, "I told you I'd be at so-and-so's house—you just didn't listen!"
- Your child's friends will back up his or her story. Since your child is using this strategy, so should you. That's why you have to talk to the other parents.

It's precisely because parents need to rely on one another that it's so important for all of us to table our filters and create a more supportive network. We need the kind of relationships that will make it easier for us to call one another up and ask, "I think my son may have had a party at the house while we were gone. Did you hear anything from your daughter?" "I heard a bunch of kids got drunk in the woods behind the school—do you know anything about it?" We've got to hope that other parents will have the courage to let us know if they see our kids stepping out of line, and we have to have that same courage to report their kids' bad behavior to them—not out of a sense of superiority but out of a sense of community.

Let's Talk About S-S-S-S-e-x

Why do we fumble so much when it comes to this subject? One of the best explanations I've read comes from Justin Richardson and Mark Schuster, authors of the wonderful *Everything You Never Wanted Your Child to Know About Sex (But Were Afraid They'd Ask)*, a book I recommend to every parent:

> *Our hunch is that by the time you finished high school, you felt you knew more about sex than your parents knew. You talked more about sex than they did. And you believed, with a little luck, that you would have more sex than they had. . . . When it came to sex, you were cooler.*
>
> *And then you had a son. Or a daughter . . .*
>
> *As it turns out, the sexual fumblings of adolescents look a teensy bit different when viewed from the other end of the kitchen table, even to someone who once had a tube top. Or pot plants growing in his dorm room.*

I hope you've managed to have several conversations with your younger child about the basics of sex—not only the mechanics but also emotional and ethical considerations. As your child gets older, you'll need to build on those discussions. Like it or not, your child is going to become sexually active at some point, and it's your job to prepare him or her for all the responsibilities that come with that. So ask yourself these questions:

- Have you discussed what you believe a responsible, healthy sexual relationship to be, and have you communicated your ideas about when someone is ready for one?
- Have you educated your child about birth control and safe sex?
- Do you know what your child's definition of sex is? Have you discussed any differences between your definition and your child's?
- If your child is dating, have you established rules about where and when he or she can entertain a romantic interest? (Is the bedroom allowed? Must the door be open? Must you or another trusted adult be present in the house?)
- Have you outlined the consequences for violating these rules?

Once you've established your boundaries, you need to help your child establish his or her own. As I suggested in *Queen Bees & Wannabes*, sometimes an ally—a trusted adult—can fill this role better than you, the parent. Ask your child to consider the following questions and know where he or she stands on each one. If he or she isn't willing to have this conversation with you and you can't find an ally, get your child a journal so he or she can write down the answers. Then let your child choose which parts to share with you.

- "How well do I have to know someone before I do something sexual with them?"
- "How do I define 'knowing someone well'?"
- "What do I feel comfortable doing with someone sexually?"
- "What do I not want to do?"
- "How will I communicate that to the person I'm with?"
- "What would make it harder for me to say what I want and don't want? How will I overcome those obstacles?"
- "What if my friends ask me about what I've done?" (This is a great opportunity to show how the boxes teach kids what they should say in those situations. For example, the "Act Like a Man" box teaches boys that they should exaggerate or lie about their sexual behavior.)
- "Whom can I go to for help if I need it?"

Problem: You Heard Your Child and His Friends Talking About Sex. Do You Tell the Other Parents?

One mother told me that she'd overheard her son and his friend talking about a girl who they'd heard engaged in a lot of oral sex. She said, "And then I heard my sweet thirteen-year-old boy say, 'Yeah, I hear she blows like a foghorn.'" She was shocked to hear something so crude come out of her son's mouth and chagrined to hear the boys passing along a rumor. How did she handle it?

I asked them if they knew what a double standard was. We talked about how a guy who gets a lot of sex is a player, but what did they call a girl who did? They told me: a slut. We talked about reputations and how unfair they could be. I also got them to admit that they had no idea whether the rumor was true—that it might have been started by an angry girl, jealous guy, etc., that it might be completely false, completely true, or somewhere in between. And that spreading that kind of rumor could be absolutely devastating to the girl. I think they really got it, but I didn't know whether I should call the other boy's mother and tell her what we'd discussed.

Should you tell the other parents if you talk to your child's friend about sex? Yes, you should. I think it's fine for you to explain your values to others, including other kids, but it's not your place to impose those values—except the idea that everyone has the right to be treated with dignity. Other parents are responsible for communicating their values to their children. Their values may be in agreement with yours, in opposition to yours, or somewhere in between. When you call the other parent and explain what you discussed, you give that parent the opportunity to open up the discussion and convey his or her values. Wouldn't you want that chance if the roles were reversed?

Another parent told me about a related—and very common—experience:

My family was hanging out with another family. There were a number of kids my son's age (fifteen). The rest of the kids went down to the basement but my son stayed with us and the other adults. I started to get really annoyed. Why couldn't he be more social? I kept pushing him to go downstairs and join the other kids. Finally he did, but then he popped right back up ten minutes later. I was a little annoyed; why couldn't I have some private grown-up time? On the ride home, he told me that all the kids were talking about blow jobs—some of the girls were bragging about giving them—and he'd felt really uncomfortable. I didn't know whether I should tell the mom.

I want to highlight a few things here. First, let's look at the mother's reaction. Kids usually know what they do that makes their parents anxious; what they don't usually know is why. It's useful for this mother to ask herself why it was so important to her that her son hang out with his peers. Did she want him to be more popular because it was important to *him* or to *her*? When her son left the group of kids so quickly, she didn't stop to consider why he might have done so. Was he generally shy, or could the particular situation have made him uncomfortable? Sometimes our natural desire to see our child well liked can blind us to the fact that we don't want him to be in a particular situation. If your child has the guts to leave a discussion because he finds it uncomfortable or offensive, consider yourself lucky.

This mother did in fact call the other mother the next day—which I think was exactly the right thing to do—and they both followed up with their kids.

Problem: You Catch the Kids "Doing It"

It doesn't matter what "it" is—if you catch your child in the act with someone else, there are three conversations you need to have: one with your child, one with your child's partner, and one with the partner's parents. The first thing you do is leave the room (or wherever you caught them), give the kids a chance to be decently dressed, and give yourself a chance to breathe.

ORAL SEX: EPIDEMIC OR EXAGGERATION?

The definitions of sex and virginity have changed dramatically since I graduated high school a generation ago. Then, having sexual (vaginal) intercourse was much more common than giving or receiving oral sex. If you were a girl, oral sex was something you rarely talked about. If word got out or rumors spread that you were willing to do it, you'd get a reputation for being a skank (which was worse than a slut).

Recently the first comprehensive surveys on sexual behavior that included questions concerning oral sex reported that more than half of American teenagers ages 15 to 19 have engaged in oral sex. In my experience working with teens, these reports accurately reflect what teens and their teachers and parents tell me. The question we need to ask ourselves is why and how can we best communicate with our children about an issue that often makes people so uncomfortable?

Today, teens consider sexual intercourse a much bigger deal than oral sex; some might not even include oral sex in the definition of having sex. In addition, not only are kids much more willing to engage in oral sex, they talk about it openly. Hearing this talk can be very upsetting for parents and teachers, many of whom see this new development as fresh evidence of the moral degradation of teens. From the way adults talk, it sounds as though children as young as twelve are engaging in oral sex whenever they get the chance.

Here's what I see going on: By the time our children arrive in high school, they've probably been educated about pregnancy, AIDS, and STDs. As a result, most teens see having sexual intercourse as a very serious decision. This is a good thing and it's a direct result of educators and parents talking with their children. Teens see oral sex as a safer alternative and often shrug off adult concerns, saying things like, "Everyone does it. It's not that big a deal." Horrified by what they see as teens' cavalier attitudes, adults often accuse teens of ignorance and/or sexual promiscuity. At that point, the conversation usually shuts down because we're so reactive and the teens are so defensive.

When I talk to teens, I don't argue with them about whether oral sex is a big deal or how often they're doing it. Instead, I ask whether the following observations ring true to them.

1. Oral sex is not reciprocal. Girls give it to guys; guys rarely give it to girls.
2. A girl is more likely to give a boy oral sex when she's competing with another girl for his attention.
3. A girl will give a boy oral sex when she's in a sexual situation that is out of her control but she doesn't want to admit it. She "offers" oral sex as a way to get out of having sexual intercourse and pleasing the guy she's with so he won't accuse her of being a tease or a prude. In her mind, this makes it more likely that the relationship will continue.
4. There are a lot of guys who know that oral sex under these circumstances is demeaning to girls. These boys might like the physical sensation, but they don't like the idea that girls are demeaning themselves to please them. The boys don't know how to talk about it because it seems so strange to them, so outside of the "Act Like a Boy" box, to admit their true—and truly confused—feelings. They know that if they

don't join in talking about it, joking about it, or asking for oral sex, they'll be suspected of being gay.

After I'm done, it gets absolutely quiet in the room and then we have a brutally honest conversation. I would encourage you to have the same conversation with your son or daughter, certainly by the spring of eighth grade, if not earlier; keep in mind that there are seventh graders who will also need this discussion.

Talking with Your Child

After you've gotten over your shock and embarrassment, you need to think things through. If you've forbidden your child to have romantic companions in his or her room, your child has broken a rule, but focus on the sex first. If this is the first time you've discovered your child is sexually active, you need to come to grips with that new reality. Your conversation needs to focus on two issues:

1. Now that your child is sexually active, he or she must take responsibility for sexually responsible decision making, including being fully informed and prepared to deal with the risks of pregnancy and STDs. If he or she doesn't feel comfortable coming to you for help on this, your child *must* go to an adult ally for support.

2. If he or she has violated a household rule, your child must accept the consequences for that; your trust has been broken and he or she will have to earn back your respect for that violation.

What if you feel your child shouldn't be having sex because it goes against your values? If you believe you should forbid your child to see his or her partner again, or take any similar action designed to stop him or her from being sexually active, my concern is that you will drive your child's sexual activity underground. If you do let your child know that you expect him or her to wait to have sex, please be sure your child knows that he or she can make a mistake (for example, get an STD or become or get someone else pregnant) and still go to you for help.

Talking with Your Child's Partner

This conversation is a variation on the one you'd give a kid you'd caught drinking or doing drugs with your child. When a child is under your roof, you consider him or her your own child, responsible for following your rules. Lay out your rules, consequences, and expectations, and explain that you'll be discussing the issue with his or her parents. For example, tell both kids involved that your rule is that they aren't allowed in the bedroom together and they aren't allowed to have sex in your house. If they violate your house rules, they'll both need to work to earn back your trust.

Talking with the Partner's Parents

Maybe you hate the whole idea of your child being sexually active. Or you hate the partner—and perhaps even blame the partner's parents for being so permissive as to raise a child who would lead your innocent down the wrong path. For the sake of your child's health and safety, you need to set these feelings aside. You don't need to like the partner's parents, but you do have to have enough of a relationship with them that you can communicate. Just be careful that that you don't slip into Perfect Parent World code language that makes the other parents feel like they are irresponsible or vice versa. Ideally, once your child starts dating someone seriously, you should make an effort to establish a relationship with the other parents. If you haven't already done so, and you've discovered that your child is sexually active, you need to have this difficult conversation right away, because it's the best way to maximize the chances that both kids will make sexually responsible decisions.

It's easy for these conversations to turn to blame:

- "You know you can't trust boys. They only think about one thing."
- "If you weren't such lax parents, this never would have happened."
- "I knew we should never have let our kid date yours; we knew her reputation."

Do your best to avoid blaming the other child or parents, and if you're on the receiving end of these kinds of hurtful remarks, take a deep breath and let them lie.

YOU: *I'm as upset as you are. This isn't something I was ready for, either. But now that we have to deal with it, I hope we can work together to make sure the kids are safe and responsible. Here's what I've told them.* (Explain your viewpoint.) *They violated our rules* (explain), *so here are the consequences we gave them* (explain). *I want to make sure you understand everything we've said and done. Could we all sit down together and figure out what else we need to do?*

Parents tell me that teaching their children how to handle alcohol, drugs, and sex is the most challenging task of their parenting careers. It's worth the effort to get it right, to be sure our children see us respecting the law and ourselves, taking responsibility, and standing firm for our values.

The Thick Envelope and the Thin

The Long March from
Gifted Preschooler to College Applicant

This party should be a good time. You like the hosts and you like their friends. But you have a child in the eleventh grade, so you're marked. No sooner do you have your wineglass in one hand and a piece of cheese in the other than a nice, seemingly reasonable parent approaches you and you have the following conversation:

OTHER PARENT: *Hi, so nice to see you!* (Two seconds of small talk.) *Emma must be a junior, right? Do I feel sorry for you! You must be going crazy deciding about colleges.*

YOU (who just had a fight with your daughter about doing homework instead of IM-ing while you're out—you're not even sure she'll graduate, let alone have a choice of where to go): *Of course, but we're keeping all her options open because we don't want her to obsess about it. We're trying to keep a healthy perspective.*

OTHER PARENT: *That's so admirable. I know there're so many parents in your class who're doing whatever they can to give their kid a leg up. It's just so competitive today. I'm sure you're already doing all that tutoring after school, getting Emma into all the AP classes, all the sports. It's so insane, but we all want to give our kids the best, right? So where are you thinking about?*

YOU (taking a deep breath): *Well—*

OTHER PARENT (interrupting): *Our Carrie just loves Duke, and Michael is thriving at Yale. Just let me know if you need any advice. Oops, will you excuse me? I need to refresh my drink. So good to catch up! Bye!*

As the other parent walks away, you suppress the desire to grab a bottle of wine and either chug it or clobber her over the head with it.

Despite appearances, I don't think people are this irritating about their kids and college on purpose. I don't believe they're trying to make you feel like a failure and make themselves look great in the process. They were probably much less irritating people before they went through the college application process with their kids. (Of course, truth be told, there are some parents who are capable of having this conversation about preschool.)

In any case, what's important is how you manage your own response to a conversation like this. Why? Because going through the college application process is one of the last opportunities you'll have to demonstrate your values while your child is still under your roof. Also, if you don't get yourself under control, then you'll morph into one of these irritating, obnoxious parents yourself, and people will talk behind your back about how much they hate you, too. If you let the process control you, your child will learn from you that education is not about its ability to make him or her a more independent, thoughtful, analytical person but rather about the status you get from putting the right bumper sticker on your car.

First acknowledge that it's normal to walk away from these kinds of conversations filled with anxiety. Feelings of being an inadequate parent or having an inadequate child will ricochet inside your head, jockeying for position with the rapidly growing checklist of ever more essential things to do: "When I get back home, I have to see if she went to that college counselor. I have to sign her up for that SAT prep course. She needs to stop playing violin and switch to viola because then she'll stand out more on her application. Better see if she's working on the first draft of her autobiographical college essay." When you have these feelings, go get a glass of wine and imagine you're on a beach far away from Perfect Parent World.

Let's also acknowledge that this probably isn't the first time you've experienced the combination of ramped-up anxiety and cutthroat competitiveness. Indeed, for many parents, their children's college application process is the culminating step in a Bataan-like death march that began the day they registered them for preschool.

> *I'll never forget when one of the women in my mommy group asked us the day after Labor Day if we'd picked up school applications. She told us that space at all the best schools was really limited, and we'd better get our applications in for the next year that very week. Our kids were two and a half.*
>
> Angelica, mother of a high school freshman

So even if your children aren't old enough to apply to colleges, this chapter is for you if you are considering placing your child in a school with a selective admissions process.

Everyone Is Gifted and Talented

> *My daughter is bright, but she's not going to get into the gifted and talented classes on her own merit. So I got to know people in the school and I found out a lot of parents do that [lobbying]. We want our kids to have the best grades or the best teacher to get those best grades.* Constance, middle school mom

Perhaps you were able to resist shelling out for *Binomials for Blastulas* or *Einstein for Embryos* or piping in Mozart to your growing fetus. But chances are by the time your offspring hits school age, the culture of Perfect Parent World has convinced you of one thing: If you don't uncover your child's special gifts and work tirelessly to develop them by getting him or her on the inside track at school, Child Protective Services will haul you away and toss you into Bad Parent Jail.

There's one fact that many parents believe is beyond dispute: Your child is doomed if he or she isn't classified as gifted and talented and put into the appropriate classes. Those GT teachers are the best, the kids are the best, everything is the best. So following that logic, it's only common sense that well-meaning parents who want the best for their children would get their kids into those classes regardless of whether they had the aptitude for them. And what if kids don't qualify by passing the right tests? Well, just get them into those classes by hook or by crook, and they'll be so motivated and enriched by the process that they'll become gifted and talented just by being there. And once they're there, let's keep them there—time to begin the endless march through every available honors and Advanced Placement (AP) course to pave the way to the widest possible menu of college options.

I'm all for challenging young people to do their best, but they have to be in an environment where that's possible. A guiding rule of good parenting is that the school, program, or teacher has to be a good fit for the individual child. Imagine that your first job after college was interning at a newspaper. Then imagine that two weeks after you got there, your parents met with the newspaper owner and somehow convinced her to make you editor in chief. Would you do a good job? Would you appreciate the efforts made by your parents to make you editor in chief?

Your child's brain is developing according to its own timetable and it might not be developmentally appropriate for him or her to take advanced-level courses. This fact doesn't make you a failure as a parent and doesn't mean that your child isn't intelligent. You might read this and think, "Of course I know that," but not so fast. Take a moment and ask yourself if your actions are consistent with your beliefs. Better yet, ask someone who knows you intimately in this area—your child—and be prepared to hear something you may not agree with.

Enrollment in a class that isn't developmentally appropriate could cause huge anxiety and frustration for your child, who might worry that if she doesn't keep up, she won't measure up in your eyes.

> *This mom told me that she and her husband paid for some expensive assemblies for her daughter's school as a way to "encourage" the school to put Irene into the gifted and talented classes. Meanwhile, Irene's telling me that she has to get tutored four times a week just to scrape by with low B's. She never gets to bed before midnight or 1:00 because she's so overwhelmed by homework, she always goes to sleep with a whanging headache, and she has to get up at 5:30 or 6:00 in the morning to start it all over again. She's a miserable kid. And she's twelve.*   Dory, middle school mom

I've seen too many parents use placement into a gifted or accelerated program as an opportunity to "other" the children who don't get in:

I was attending a mother-daughter party around Mother's Day at a friend's home. There were probably twenty moms (only the cool ones were invited, I must say). The kids had been in testing for a week and had just received their scores for the test for the Gifted and Talented Exam that places kids in GATE sections at magnet schools. It was all anyone could talk about. A few of the moms whose children would be considered GATE were telling everyone what their child's score was and how excited they were. Of course the moms whose children did not test [well] felt awful. One mom in particular, who believes her child is perfect even though she is a perfect brat, chose to share the child's score with her child. This child told everyone how smart she was and told my child she was stupid. I made the mistake of telling the mom this (as I thought we were close friends) and the mom didn't believe me and made me feel ridiculous. Her response to my concern about kids has always been, "All kids do that."

                                                    Fran, middle school mom

What's going on here? This is an extreme Perfect Parent World sport in which everybody who can brags about their child's test scores while simultaneously expending tremendous amounts of energy to look like they aren't. This is also a typical conflict between a Wannabe or Sidekick Mom and a Queen Bee Mom. Fran assumes that "because they're close friends," she can tell this mother about a problem she had with her daughter. The other mother's response left her feeling ridiculous and dismissed—which will make it really hard for her to confront this woman again. Fran then uses the other mother's reaction as further justification to blame her rather than to look at her own behavior. Her statement that the other mom "believes her child is perfect even though she's a perfect brat" indicates that she's been sitting on her bad feelings toward the other woman for a while and letting them build—a classic illustration of how mothers often handle conflict poorly. She then overreacts and the other mother dismisses her. Meanwhile, these women will continue to compete against each other—one to prove her self-worth, the other to assert it—and one of the arenas will be their children's educational experiences.

Let me be clear: I am *not* saying that you shouldn't apply for a slot in a GT program if it's a good fit for your child's talents and interests. But I am asking you to examine your motives and move ahead with your child's best interests in mind. You might already have had a meeting with your child's guidance counselor or head of school to discuss the issue of gifted classes, honors programs, and the like. That educator probably advised you to be sure that your child had a real passion and aptitude for classes that will require greater effort and generate more homework. You probably listened thoughtfully. And then perhaps you said to yourself something like this:

- "A real passion for study? The only thing my kid has a real passion for is his Xbox. Does that mean I shouldn't encourage him to do his best?"
- "My kid never thinks she wants to go the extra mile, but once she's in a class she always rises to the challenge."
- "My kid would be bored in regular classes."
- "All the parents of older kids say the best teachers teach the honors classes."
- "I've heard that the honors classes get the best resources and more of the school's budget. I'm afraid my kid will get left behind if she doesn't get into those classes."
- "Isn't it my job as a parent to set the bar high for my kid? I'd rather my child get a B in an honors program than an A in regular classes."
- "It's my job to keep my kid's options open, and that includes colleges. I want to give him the best shot possible at going wherever he wants to go."
- "I always regretted that my parents didn't push me harder; I would have gone further. I want my child to have the opportunities I never had."

Any or all of these points may be true — or they may be rationalizations. You won't know unless you check in with yourself and your child. What evidence do you have to support your child being in these classes? Has someone in the school shared a different opinion with you? What was his or her perspective? Was there something he or she said that set you off? Why?

Sometimes kids will surprise you:

My son came home his freshman year in high school and told me that he'd gone to his guidance counselor and gotten himself transferred into honors math. I told him I thought it was too much; he had three other honors courses already. "Mom," he said, "I figure if I'm gonna be here for four years, I want to be challenged and learn all I can." "Wow, honey," I told him. "That's so mature!" "Just playing you, Mom," he said. "There's a really cute girl in honors math."

Betsy, high school mom

If they're up to the task, it doesn't matter why they want to be there. Take motivation where you can get it. Keep monitoring your child's progress in honors classes. If he has to stay up till the wee hours every night or get constant tutoring or other extra help to keep up with his peers, what's the real message he's getting: that learning must necessarily be fraught with suffering, or that he's not good enough if he's not an honors student? Listen to your child's teachers and guidance counselors with an open mind. If they're telling you that a different class would be a better fit for your child, consider it.

THE DREADED "PERMANENT RECORD"

In addition to shoehorning kids into accelerated classes for which they're not suited, the other mistake I often see parents make is shielding kids from the consequences of their bad actions lest the incidents become a matter of public record and tarnish the kids' transcripts. In Chapter 5, I warned you that your natural protectiveness might lead you to protect your child from failure, disappointment, or being held accountable. Protecting a child's pristine school record is a major temptation.

Here's what I now know from principals. While a child's serious infractions are—and should be—part of his or her school record, they need not sound the death knell for college admission or other future plans. Listen to this principal:

I don't think getting suspended freshmen and sophomore year is held against them. The student has makeup time to prove himself. If the student does something senior year and even spring of junior year (because there's such a maturity difference between fall and spring of junior year), the colleges think, If this kid is doing this now, what is he going to do when he gets here?" Cheating is the worst offense. Drinking, even plagiarism, isn't as bad because, honestly, some kids may not realize what they're doing. But cheating is different because if you're caught and it's proven, it shows that you put in planning and preparations for cheating.

Penny, high school principal

What's important is how your child behaves after he or she has been punished. Did your child take responsibility for his or her bad behavior? Make amends? Keep a clean record from that point forward? What did he or she learn from that mistake, and how did it shape his or her character?

But that's not the question most parents want to talk about. What they want to know is whether the child should tell the colleges to which he's applying that he's been disciplined for any reason. Most college applications ask a student to report any suspension and explain why. It's very important for students to answer that question honestly for two reasons. First, many schools have an honor code that mandates that if the student attempts to hide a suspension on an application, the high school is ethically bound to tell the college.

Second, as the following story makes clear, Mom was right: Don't lie, because you're bound to get caught—and then you're in even worse trouble than you were for doing the thing you were lying about in the first place.

We had a kid who lied on the school application when it asked if he'd been suspended. But the recommendation I wrote for him included what he had learned from his suspension. The college rejected him and they told him that he would have been accepted if he had been honest.   Darryl, upper school dean

I've seen dozens of "side letters" that principals have sent to colleges explaining how students have grown from taking responsibility for their mistakes. I know you may be reading this and thinking. "Yeah, right, there's no way those letters work." Don't take my word for it—listen to some college admissions officers:

If I get a fabulous letter where the student has made a mistake, even a really big mistake, and I see that she is taking responsibility, the application does stand out. And I'll also tell you what essay I hate to see the most in an application. When parents send their kid off to Guadalajara to build an orphanage and their essays are basically, "I went to Mexico and learned that poor people are nice, too." I hate those applications.   Candace, college admissions officer

I went to a college to see the other side [of the admissions process]. They gave us three applications—one to accept, one to defer, and one to reject. Our decision was the opposite of what the college actually did. We accepted and deferred two candidates with the best academic records but in actuality the college had rejected them. They chose to accept the student who wrote the best essay but was not as strong academically because he came across as genuine.

Kyle, high school principal

In an effort to dispel the mystery behind these letters, I asked a school colleague to share an example of a letter he sent to a school.

To whom it may concern:

I am writing on behalf of X's application to _____ University. I am presently dean of student life at ____ School and serve as the faculty sponsor for the Honor Council. At the end of second semester of her junior year, X plagiarized her final paper in her religion course. At the beginning of this year she appeared before the Honor Council and received an F on the final paper, which gave her an F for the course. In addition, she received a two-day out-of-school suspension. When she appeared before the Honor Council, X took full responsibility for her actions and showed true regret by giving a sincere apology.

Since her appearance before the Honor Council, X and I have had several conversations about her infraction of the Honor Code and her actions since then. I believe that she learned from her mistake and that she has shown a remarkable personal growth and maturity during her senior year. The best example of her growth as an individual was her single-handedly taking on the responsibility of organizing students to help the homeless. She organized the student participation from our school with the students from several other schools. The end result was a very productive community service project that involved a great many of our students and helped several homeless families. X's leadership in this project shows her ability as a student and a person to take on a difficult task and be successful, much like the task of learning from her mistake and making herself a better person.

If you have any questions regarding X's record or my recommendation, please feel free to contact me. Thank you for your consideration of her application.

I've seen more than a few letters of this kind, many of which resulted in admission to the child's college of choice. (And yes, I'm mildly concerned that some particularly gung-ho parents will see this as an opportunity to encourage their child to "use" his or her bad behavior in a college essay.) However, I know there'll be people reading this book who will think, "Of course, those side letters are all well and good in an ideal world, but I'd prefer we keep this little incident to ourselves—no need for the school to get involved." No problem; instead, let's just focus on your child's safety.

Imagine that your child has gotten into Harvard on merit. All those AP classes have paid off—not to mention lettering in five sports while starting a preschool for underprivileged children on two hours' sleep a night for four years. When other parents ask you where your kid is going to school, you can say "Cambridge" with a hint of modesty and a dash of pity for the poor souls who don't know that's code for "My kid got into Harvard." You're looking forward to spending the billions of dollars in tuition.

Now think of the parents who threatened, bribed, and threw huge tantrums to make sure that their child's disciplinary record wasn't included in his or her high school transcript. I want you to imagine the most Entitled, bullying parents possible. And now I want you to think of their child. Time and time again I've seen children who have violently hazed, sexually assaulted, and bullied other children in their schools and gotten away with it—meaning that their schools capitulated and didn't mention their bad behavior or the disciplinary actions in their high school transcript. These bullying kids have been accepted by prestigious schools often because those universities are in the dark about their behavior.

We know that some independent schools are changing their policies so that certain disciplinary procedures will not be shared with us as a matter of course—that's when I close my office door and get on the phone with the college admissions people at the school."
April, college admissions officer

Now imagine that it's freshmen orientation week. Your child is off to her first mixer, far from home and your supervision. She's surrounded by people she doesn't know, but she has a sense that they're already family. Your daughter's beginning to have feelings of loyalty toward these strangers; she assumes they all share common values.

From across the room your daughter spies the boy of her dreams, the personification of the "Act Like a Man" box. He comes over to say hello. Not only does he look good, he knows exactly what to say to sweep her off her feet. In the spirit of all college orientation parties, she drinks too much and trusts too much. She goes back to this guy's dorm room and wants to hook up with him but doesn't want to have sex. But he's grown up to be deaf and blind to other people's needs and he doesn't really care anyway because he's never been held accountable when he hurts others. His parents did whatever it took to erase any sign of bad behavior from his record because to be held responsible would "ruin his chances." This boy has bullied, disrespected, and degraded people throughout high school and has no reason to operate differently now—and let me assure you that'll include your daughter, who is now in his bedroom.

If you're the parent of the girl, what can you do about it? You can't transport yourself into that dorm room and spirit your daughter to safety, but you can stand up to those bullying parents of misbehaving students now, while your child is still in high school. You can tell your school leaders that you'll support them when and if they hold powerful students who have broken school rules accountable, along with their parents. You can speak out in parent meetings when bullying parents try to set the school's agenda.

If you're the parents who have fought tooth and nail to get your child's record wiped clean, I understand that your actions were based on wanting the best for your kid. But I'm asking you to look hard at your actions and to be the parent your child deserves by letting him take the fall. I want you to envision the relationship you hope you have with your child when he or she is an adult. You want to be proud of your child. If you're bent on wiping your child's record of misbehavior clean, are you teaching him or her to treat you or anyone else with respect, dignity, and fairness? How will that perspective affect the choices he or she makes in relationships or on the job?

There are few issues more contentious and difficult to think through clearly—for both the school and the parents—than the expulsion of an aggressive, severely misbehaving student. If the student's parents are obsessed with their child's permanent record, the situation can easily get out of hand. If you are that parent and your child is facing serious long-term consequences, how can you keep your cool and think clearly?

> *We had an excellent student who was also an accomplished athlete. He was accepted to a very prestigious university but he was also caught drinking on campus. We had had other experiences with this student before where he was held accountable in a way we thought was appropriate but he just wasn't getting it. So we did have him write a letter to the university and it got ugly with his parents. But we stuck to our position and he was denied admission for that year. But they told him that if he worked hard and proved his merit they would accept him for the following year—which they did.*
>
> Alex, private school dean

> *I think colleges distinguish between different kinds of behavior. Honor offenses like cheating and stealing are really serious. One of our students last year was arrested for shoplifting and then was suspended. She was incredibly remorseful and of course there was a lot more to it. The college did not reject her; they deferred her. In addition, we need to get some of these kids help. We always do an assessment by the counselor if a student is found guilty of a drinking offense.*
>
> Rozelle, high school dean

If you were the parent in this situation, would you be tempted to jump up and down at this school and say the punishment was too harsh? Yes, the kid made a mistake, but should this one mistake ruin her future? How could the school do this to her? Here's what I think stands the greater chance of ruining your child's future: never punishing him or her in a way that really hits home. In this situation, the student learned that she had to take responsibility for herself, that she could face a bad situation and do something about it. Which child would you want attending that university—the kid who thinks she can get away with whatever she wants, or the kid who knows that she's a part of the community and has responsibilities toward that community? Which child do you want going to parties with your child?

> *We had a student that received a four-year full ride to a very prestigious university. Shortly after, he came to a basketball game drinking. We had to tell the school and the school took away the $250,000 scholarship. The parents were so angry at us, it actually got a little hard to advocate for the student—which we did. We had to tell the university but we also wrote letters, called, but they stood their ground. So we worked really hard with the student and he got another scholarship to another equally good school.*
>
> Dennis, high school dean

Take This Application and Shove It

Let's go back to that party I described at the beginning of the chapter. Why does even the most benign conversation about the application process make you so nuts? Of course, it's a challenge to jump-start a kid already overwhelmed by a million activities to send away for and fill out all those forms on a rigid schedule, not to mention squeeze in all the requisite testing, begging for letters of recommendation, etc. Still, why are you curled up into such an anxious ball about the whole experience? What's really going on? I think we're insane about this application stuff for good reason, and I have a few ideas about what makes it feel so intolerable:

- Constant conversations, some would say gossip, among parents make us feel like we can't escape. And the more we talk (i.e., gossip) about college, the more anxious we become. It seems as if every parent has heard some version of "They used to let 40 percent of kids into College X; now they're only taking 7 percent of applicants."

I know there are colleges where they say to prospective students vis-
iting the school, "Look to your right and look to your left. Only one of
you will make it—if you're lucky." Or "Don't even think of applying
here unless you have taken five AP classes." I don't admit people on
that basis. I always remember what my first dean of admissions told
me: "Of course we want a few students who get all A's but we also
want to admit the kind of student that you can have a conversation
with at 3 a.m. in your dorm when you can't sleep."

Adele, college admissions officer

- We're being made fools of. All schools, from preschool to universities, love it when parents talk about how there are so many applicants for a shrinking number of spots. The more difficult it appears
  to be to get a spot in their school, the more people apply. And the
  more grateful parents are to get their kids in, the meeker they'll be
  once their kids are in the school (except for the Entitled parents,
  who consider it their inalienable right to have their children in that
  school and will have no problem speaking out).
- You get so amped up about where your child chooses to go to college (or if he or she chooses to go at all) because this is one of the
  last official big decisions in which you have a lot of say. If you postpone the joy now, you'll have to wait until your son or daughter
  gets married to make your kid miserable.
- Word is out to those upper-middle-class families (meaning you
  come from a couple of generations of wealth but don't like to
  admit it) that the "gentleman's C" might not cut it anymore. It
  used to be that if you were from the upper middle class and white,
  you would get a free pass into the best colleges even if you didn't
  deserve it based on your grades and activities. It's still true that
  these well-connected families have more of an inside track, but
  now these families have to work harder (sometimes in the form of
  donating more and more money). Listen to the head of a prestigious New England boarding school:

There's this feeling in the upper classes in this country that they can't
get their kids into these schools like they used to and it makes them

very uneasy. You used to pass on a gentleman's C and now you can't. It feels like anyone can take your place.

Monroe, dean of private high school

Basically, everything about today's college application process underscores the notion that it's a zero-sum game: more kids applying for fewer slots, which translates to "Your kid's admission is my kid's shrinking chances." So when people talk about the world being more competitive today, they really believe it.

Is it true? David Anderegg, author of *Worried All the Time,* points out that there are sixteen colleges in the top fifty with acceptance rates of more than 50 percent. (He used *U.S. News & World Report*'s annual college ranking as a guide to top colleges.) He also noted that while going to one of the most prestigious schools might increase one's lifetime income, it does so by a smaller percentage than people suppose. In other words, it's not as hard to get into a good school as parents suppose, and it's not such a big deal if you can't paste that Harvard or Yale bumper sticker on your car.

WHERE TO APPLY?

"I just want you to have the opportunity to go to [insert name of your favorite school]." It's human nature to warm to the thought of your child attending the college you loved so much, or to want him or her to have the privilege of attending an elite college with famous professors, vast resources, and an incredible menu of educational opportunities. However, with these loving intentions come temptations. Remember Chapter 5. Just as the desire for your child to have the "best" can influence the degree to which you're willing to bend the rules to ensure that he or she gets into all the "right" classes, the desire to have your child attend the "right" college can lead to you putting your wants and needs before those of your kid.

My dad really wants me to go to the Naval Academy. I have never expressed interest in the Naval Academy but he tells me, "I had the opportunity to go and I didn't, so I want you to go."

Arlene, high school senior

My dad tried to bribe me any way he knew how—a new car, a trip—but it really didn't matter to me. I didn't want to go to the schools he wanted me to. If I did, it would have been like never graduating from high school because all the same people in high school went to the same college.   Carmen, college sophomore

We [the guidance counselors] tell the parents, "You have a right to have major involvement"—it's their nickel and they're not a potted plant. Parents are a vital part of the process and have the right to set the parameters. Those parameters can be financial, geographical, or religious. For example, you won't want your kid to go to California because they'll fall off the face of the earth. You have that right but once you set your parameters, get out of the way.
                    Mara, high school guidance counselor

Again, what matters most about where your child goes to college is goodness of fit—the match between your child's abilities and interests and what the school has to offer. If your school has a college counselor, they'll probably give you a list of "reaches," "likelies," and "safeties." If you're disappointed by the list or you think the counselor isn't a good advocate for your child, first ask her to explain her criteria for developing the list. If you don't feel that your conversation is productive, you can always ask for a second opinion—but before you go spending lots of money on a professional college advisor, ask someone within the school who knows your child.

DECODING APPLICATION-SPEAK

It's a toss-up as to which is more horrible: watching those application deadlines bear down on your hapless child (all the while forcing yourself not to swoop in and take over) or dealing with squads of other equally anxious parents in the same boat. It helps to arm yourself with a little verbal self-defense. Let's start with some code breaking.

"Where Are You Thinking About Applying?"

Decoded, this means: "Are you a member of Perfect Parent World or are you a loser?"

Too many parents think their responses will reveal the sum total of their success as parents and the absolute worth of their child. I believe that there's no good reason to ask this question. For one thing, people don't honestly care where your child goes to school—unless they're worried that your child might be applying to the same school as their child and want to assess the competition.

> We live next to a very wealthy town famous for its elite school system. Some parents there won't tell other parents where their kids are applying, since only a certain number of kids from the high school are allowed to apply to a given school to maximize the chances for admission. So everybody there keeps it a big secret.
>
> Miranda, mother of high school freshman

Second, why would you want to ask someone a question that is nearly guaranteed to make him or her feel inadequate?

I suggest you stop asking or answering this question and urge your child to do the same. Remember that one child's "safety" school (the one she's a shoo-in for) is another child's "stretch" school (the one she has a slim chance of gaining entry into but is going for anyway). It can be humiliating for parent and child alike to discover that their "stretch" school is someone else's "safety."

What do you say when someone asks you? Of course you can't be rude, and you don't need to be. Smile and say, "You know, the college application process is so stressful that we decided as a family that we weren't going to talk about it outside the family." Then change the subject. You'll send the clear signal that the topic is off the table. When in doubt, always ask people about themselves and they won't be offended by your refusal to discuss your child's school choices with them.

And when they tell you, "Oh, we're applying to ____, ____, and ____," just smile and say, "I wish you all the best." Then take a private moment to remind yourself that "we" aren't applying anywhere; this is your child's journey, not yours. Your role is to coach and encourage, insisting that your child take the lead.

LANDMINE!

Don't use the word *we*—as in "We got a 1350 on our SATs"— when discussing your child's applications to colleges. I've asked college admissions people around the country what percentage of parents use *we* when describing their child's college application—they say about 60 percent! So if you catch yourself thinking or saying it, take a moment, laugh at yourself, and then change your pronoun.

"Oh, I'm Sure Jenny Will Get In—She's a Legacy."

Decoded, this means: "The fix is in; Jenny doesn't have a chance to get in on her own merit."

Some parents think that schools automatically accept the children of alumni, but don't consider this a guarantee until you've done your homework and can separate fact from fiction. Some schools guarantee only that a legacy application will get a closer reading. Some schools have codes and rules in their mandates about legacies and in-state acceptance rates. Read the school's covenant and educate yourself.

"Your Child Has No Chance to Get Into a Decent College Unless She Takes Advanced Placement or International Baccalaureate Classes"

Decoded, this means: "Load up your kid's transcript or the game's over."

Look, students apply to our college even if their school doesn't offer AP classes—and we can't penalize them for that. We always look at their grades in the context of their classes.   Mark, college admissions officer

First of all, ask yourself what you really mean by a "decent college." I would urge you to make a list of the qualities you want in a school. You'll most likely be giving a huge amount of your hard-earned money to this institution, so it had better measure up.

Worrying about whether your child should take a regular class and get an "A" or an AP class and get a B?

> *Parents think that colleges are looking for the "well-rounded student." That was true twenty years ago, but it's not true today. Now they're looking for a well-rounded student body. They want to see students who have a couple of things that they are passionate about.*
>
> Luke, college counselor

Here's a sampling of the kinds of things parents tell school administrators in their drive to get their kids on the slickest, fastest inside track to their dream colleges:

"I don't care if he needs to be tutored every day, David *has* to be in AP calculus."

"My husband was a math major; he can work with Lauren."

"Can't you just make the course easier so that all the students can take it?"

"I'm not paying $15,000 a year for my daughter to miss out on calculus."

"I'm not paying $15,000 a year for my daughter to go to the state university."

"I'm not paying $15,000 for my son to get a C." (*Which begs the question: Should the school then give all its students A's and call it a day?*)

"So what if she's not ready? Just place her in the class! If she can't hack it, she can drop it, but at least it'll show up on her transcript."

"She's applying early decision and she needs the course to get into an Ivy League college."

"Can't you offer a precalculus course to seniors and call it calculus?"

"I don't care what the course content is. Colleges want to see AP History on the transcript."

If you catch yourself engaging in any kind of this special pleading on behalf of your child, ask yourself how your community's version of Perfect Parent World may be influencing your behavior. Remind yourself that your primary goal here is helping your child find a school that fits *her*, not the person you think she should be.

Paperwork-for-Hire

Given the competitive atmosphere, parents are often tempted to job out the most challenging aspects of the application process to maximize their child's chances. "Admissions counselors" abound; for a modest four or five figures, they'll work all available angles to ensure a child's best shot at the most elite institutions. For a fee, consultants can be hired to provide SAT tutoring, massage a college essay, corral letters of recommendation, and so forth.

Should you buy—and buy in to—these services? This is a huge issue, and one about which I have mixed feelings. I can understand parents wanting to help their children, but in practice it's unfair because some parents can afford to extend this advantage while so many cannot. Some kids with organizational challenges truly need help pulling all the elements of a college application together. But I have a huge problem with professionals who essentially do the application for the student. Talk with your child's guidance counselor to help figure out a balance between a helping hand and someone doing your child's work.

I think it's fine for you to read over your child's application and/or essays to offer suggestions, but writing the essays for him or her isn't ethical. It's your *child's* skills the colleges need to assess, not yours. And what's your plan if your child is admitted somewhere on the strength of your work? Are you going to attend classes with him or her and write all those college term papers yourself? If you even paused and thought about that last question, you seriously need to take a step back and laugh at yourself. Look at the application process as a major step your child is taking toward independence. Your child will never become a fully functioning, competent adult if you do the work for him or her. Besides, admissions officers can smell your interference a mile away:

If the application is too perfect, I look at it more closely. Sometimes I just get this feeling. I can't quite put my finger on it but I just know. That's why it's so important to have good relationships with the college counselors. I'll call them up and ask them if the student or the parent did the application. So then I ask for a graded paper from the student.   Nancy, college admissions officer

Stop doing their applications for them! I see it much more with moms doing the applications for their boys. Why? Because mothers take care of their sons. Moms will say to me, "But then they won't do it!"
                    Ryan, high school guidance counselor

My daughter really messed up her junior year of high school and then she basically did nothing for a year and a half after she graduated. I could have helped her—filled out her applications, sent in the fees on time (she never sent anything on time)—but I made a pact with myself that I wasn't going to do it. I wasn't paying for her to party and fool around at a college. But it was hard—and it was embarrassing when my friends talked about what their kids were doing in college. Finally in the last year, she has gotten herself into school and she's taking it seriously.   Trini, high school mom

If you're doing your child's applications, you're not letting him learn about the importance of meeting deadlines and the possible consequences of not taking them seriously. It could be that your child isn't ready to go to college, and not being able to fill out an application is a clear indication of that.

EMILY POST V. 2.0: ADMISSIONS ETIQUETTE

For more than ten years, I've been telling parents to mail their children's party invitations to invitees' homes rather than allow their kids to pass them out at school, unless the entire class or school is being invited. The same discretion is a good idea when college acceptances begin to arrive. By all means, if your child got into a favored college, it's time for a family celebration. But please urge him or her to use good judgment in sharing the news at school. Of course, good friends must be told, but your child should be mindful of kids who didn't get the news they were hoping for. And if your child gets rejected by his favorite college and his best friend gets into his first pick? Encourage him to have the grace to congratulate the friend on the payoff for all his hard work.

Your child isn't likely to be discreet if you don't model discretion yourself. That means sharing the good news with dear friends and family but not plastering your car with bumper stickers or sporting that new university T-shirt. It's especially tough when your best friend's child is rejected from the same school your child got into; you'll be bursting to talk about your good news even as you feel for your friend.

> *My daughter got into a school that was her best friend's first choice—and that girl got rejected. These girls had been friends since they were ten years old. They had become a part of the other's families, but after my daughter got into that school and her daughter didn't, it was never the same. The girls were fine but the mother was never friendly with my daughter again.*   Rosanne, high school Mom

The situation described above would be awkward for anyone. So if your child is the one who got in, immediately express your condolences to the other parent and/or kid and say something like, "I'm so sorry they didn't accept you. They have no idea what an incredible, amazing person they are missing out on."

Speaking as someone who didn't get into her first-choice college, I vividly remember the feeling of being left behind as I watched close friends get into higher-ranked schools. If you or your child is going through that, it's really hard to not be beaten down by those feelings. However, I can also report that I bounced back from my initial disappointment, got a terrific education at a college I came to love, and felt supported by my parents the whole way. How you help your child weather this same journey matters every bit as much as the name on your graduate's diploma.

Epilogue

I live in a small community in Utah and we have serious problems with bullying. I thought people would blow me off if I tried to do something about it, but now the whole town's behind it. I have to tell you how scary it was to speak out. I mean, this is a small community in Utah, but we are working on it, and I feel like I am really doing something to make this a better place for my children.

Beth, high school mom and community leader

I'm ashamed to admit this but I forbade one my son's friends, a girl, to come over to our house because I listened to nasty gossip about her from the other parents. I even spread some of the gossip myself. Now I look at what I did and think to myself, "This girl is thirteen—she may look a lot older but she really is a thirteen-year-old girl." Then her mom called me and said some really hurtful things to me but at some point in the conversation I realized that I was acting like I was thirteen and that's not right. I don't think of myself as a cruel person and the last thing I would want to teach my son is that it is acceptable to be cruel or exclude someone because of gossip. Just in that moment the embarrassment of my behavior made me realize that I had an obligation to do better.

Sarah, middle school mom

This book is my best attempt to ask you to work with me in the same way: to teach children by example that courage is speaking out when your impulse is to be silent. By doing so, you're teaching children to admit when they have wronged someone else. You're demonstrating that your actions are consistent with your values. I believe this is our responsibility to our children.

This is not to say that we all don't have moments of temptation when we really want to act badly. And it's completely acceptable to admit to ourselves that we have these temptations. What's not acceptable is to allow them to guide or justify our actions. When I have moments of temptation like these, here's what I remember:

1. If my sons experienced the problem I'm muddling my way through, how would I want them to act?

2. Parenting isn't an excuse for bad manners—mine or anyone else's.

3. My theme song, which I mentioned in the introduction: Stevie Wonder's "Isn't She Lovely."

Finding this kind of courage couldn't be more difficult. We live in a culture that loves to talk about family values but rarely asks us to look inward to be sure our actions are truly consistent with our words. We love to feel invincible, fearless, and independent. But we rarely have the courage to show humility, apologize, or acknowledge wrongdoing.

If you doubt your ability to make a difference, remember that you don't have to walk down the street with banners to make the world more socially just. What makes more of a difference in a child's life, marching down the street with a sign or protecting a child's dignity in your home, the classroom, on the playground, or on the athletic field? When you step up, you are working to safeguard the well-being of your community. You are teaching children that bravery includes admitting when they have wronged someone else. I believe there is nothing more sacred that you and I will ever do.

Acknowledgments

Inspiration can come from anywhere. About a year after the publication of *Queen Bees & Wannabes*, a good friend of mine went home for a family reunion and struck up a conversation with his fourteen-year-old cousin that went something like this:

MY FRIEND: *I think my friend Rosalind Wiseman spoke at your school this year!*

COUSIN: *Rosalind Wiseman is your friend? Well, I'm sure she's a nice person as a friend, but personally I couldn't stand her. She ruined everything.*

MY FRIEND: *Ruined everything? What do you mean?*

COUSIN: *Now all these pathetic girls in my class think they can complain when we do the least little thing to them.*

When my friend related this experience to me, I couldn't stop laughing. What an affirmation of my work! How dare I ruin this girl's ability to make other girls miserable! So before moving on to all of the people who helped me write this book, I would like to thank my friend's cousin because I often remember her when I need to focus and maintain my sense of humor.

First and foremost, I must thank the hundreds of parents, school administrators, teachers, counselors, coaches, teens, and children who contributed to what you just read. I have disguised almost everyone's identity because many people took great risks sharing their experiences with me, and I greatly appreciate that they did. If these people hadn't been so honest and willing to share the challenges they faced, this book couldn't have been written. I hate that I can't write all of your names down here. So to all of you: Thank you for believing I would do right by you. It has been a pleasure and honor working with you.

I also want to thank my support system—those who make me sit at my desk and get the job done. For the second time I had the opportunity to work with Betsy Rapoport, and it was a collaboration in the best sense. Thank you for making me stay the course. To my assistant, Jennifer Howard, thank you for keeping me calm and focused (a full-time job). Thank you to Emily Horowitz for finding wonderful people to interview. Thank you to my editor at Crown, Rachel Klayman, and my "in-house" editor, Steve Wiseman. I also had critical last-minute editorial help from Julie and Corey Holter. When I write a book about boys, Corey will be drafted for full-time assistance.

As always, I am so grateful to Jim Levine and everyone at Levine Greenberg Literary Agency. If anyone is interested in finding the best agent in the world, look no farther. Likewise, thank you to everyone at Empower: Shanterra, Marlon, Susan, Betsy, Kristen, Dop, and Rusty (although you are no longer at Empower, I appreciated your nagging). Couldn't and wouldn't do it without you.

I need to thank my community of friends. Leah, who is in charge of music and making sure I don't procrastinate. Everyone needs a friend who calls you when you are supposed to be writing and when you answer yells at you to get off the phone. Thank you to all my friends who ask me, "How's the book doing?" and then suffer through my incomprehensible explanations.

This book gave me the opportunity to learn from many religious leaders and lay people of varied faiths. I have been deeply touched by the warmth, open exchange of ideas, and feeling of inclusiveness I have experienced. In my own home community, I would like to thank Rabbi Daniel and Louise Zemmel, Meryl Weiner, and everyone at Temple Micah for helping me to rediscover the good in my own religious roots.

Living with a writer isn't easy. We walk around in our pajamas pulling our hair out, a tad self-absorbed and distracted. I am very grateful that my husband, James, supports me through the process. Last, I want to thank my sons, Elijah and Roane, who remind me on a daily basis that I will never be an expert in my field.

RW

I'm exceptionally grateful to Rosalind Wiseman, on whom I leaned shamelessly for her brilliant—and free—advice on coping with numerous adolescent and parental dilemmas while I was supposed to be helping her on the manuscript. Ross, your work with adolescents is visionary, and I'm honored to be your collaborator. Thanks also to Rachel Klayman for her sharp line editing and helpful organizational ideas. I'm very grateful to Rabbi Tom Weiner of Congregation Kol Ami for his insightful comments on bar and bat mitzvahs. I'm so deeply grateful to Janet Pietsch and to the "Temple Belles"—Felice Baritz, Dana Billman, Laurie Cole, Shelley Lanman, Stacey Matusow, and Patti Stracher—for endless parental support and advice. Martha Beck, Karen Gerdes, and Susan Edsall, my most ardent writing mentors, were relentlessly encouraging. My mother, Mary Ann Rapoport, has been my lifelong role model for unconditional love and magnificent mothering; I'll cherish her memory forever. My father, William Rapoport, is the embodiment of a proud papa. Thanks most of all to my husband, Ken Weiner, and our kids, Sam and Kate, for all the love and cheerleading, and for allowing me to steal their best lines.

ER

Index

A

Acceptance, definition of, 253
"Act Like a Boy" box, 64, 123, 185, 297–298
"Act Like a Dad" box, 33, 123
"Act Like a Man" box, 32–33, 64, 136, 158, 159, 198, 201, 294, 311
"Act Like a Mom" box, 30–32, 123, 228
"Act Like a Woman" box, 29, 32, 61, 136, 198
Adolescence, reliving, 23
Advanced placement courses, 116–117, 303–307, 318–319
Aggression, 43
AIDS (acquired immunodeficiency syndrome), 100, 297
Alcohol use, 121, 272, 273

ambivalence toward, 280–281
conversation with other parents about, 277–278, 282–283, 287, 292
conversation with your kid about, 274–277
discipline and, 283–285
out-of-town parents and, 289–291
typical problems, 281–292
under-my-roof parents and, 278–279
zero-tolerance parents and, 279–280
All-Boy Moms, 57–58
All-Girl Moms, 58
Alternative proms, 265–266
Anderegg, David, 112, 120, 315
Anger, expression of, 73–76, 125 (*see also* Confrontation)
Anti-Semitism, 93

Apologies, 147, 261
  definition of, 148–149
  male vs. female, 149–151
  as tactic for manipulation, 75
Appearance (*see* Personality profiles)
Astrology, 85
Athletics (*see* Sports)
Awards and tributes, 118–119

B

Baby boom generation, 97–99
Back-to-School Night, 1–3, 24–27
Backups, 68
Banker Dads, 69–70
  personality profile of, 80
Banker Moms (*see* Starbucks & Sympathy Moms)
Bar and bat mitzvahs, 268–271
Baron, Julie, 180
Belonging, need for, 25, 26
Benign Neglect Moms, 57
Best-Friend Moms, 59
Birth control, 293
Birthday parties (*see* Parties)
Birth order, 85
Black History Month, 86
Black parents, 87–92
Blakely, Mary Kay, 240
Blind spots of parents, 14–15
Body language, of Queen Bee Moms, 43
Boobs-on-Parade Moms, 61
Boy World, 3–4, 17, 28, 64, 65, 68, 69, 73, 75, 199, 201
"Bulletins from the Front," 64, 80–85

Bullying, 5, 8, 20, 185–188, 311–312
  blowing off or challenging, 74
  by coaches, 199–204
  committee members and, 231–232
  cyber, 115

C

Candle-lighting ceremonies, 267, 268
Carville, James, 131
Caveman Dads, 71–72, 132
Cell phones, 111–115
Christian parents, 94
Class (*see* Socioeconomic status)
Class parents, 236–237
Cliques, 4, 6
  definitions of, 36
  mom (*see* Mothers)
  teen, 36, 37
Closed-Book Dads, 79–80
Closed-Book Moms, 56, 79
Coaches, 197–204
  bullying by, 199–204
  characteristics of bad, 198
  characteristics of good, 197–198
  common problems with teams, 204–209
  discipline and, 207–209, 216–217
  on parental behavior, 11, 217–218
  parents as, 209–211
  principals and, 199, 203
  spectators and, 215
College application process, 116–117, 120, 301–322
  acceptance rates and, 313–315

admissions counselors, 320
  gifted and talented classes and,
    303–309
  legacy applications, 318
  school record and, 307–313
  side letters and, 308–310
  telling news of acceptance,
    321–322
  where to apply, 315–318
Comfort, in friendships, 140
Committees (*see* Volunteering)
Communication, 102–127
  "I don't know what I did to deserve
    such a good kid," 120–122
  "I hear that Aretha got a 5 on her
    AP Physics test—how nice for
    you," 118–119
  "I'm my child's best advocate—I'm
    acting in the best interests of
    my child," 108–109
  "It's so competitive today," 120
  "I want to give my kids every
    opportunity I didn't have,"
    115–118
  listening, 124–126
  "My biggest priority is my kids,"
    107–108
  "My child and I have an open rela-
    tionship—she tells me every-
    thing," 122–123
  "My child needs a cell phone so
    that if anything goes wrong she
    can get in touch with me,"
    111–115
  "My job as a parent is to protect my
    kids," 109–111
Competitiveness, 4, 6–7, 119, 120
  in sports (*see* Sports)

Conflict (*see* Communication; Con-
    frontation)
Confrontation, 128–153
  anger mismanagement, 136–139
  apologies, power of, 147–151
  avoidance of, 46, 47, 76, 133–136,
    139
  death threat example, 129–133
  fathers and, 73–76
  location of, 152
  script for, 152
  SEAL (Stop, Explain, Affirm and
    Acknowledge, and Lock
    In/Lock Out) strategy and,
    142–147, 151
  successful, 136
  timing of, 151–152
Counselors
  confidentiality and, 176
  dealing with, 173–177
  good vs. bad, 174–175
  parental memories of, 159–160
Crick, Nikki, 43
Crozier, Brad, 178–179
Cultural definitions of femininity and
    masculinity, 28–29
Cultural norms, 26–27
Cultural rule breakers, 27
Culture (*see also* Filters)
  defined, 26
Cyberbullying, 115

D

Dads (*see* Fathers)
Dad Totem Pole, 62–83
  Banker Dads, 69–70, 80

Dad Totem Pole (*continued*):
　Caveman Dads, 71–72, 132
　Desperate Wannabes, 70–71
　Floater Dads, 72, 75, 78, 80, 213
　Invisible Dads, 17, 73, 80, 204
　Kingpin Dads, 17, 65–68, 70, 71,
　　75, 78–80
　Outcast Dads, 73
　Reformed Dads, 72, 75, 78, 80, 213
　Sidekick Dads, 68–71, 75, 78, 79
　Stay-at-home dads, 76–78
　Torn Wannabes, 70–71
Date rape, 100
Desperate Wannabes
　female, 45–47, 221, 251
　male, 70–71
Diet pills, 286
Discipline, 90–91, 98–99
　alcohol and drug use and, 283–285
　college application process and,
　　307–308, 310–311
　in sports, 207–209, 216–217
Discrimination, 34, 35, 92
Divorce, 50, 86, 143
Dominators, 4, 65, 68
Don't-Ask, Don't-Tell Moms, 56–57
Drug use, 100, 121, 181–182, 263
　ambivalence toward, 280–281
　conversation with other parents
　　about, 277–278
　conversation with your kid about,
　　274–276, 282–283
　discipline and, 283–285
　typical problems, 281–292
　under-my-roof parents and,
　　278–279
　zero-tolerance parents and,
　　279–280

E

Elite (select) teams, 195, 204
Empathy, 125
Empower Program, 4, 32, 115
Entitled parents, 48, 50, 64, 116,
　　188–189
　Banker Dads, 69–70
　college applications and, 310
　Kingpin Dads (*see* Kingpin Dads)
　Queen Bee Moms (*see* Queen Bee
　　Moms)
　Sidekick Dads, 68–71, 75
　Sidekick Moms (*see* Sidekick
　　Moms)
　sports and, 199, 203–204, 213
　Starbucks & Sympathy Moms,
　　44–45
Ethics and morals, 12, 15
Ethnicity/race, 86–92
*Everything You Never Wanted Your
　　Child to Know About Sex (But
　　Were Afraid They'd Ask)*
　　(Richardson and Schuster),
　　293
Extracurricular activities, 116–117

F

Fathers, 6, 15–17 (*see also* Dad Totem
　　Pole; Personality profiles)
　Closed-Book Dads, 79–80
　Hip Dads, 78–79
　Lock-Her-in-a-Closet Dads, 78
　lunch-making by, 82–83
　Maverick Dads, 79
　moms on, 60–61

No-Excuses Dads, 80
Outcast Dads, 73
Sideline-Star Dads, 79
Silent Presence Dads, 80
Throbbing-Vein Dads, 79
traditional authoritarian role of,
    16, 76
volunteering and, 221, 226,
    238–240
Femininity, definitions of, 28
Filters, 18, 84–101, 144, 221, 227
generation gaps, 84, 97–100
marital status, 84, 85–86
multiple, 100–101
race/ethnicity, 84, 86–92
religion, 84, 92–94
socioeconomic status, 84, 95–97
Floater Dads, 72, 75
personality profile of, 78, 80
as sports spectators, 213
Floater kids, 47, 48, 72, 264
Floater Moms, 47–48, 75
personality profile of, 57, 58
Friendship Bill of Rights, 140–141, 203
Fund-raising, 223–224

G

Generation gaps, 84, 97–100
Generation X, 97, 99–101
Generosity, in friendships, 140, 141
Getting into college (*see* College
    application process)
Gifted and talented classes, 303–309
Gifts, cost of, 264–265
Girl World, 3–4, 17, 28, 32, 64, 75,
    199, 225, 232

Gordon, Thomas, 124
Gossip, 4
definitions of, 39
Goto-Hirai, Linda, 241
Grades, 161–167
Group projects, 167–170

H

Happy Hollow Elementary School,
    178–179
Hazing, 4, 68, 69, 98
Hip Dads, 78–79
Hip Moms, 55, 78
Honesty, in friendships, 140–141
"Housewives, Try This for Des-
    peration: Stay-at-Home
    Fathers Face Isolation and
    a Lingering Stigma"
    (Medina), 77
Hovercraft Moms, 55, 71
Humor, sense of, in friendships,
    140, 141

I

Imaginary Audience Syndrome,
    194
Inner Wimp, 134
Internalized racism, 89
Internet, 99
pornography sites, 157–159
Interruptions, 125
Invisible Dads, 17, 73, 204
personality profile of, 80

Invisible Moms, 17, 49–50, 73, 204,
    225, 232, 254
  personality profile of, 57, 59
"Isn't She Lovely" (Wonder), 19, 324
"I"-statement strategy, 124–125

J

Jewish parents, 93, 94

K

Kingpin Dads, 17, 65–68, 70, 71, 75
  personality profile of, 78–80

L

Left Out, 40, 64, 65
  Invisible Dads, 17, 73, 80, 204
  Invisible Moms, 17, 49–50, 57, 59,
    73, 204, 225, 232, 254
  Outcast Dads, 73
  Outcast Moms, 49, 50, 55, 58, 59,
    73
  Socially Challenged Moms, 51
Legacy college applications, 318
Life Skills (Williams and Williams),
    125
Listening, 124–126
Lock-Her-in-a-Closet Dads, 78
Lord of the Flies mentality, 74
Losing (*see* Sports)
Loyalty, 27
Lunches, 82–83
Lying, 291–292, 308

M

Machiavelli, Niccolò, 135
Marital status, 84, 85–86
Martin Luther King Jr. Day, 86
Masculinity, definitions of, 28–29,
    65–66
Materialism, 96
Math and science, 116
Maverick Dads, 79
McBride, Shanterra, 9
Mclean School, Potomac, Maryland,
    180
Medina, Jennifer, 77
Middle Men (*see* Dad Totem Pole)
Middle of the Pack (*see* Mom cliques)
Moms (*see* Mothers)
Mormon parents, 94
Mothers, 36–51
  All-Boy Moms, 57–58
  All-Girl Moms, 58
  Benign Neglect Moms, 57
  Best-Friend Moms, 59
  Boobs-on-Parade Moms, 61
  Closed-Book Moms, 56, 79
  Desperate Wannabes, 45–47, 221,
    251
  Don't-Ask, Don't-Tell Moms,
    56–57
  Floater Moms, 47–48, 57, 58, 75
  Hip Moms, 55, 78
  Hovercraft Moms, 55, 71
  Invisible Moms, 17, 49–50, 57, 59,
    73, 204, 225, 232, 254
  Mousy Moms, 59
  No-Privacy Moms, 58
  Outcast Moms, 49, 50, 55, 58, 59,
    73

Proud-to-be-a-Pain Moms, 56, 213
Pushover Moms, 59, 61
Queen Bee Moms (*see* Queen Bee
Moms)
Reformed Moms, 48–49, 56, 58, 72
Sidekick Moms, 40, 43–44, 49, 55,
57–59, 232, 305
Socially Challenged Moms, 51
Sound-the-Alarm Moms, 58–59
Spirit Moms, 57
Starbucks & Sympathy Moms, 17,
44–45, 56, 69, 254
stay-at-home moms, 51–54,
225–228
Steamrolled Moms, 47
Torn Wannabes, 45–47
working moms, 51–54, 227–228
Mousy Moms, 59

N

New York Times, 77
No-Excuses Dads, 80
No-Privacy Moms, 58

O

Odd Girl Out (Simmons), 115
Open mike night, 268
Open relationships, 122–123
Oral sex, 294, 296–298
Outcast Dads, 73
Outcast Moms, 49, 50, 73
personality profile of, 55, 58, 59
Overprotective parents, 7, 14,
110–111

P

Parental involvement, myth of, 6–8
Parents, Drug use; Fathers; Mothers
(*see also* Alcohol use; Sports)
accountability of, 8
bad behavior of, 8–12
black, 87–92
blind spots of, 14–15
as coaches, 209–211
competitiveness, 4, 6–7
entitled (*see* Entitled parents)
insecurities of, 4–6
religion and, 93–94
single, 85–86
social hierarchies and, 17–18
social power and status, 5–7
Parent-teacher conferences, attendance at, 15
Parent volunteerism (*see* Volunteering)
Parties, 5, 18, 92–93, 96–97, 122–123,
242–271
alcohol and drugs at (*see* Alcohol
use; Drug use)
alternative proms, 265–266
bar and bat mitzvahs, 268–271
control of pre-party chatter,
246–247
cost of, 264–265, 267
exclusion from, 244–246, 250–261
favors, 247, 248
games at, 261–262
guest list, 245, 246, 248–249,
254–261, 271
honoring commitment to attend,
262–264
hosting responsibilities, 246
no-shows at, 264

Parties *(continued)*:
  out-of-town parents and, 289–291
  rules for, 245–246
  on same date, 249–250
  sleepovers, 286–287
  special-event, 266–271
  theme, 266–267
  videos, 267–268
  withdrawing invitations to, 261–262
Peer pressure, parental, 6, 16
Percocet, 286
"Perfect" friendships, 31–32
Perfect Parent World, 3–4, 17, 23–35,
      64, 193, 194, 221, 244, 266,
      269, 277, 299, 303
Personal filters *(see* Filters)
Personality profiles, 54–61
  All-Boy Moms, 57–58
  All-Girl Moms, 58
  Benign Neglect Moms, 57
  Best-Friend Moms, 59
  Boobs-on-Parade Moms, 61
  Closed-Book Dads, 79–80
  Closed-Book Moms, 56
  Don't-Ask, Don't-Tell Moms, 56–57
  Hip Dads, 78–79
  Hip Moms, 55
  Hovercraft Moms, 55
  Lock-Her-in-a-Closet Dads, 78
  Maverick Dads, 79
  Mousy Moms, 59
  No-Excuses Dads, 80
  No-Privacy Moms, 58
  Proud-to-be-a-Pain Moms, 56
  Pushover Moms, 59, 61
  Sideline-Star Dads, 79
  Silent Presence Dads, 80
  Sound-the-Alarm Moms, 58–59

  Spirit Moms, 57
  Tennis Skirt Mom, 54–55
  Throbbing-Vein Dads, 79
Pipher, Mary, 194
Pleaser kids, 47
Popularity, definitions of, 37–38
Pornography sites, 157–159
Power system, 4, 5
Pregnancy, 52, 297, 298
Prince, The (Machiavelli), 135
Principals, 18
  changing minds, 182–183
  coaches and, 199, 203
  examples of problems, 181–187
  going over head of, 185, 187
  good vs. bad, 178–179
  meeting guidelines, 180–181
  on parental behavior, 8–10
  parental memories of, 159–160
  write-in campaigns, 188–189
Privacy, 12, 122
Proud-to-be-a-Pain Moms, 56, 213
PTA associations *(see* Volunteering)
Punahou School, Hawaii, 240–241
Pushover Moms, 59, 61

Q

Queen Bee Girls, 3, 4, 38–40, 42,
    131–133
Queen Bee Moms, 40, 43, 48, 50, 65,
    138, 221, 224, 225, 232–233,
    235–236
  apologies and, 129, 131
  body language of, 43
  characteristics of, 41–42
  death threat example and, 129, 131

gossip and, 44
parties and, 254–255
personality profile of, 55, 56, 59
stay-at-home, 226
test scores and, 305
Queen Bees & Wannabes (Wiseman),
3, 4, 18, 40, 54, 104, 262, 291,
294

R

Race/ethnicity, 84, 86–92
Racism, 86–92
Reflective listening, 124–125
Reformed Dads, 72, 75
personality profile of, 78, 80
as sports spectators, 213
Reformed Moms, 48–49, 72
personality profile of, 56, 58
Rejection, 38–39
Religion, 84, 92–94
Religious schools, 190
Reviving Ophelia (Pipher), 194
Richardson, Justin, 293
Rites of passage, 18
Back-to-School Night, 1–3, 24–27
parties (*see* Parties)
Role reversal, sports and, 194
Rood, Gregg, 77

S

Safe sex, 293
School functions, attendance at, 15,
81–82
Schuster, Mark, 293

SEAL (Stop, Explain, Affirm and
Acknowledge, and Lock
In/Lock Out) strategy,
142–147, 151, 162–163, 170,
171, 202–203, 215, 233,
255–256
Sexual activity, 121, 123, 273,
293–300
"catching in act," 296, 298–300
conversations about, 293–296,
298–300
oral sex, 294, 296–298
Sexual games, 261–263
Sidekick Dads, 68–71, 75
personality profile of, 78, 79
Sidekick Girls, 43, 131–133
Sidekick Moms, 40, 43–44, 49, 232
personality profile of, 55, 57–59
test scores and, 305
Sideline-Star Dads, 79
Silent Presence Dads, 80
Silent Sundays, 215
Simmons, Rachel, 115
Single parents, 85–86
Sleepovers, 286–287
Socially Challenged Moms, 51
Social skills deficits, 51
Socioeconomic status, 84, 95–97
Sound-the-Alarm Moms, 58–59
Spirit Moms, 57
Sports, 18, 43, 45, 192–218
coaches (*see* Coaches)
common problems with teams,
204–209
discipline in, 207–209, 216–217
elite (select) teams, 195, 204
psychology, 198
role reversal and, 194

Sports (continued):
  spectators, 11, 12, 211–216
  winning and losing, 196
Starbucks & Sympathy Moms, 17,
    44–45, 69, 254
  personality profile of, 56
Stay-at-home dads, 76–78
Stay-at-home moms, 51–54, 225–
    228
STDs (sexually transmitted diseases),
    100, 297, 298
Steamrolled Moms, 47
Stereotypes, 85, 92, 93, 137
Stuck and Silenced, 71, 72
Super Mom image, 32
Superstar archetype, 119

T

Talk-show psychology, 85
Targets, 50
Teachers
  child's harassment by other kids
    and, 170–171
  grades, 161–167
  group projects, 167–170
  housing and, 97
  name-calling by, 171–172
  parental memories of, 159–160
  threats toward, 165
  working effectively with, 161–173
Team sports (see Sports)
Three-strikes-and-you're-out philoso-
    phy, 146–147
Throbbing-Vein Dads, 79
Title IX, 195
Torn Wannabes

female, 45–47
male, 70–71

U

Unicel, 115

V

Vaginal intercourse, 296, 297
Valium, 286
Vandalism, 263
Vicodin, 286
Videos, at parties, 267–268
Volunteering, 5, 41, 219–241
  appreciation, expression of,
    228–229
  class parents, 236–237
  common problems on committees,
    230–236
  fathers and, 221, 226, 238–240
  fund-raising, 223–224
  leadership and, 222–229, 232–236
  micromanagement and, 224–226
  recruitment strategies and, 226

W

Wannabe parents, 49, 75, 188–189,
    232, 254
  Desperate Wannabes, 45–47,
    70–71, 221, 251
  personality profiles of, 55, 57–59,
    61, 78
  sports and, 204

test scores and, 305
Torn Wannabes, 45–47, 70–71
Weapons, 188
Weiner, Tom, 269–271
Williams, Redford, 125
Williams, Virginia, 125
Winning and losing (*see* Sports)
Wonder, Stevie, 19, 324
Work/home balance, 16
Working moms, 51–54, 227–228
*Worried All the Time: Overparenting
in the Age of Anxiety and How
to Stop It* (Anderegg), 112, 315

Write-in campaigns, 188–189

X

Xanax, 286

Z

Zero-tolerance policies, 188, 276,
279–280

About the Authors

ROSALIND WISEMAN is the co-founder of the Empower Program, a nonprofit organization that empowers youth to stop the culture of violence. She is the author of *Queen Bees & Wannabes: Helping Your Daughter Survive Cliques, Gossip, Boyfriends, and Other Realities of Adolescence*. She lives in Washington, D.C., with her husband, James, and two sons, Elijah and Roane.

ELIZABETH RAPOPORT was the editor of Rosalind Wiseman's *Queen Bees & Wannabes*. A full-time editor, writer, and life coach, she lives in White Plains, New York, with her husband, Ken, and their two teenagers, Sam and Kate.